Language Myths, Mysteries and M

Also by Karen Stollznow

GOD BLESS AMERICA: Strange and Unusual Beliefs and Practices in the United States

HAUNTING AMERICA: The Truth behind Some of America's "Most Haunted" Places

Language Myths, Mysteries and Magic

Karen Stollznow

University of California, Berkeley, USA

First published 2014 by
PALGRAVE MACMILLAN

Palgrave Macmillan in the UK is an imprint of Macmillan Publishers Limited, registered in England, company number 785998, of Houndmills, Basingstoke, Hampshire RG21 6XS.

Palgrave Macmillan in the US is a division of St Martin's Press LLC, 175 Fifth Avenue, New York, NY 10010.

Palgrave Macmillan is the global academic imprint of the above companies and has companies and representatives throughout the world.

Palgrave® and Macmillan® are registered trademarks in the United States, the United Kingdom, Europe and other countries.

ISBN 978–1–137–40484–8 hardback
ISBN 978–1–137–40485–5 paperback

This book is printed on paper suitable for recycling and made from fully managed and sustained forest sources. Logging, pulping and manufacturing processes are expected to conform to the environmental regulations of the country of origin.

A catalogue record for this book is available from the British Library.

Library of Congress Cataloging-in-Publication Data
Stollznow, Karen.
    Language myths, mysteries, and magic / Karen Stollznow, University of California, Berkeley, USA.
       pages cm
    ISBN 978–1–137–40484–8
    1. Language and languages—Miscellanea. 2. Language and languages—Usage. 3. Alphabet—Miscellanea. 4. Magic. 5. Incantations.
    6. Historical linguistics. I. Title.
    P107.S75 2014
    401—dc23
                                                               2014019091

Contents

Part V   Therapeutic Language

Acknowledgments

With sincere thanks to the following people for their invaluable assistance, advice, and support during the writing of this book: Joe Anderson, Banachek, Matthew Baxter, Bryan Bonner, Rick Duffy, Reed Esau, Gary Goldberg, Stuart Hayes, Jamy Ian Swiss, Mark Newbrook, Lynne Kelly, Nikolas Kovacevic, Scott Lilienfeld, Kim Scarborough, Aiden Sinclair, Blake Smith, Gaye Stolsnow, Paul Turner, Robert Walker, and Karen Woodman.

Introduction

For some people, language is about more than everyday communication. Words have a greater purpose than to make small talk about the weather, tell a joke, or try a pick up line. They believe that language can transcend the normal and enter the realm of the paranormal. Language is thought to have special powers and can be used to communicate with gods, demons, monsters, aliens, and the dead. From ancient curses carved on tablets to modern-day affirmations, supernatural language is used in an attempt to predict the future, diagnose and cure disease, attract good luck, repel bad luck, and to charm and curse.

Language Myths, Mysteries and Magic explores this mysterious side of language. We encounter a fascinating collection of strange phenomena involving language, including folklore and mythology, superstitions and scams, customs and ceremonies, religious doctrine and rituals, and popular paranormal beliefs and practices. As we will see, language is connected to all aspects of the supernatural.

Unusual claims about language appear frequently in the media. We've all heard the story about the woman who goes to bed with a headache and wakes up to discover she has a foreign accent. We've all received emails from princes, presidents, and rich widows promising us millions if we provide them with our banking information. We've all wondered if there are experts who can really tell if we're lying by reading our body language.

As a linguist, I'm often asked about weird language. Can hypnosis increase the size of your breasts or penis? Can personality be interpreted through our handwriting style? Is there a "brown note" that causes a loss of bowel control? Can psychic mediums speak with our deceased loved ones? Can animals talk? If we don't forward that chain email will it result in death and destruction? So, what is true and what is false about these topics?

Many of the subjects in this book will be well known to you, including the Bible Code, Nostradamus predictions, the supposed healing power of prayer, and whether Elvis is dead or not. Rather than repeating the same old theories I'll be providing new insight into these classic phenomena. This book also digs into topics about which little has been written, such as chain letters, blasphemy, neurolinguistic programming, alien and monster languages, devices that seem to be able to contact the dead, and talking dolls.

We look at some bizarre real-life cases, including the story of a twentieth-century English woman who suddenly began speaking in an ancient Egyptian dialect. We hear about a song that is so depressing it is said that it drives people to commit suicide. We check out the idea that if you fall asleep on a book you can absorb its contents without having to read it. We also delve into the tale of a grim-reaper cat that seems to predict the death of residents in a nursing home.

This book is a magic shop of mystical beliefs and practices. From satanic messages in music to speaking in tongues, these topics are diverse but each involves communication, whether it is talking, writing, drawing, reading, listening, or thinking. As you read through the book you'll see a web forming of myths, mysteries, and magical stories that are all interwoven by the thread of language.

Part I
Magical Language

Introduction

It's tempting to think that a belief in magic isn't common anymore, although we reveal a tradition of superstitious thinking in our everyday language. We expose our linguistic past in our present when we respond to a sneeze with "Bless you!", when we insult someone with "Damn you!", or we tell them to "Go to Hell!".

Language is a crucial catalyst in magical belief, thinking, and performance. From ancient Greece to modern America, these chapters explore language believed to have miraculous powers. Spells, St Jude novenas, affirmations, and online prayer requests are hoped to change the world around us. Divination and prophets are believed to predict the future, while charms attract good luck and repel bad luck. Blasphemy, curses, and chain letters are thought to have the ability to harm, and a sentimental song is said to drive people to commit suicide.

1
Curses, Charms, and Taboos

Spells and incantations are written or spoken words and formulas that are believed to have magical powers. A spell isn't inherently positive or negative, although specific kinds of spells do have connotations of good or evil. Charms, cures, and blessings are specifically intended to be good, or are hoped to counteract bad spells. Curses, hexes, and jinxes are always underpinned by bad intentions, like wanting someone dead, or wanting them to become fat.

Charm your pants off

Nowadays, "charm" tends to conjure up images of jewelry, or a rabbit's foot carried for good luck. We might think of "to charm", that is, to win someone over, or a charm school that teaches outdated etiquette. We might even picture the Prince Charming of fairy tales, or a snake charmer sitting cross-legged as he plays his flute to a cobra that looks ready to strike. If something has a "certain charm" it doesn't really have any charm at all.

Medieval charms

Before there were charm bracelets, lucky charms, and breakfast cereals by that name, early charms were spoken or written magical spells intended for a range of purposes. It became common practice to write down a charm and place it into a pendant, ornament, stone, or other kind of amulet, an object used for protection or to attract good luck. The charm itself might be a picture, such as a pentagram or astrological symbol. It might be a word, name, or phrase, written in Latin, Greek, Hebrew, or gibberish if you couldn't spell. The charm was drawn on papyrus, parchment, or paper; or inscribed on communion hosts, leaves, sticks, knife handles, metal, or gemstones. These charmed amulets were worn or carried close to the body for many specific or general purposes: to attract good luck, exorcise demons, cure illness, ensure safe travel, improve memory or sexual prowess, to rid oneself of vermin, to guard against wild animals, avoid sudden death, protect against evil spirits, protect property, to bind thieves so they couldn't enter a house, or to ensure protection from general misfortune. A form of white magic, charms were created for good, not evil.

A charmed life

Healing charms were probably the most common type of charm. In those days, without doctors, charms were intended to alleviate pain or cure disease. Protective charms were prophylactic: to ward off disease, and to protect a pregnant woman against miscarriage, a difficult birth, or having disabled children. Healing charms were like the folk remedies and old wives' tales that still do the rounds today, such as "feed a cold and starve a fever", and the belief that you can scare away hiccups with "Boo!".

Scripture was popularly used in healing charms. Religious texts are often believed to be divinely inspired and holy books are credited with miraculous powers, especially the ability to heal. The alleged curative powers of these divine texts were transferred through contact with the body, so a copy of the Bible, Torah, or Qur'an would be placed against the afflicted body part. Many of these cures were forms of sympathetic magic, that is, the cure would somehow imitate the problem. For example, the Gospel of John contains a number of miracles and healings, and so this book was used as a pillow to cure headaches (Segal, 2006).

To be most effective, charms were kept close to the body at all times. In ancient Egypt spells from the Book of the Dead were written on amulets and wound into the wrappings of mummies. Even the living could benefit from carrying or wearing healing charms for prevention or treatment. These charms included prayers or biblical quotes written on paper or parchment and often bandaged around the affected body part. Charms taken from scripture were somehow relevant to the problem at hand, but sometimes, the "scripture" wasn't even scripture. Many charms used narratives involving biblical figures that had no scriptural source. These apocryphal tales are known as "narrative charms". A fourteenth-century cure for a toothache petitions St Apollonia, a virgin martyr who was tortured by having her teeth torn out. For this reason, she is the patron saint of dentistry. The following charm was written on material and wrapped around the patient's head.

> In the city Alexandria rests the body of Blessed Apollonia, virgin and martyr, whose teeth the wicked extracted. Through the intercession of Blessed Maria, virgin, and of all saints and blessed Apollonia, virgin and martyr, free, Lord, the teeth of your servant from toothache. Saint Blaise pray for me. In the name of the Father, etc. Our Father. Ave Maria. And let this charm be tied upon the head of the patient.
>
> (Olsan, 1992)

Charms were usually a blend of Christian and pagan practices, and surprisingly, the Church adopted many pagan practices. Milk and honey were blessed by Bible passages such as "be fruitful and multiply", while if farmland was barren prayers were said over the property to make it fertile (Blake, 2010). As a result of this crossover, many charms were composed of Christian elements, and included fragments of Catholic liturgy, prayers, and saints' legends.

To bring the healing text into closer contact with the sufferer, the words might be written directly onto the patient's body. For example, the Veronica charm was used to control chronic bleeding, such as excessive menstruation. This idea comes from the biblical story of a woman who touched Christ's robe and was cured of a 12-year bout of hemorrhaging (Matthew 9:20, Luke 8:40, Mark 5:21). To use this charm, "Veronica" was written on the patient's forehead with his or her own blood, to stem the bleeding. This charm is also linked to the mythical story of Veronica who wiped Christ's brow as he carried his cross to Calvary. This left an imprint of Jesus' face on her cloth, much like the Shroud of Turin. Known as the Veil of Veronica, it was said to have miraculous powers to be able to cure blindness and raise the dead. This fabled cloth became a popular holy relic in the middle ages, and there were many of them, even though it never existed.

Wear your prayer

To this day, some Jewish people wear their prayers. This is not for protection, but to remind them of their religious rules of conduct. Torah passages in Exodus and Deuteronomy say that the story of the Exodus should be kept constantly in mind: "You shall put these words of mine on your heart and on your soul; and you shall tie them for a sign upon your arm, and they shall be as *totafot* between your eyes"

(Deuteronomy 11:18). It is likely that the texts were symbolic but some chose to take them literally. Observant Jews wear *tefillin* on their head and arms during prayer. These are small black leather boxes containing scrolls inscribed with passages from the Torah. A modern version is to wear religious jewelry, such as medals and rings inscribed with verses of scripture. Some people display sacred and inspirational texts around the house and garden like amulets for the home, such as "Bless this House" or "Bless this Mess".

Another kind of charm involved speaking or writing powerful words and names. This was believed to somehow command the attention of a corresponding deity and get their help. A medieval charm was to write the name of "Ishmael" (the first-born son of Abraham) on a laurel leaf to cure insomnia caused by elves. The healing names could also be recited over the patient's body. A healing charm from the fourteenth century involved listing Latin, Greek, and Hebrew epithets of Christ over the patient, including *Messias* "Messiah", *Sother* "Savior", and *Adonay* "my Lord" (Olsan, 1992). Biblical figures and patron saints were invoked by name to intercede in matters related to their special concern. People petitioned Job to cure their worms because the Book of Job (19:26) says, "And though after my skin worms destroy this body, yet in my flesh shall I see God." St John survived an attempted poisoning by a drink of snake venom, so he was asked to treat cases of poisonings and snake bites. Invoking the saint's name was believed to establish a connection between the sick and the special power of the holy person. Of course today, St Christopher, St Jude, and other saints are worn on medals and petitioned for help.

Eat your words

Prayers and charms could be recited over the patient or they could be recited *into* the patient. Charms might be whispered into the patient's ears or mouth or spoken to the afflicted body part. Sometimes it's okay to eat your words. To further facilitate the charm's penetration into the body, the patient would eat or drink the powerful words. The name of Christ or a short spell was scratched onto apples, butter, or sacramental bread and swallowed by the patient like medicine. A fourteenth-century English manuscript includes a birthing charm that was written on bread or cheese and then eaten in the hope that the mother-to-be would ben-efit from the words literally. A medieval remedy to treat a rabid dog or someone bitten by one was to write *quare uare brare arabus arabris albus abbris rew few* on a piece of food and feed it to the sick (Skemer,

2006). Another medieval practice was to wash sacred texts, wring out the iron-gall ink from the pages of the book, and drink it as a tonic.

During the Christian celebration of the Eucharist, the celebrant turns bread (or wafers) and wine into the body and blood of Christ using the words, "This is my body", and "This is my blood". This Holy Communion is a reenactment of the Last Supper where Jesus performed this rite with his disciples. According to the doctrine of transubstantiation, the bread and wine literally metamorphose into the body and blood of Christ. This theory is controversial, and many Protestant denominations consider the act to be symbolic, although they believe that Christ is present at the Eucharist. When the bread has been consecrated by this ceremony it has become powerful. In medieval times, these "hosts" were stolen by parishioners and sold to cure illnesses in humans or animals or to ward off disease. To increase its potency, biblical texts were sometimes written directly onto the bread.

Worked like a charm

Like the mad dog charm above, many charms have melodic sound patterns and they usually had rhyme and alliteration. Exotic words simply sound powerful so many charms included a mix of words from classical languages and even nonsense words. *Rex pax nax* was a tenth-century toothache cure, *max max pax pater noster* was used to stop bleeding, and *arex, artifex, filia* was believed to relieve insomnia (Olsan, 1992). A few examples of sound play still exist. The magical exclamations "abracadabra!", "alakazam!", "hocus pocus!", "presto changeo!", and "ta da!" are still used in corny magic tricks today.

Word games also made charms seem more potent. A common one was the palindrome (it reads the same ways backwards) phrase *sator arepo tenet opera rotas*. This was usually abbreviated to "Sator". It was considered magical because it was reversible and it was hoped that saying or writing Sator would likewise reverse any bad circumstances. In medieval handbooks of women's medicine known as the Trotuala texts, a childbirth charm involved writing "Sator" on a piece of cheese or butter for the woman to eat (Skemer, 2006). To increase its effects, the formula is often written in a word square. The Sator square was considered extra magical because it is readable from every direction.

S A T O R

A R E P O

T E N E T

OPERA

ROTAS

Shaping text into a potent pattern is a common feature in magic. The most popular magic shape was the shrinking word formula. These are magical words gradually reduced in letter size to form an inverted triangle. Abracadabra is probably the most famous example of a shrinking word. Instead of being used to pull a rabbit out of a hat, "Abracadabra" was written down and worn as a charm. The origins of this famous magical word are unknown, but it may be related to "abrasax", found engraved on gemstones and used as an amulet. Another theory is that abracadabra is derived from a Hebrew expression paraphrased as, "I create as I speak".

"Abracadabra" is a clichéd word that no respectable magician would use today but the first person to use it was a physician, not a magician. Quintus Severus Sammonicus was a third-century Roman physician who used it as a shrinking word in his poem "Praecepta de Medicina". The word was arranged into a magical-looking triangular pattern, shrinking the word from 11 letters to just one.

ABRACADABRA
ABRACADABR
ABRACADAB
ABRACADA
ABRACAD
ABRACA
ABRAC
ABRA
ABR
AB
A

This poem was a healing charm to treat toothache, fevers, and other ailments. In another example of sympathetic magic, it was believed that shrinking the word would somehow shrink the illness. "Abracadabra" was written on parchment, folded into the shape of a cross, and worn around the neck for nine consecutive days. To increase their efficacy, and get God on side, medieval charms were often written in the form of a cross. The written word itself increased the apparent potency of the spell. These were days when illiteracy was high, so handwriting held a mystique for those who couldn't read or write. Even more powerful was an exotic language they couldn't understand, especially a sacred or ancient one, such as Hebrew. A dead language is even more mystical still. To this day, Wiccans use fragmented Latin in their spells. This is nothing new; Roman pagans used Etruscan in the same way, when it was already a dead language.

Reading a charm aloud was also believed to further enact the words in the spell. This way, the intervening spirits and gods could hear the petition. Also, text set to verse could be more easily committed to memory and repetition was also believed to be necessary for charms to take effect. Prayer wheels were designed to enable this repetition. These are cylinders inscribed with prayers, scripture, wishes, mantras, magical words, or charms. Like a perpetual motion prayer, spinning the wheel is believed to repeat the prayer, and to have the same effects as oral recitation. Prayer wheels were used in ancient Greece and Rome. They are still used in modern Buddhism and for ornamental purposes in gardens. We can also find online prayer wheels and prayer wheel apps. To reinforce the intention, repetition is a feature of modern litanies, prayers, novenas, spells, and positive affirmations; and in a more secular setting, naughty school kids are forced to write lines as a form of discipline.

Ancient and modern curses

On November 4, 1922, Lord Carnarvon and Howard Carter made one of the greatest archaeological discoveries of the twentieth century – the nearly intact tomb of King Tutankhamen. Soon thereafter, Carnarvon died under mysterious circumstances. According to media reports, Carnarvon was a casualty of an ancient curse written in hieroglyphs at the entrance to the tomb: "Death will come swiftly to those who disturb the tomb of the king." Many other members of the archaeological dig quickly became victims to this curse.

Carnarvon died eight months after the discovery of the tomb. The circumstances were certainly weird; he suffered an infection after he snagged a mosquito bite while shaving. However, it appears that Carter started the legend to keep the press at bay, or as a prank. Carter, who was the one to actually discover and open the tomb, lived for another 16 years without incident. In fact, the average duration of life for the rest of the party was 23 years (Randi, 1995). Most damning of all to the legend, there is no artifact inscribed with a curse among the thousands of treasures found in the tomb. Simply, there is no curse of Tutankhamen.

Surprisingly, tomb curses are rare, especially during Tutankhamen's New Kingdom era. There are some examples from the Old Kingdom, but they aren't great sound bites like the fabricated curse above. Here's a warning against priests who might otherwise eat fish before entering the tomb of the official buried within.

> As for all men who will enter this my tomb of the necropolis being impure, having eaten those abominations that good spirits who have journeyed to the West abominate... an end for him shall be made for him concerning that evil... I shall seize his neck like a bird... I shall cast fear of myself into him.
>
> (El Mahdy, 1989)

Tomb curses are legendary threats. Another infamous curse of this kind is the folkloric Gypsy curse, "May you wander over the face of the earth forever, never sleep twice in the same bed, never drink water twice from the same well and never cross the same river twice in a year." Another type of curse is a legendary warning. The curse of Tippecanoe warns that US presidents elected in years ending in zero will die during office. Abraham Lincoln, Franklin D. Roosevelt, and John F. Kennedy fulfilled the criteria for this "curse", although Ronald Reagan and George W. Bush survived their full terms, despite assassination attempts made on their lives. Some dangerous places are allegedly cursed, such as the Bermuda Triangle, given the frequency of shipping and aircraft accidents in that region. Some unsuccessful sports teams are allegedly cursed, such as the Boston Red Sox baseball team, which didn't win a single World Series between the years 1918 and 2004. Some curses are tongue-in-cheek, such as the "curse of Eve", the "monthly curse", and other euphemisms for menstruation.

A pox on your house!

Few of us would consider "Damn you!" or "Curse you!" as sincere or harsh curses, but in some cultures, insults can be wielded as curses. In Dutch, diseases are wished on people as insults. Nasty archaic and mostly eradicated diseases are preferred, such as plague, leprosy, cholera, smallpox, tuberculosis, and typhus (Burridge, 1999). They don't believe that saying the name of the sickness invokes the sickness itself, but they are showing how angry they are. Today's English equivalent is to wish an incurable disease on someone, "I hope you die of AIDS!". This is one of the strongest expressions of contempt reserved for people who've committed the worst social crimes. The equivalent in early modern English was to curse someone with, "A pox on your house!".

A classic curse is a spell or prayer to a god, natural force, or spirit made in writing, speech, or thought that is believed to have a negative causative effect. The opposite of a blessing, a curse attempts to bring misfortune to a person, place, or animal, and usually to exert power or control over them. The curse is either placed directly on a specific person, or, like the tomb curses, it is placed indirectly on an object to affect strangers sometime in the future. A belief in curses is still popular today, especially in Afro-Caribbean religions such as Voodoo and Santeria, Hoodoo folk magic, and the paranormal community. Other ways to curse someone are to jinx, hex, trick, bind, hot foot, cross, or goofer.

Curses are not frivolous bad intentions, such as wishing someone a bad hair day, or telling someone to "Go to hell!". Curses have an extreme and evil edge to them, as they impose disease, disaster, or death on the victim, and maybe even a doomed afterlife. A dark ages curse was to name a living person during a Mass for the Dead, hoping it would cause them to die (Cavendish, 1967).

Curse tablets dating from the fifth century BCE to the fifth century CE have been discovered from Africa and Europe, but mostly from ancient Greece and Rome (Gager, 1999). These curses or binding spells are known as *devotianes* or *defixiones* and were dedicated to a god or spirit. They were intended to bring people under power and control. These tablets contained mysterious words, including garbled words from Hebrew and Egyptian inscribed on thin sheets of lead. These were buried near the victim's home, or placed in a grave to enlist help from the dead. The curses were directed at adversaries in business and courts, and against competitors in sport, such as chariot racers and their horses. Some curses aimed to exact revenge against thieves, either known or unknown, and to retrieve any stolen items. Other curse tablets hoped to get rid of an unwanted partner or a bad neighbor. Even ancient people hated their neighbors.

Evil prayers

Curses are like evil prayers, not that all prayers are positive. A 1994 Gallup poll revealed that 5 per cent of Americans admitted to praying for the harm of others (Dossey, 2011). Some people believe that sticks and stones can break bones, but that words can also hurt us. Dossey, the author of *Be Careful What you Pray For, You Might Just Get It*, believes that negative words, thoughts and wishes towards others are everyday curses that he calls "negative prayers". They are often offhanded and launched unintentionally, but powerful nonetheless. He claims that these bad prayers are the cause of our daily accidents and mishaps. Losses at sports events are explained as bad wishes coming from the fans of opposing sports teams. Negative prayers are also the cause of sickness. Dossey recommends that to counteract these malevolent prayers we need to recite protection prayers. There are studies testing intercessory prayer (see Chapter 4) but there aren't any experiments testing negative prayer. Try getting that one past the ethics committee!

In the American Navajo culture it is believed that thought and language have the power to shape reality and control events. They believe that it is important to think and speak in a positive way, because negative talk incites a negative outcome. These beliefs are encoded in the common phrases "Think in the beauty way" and "Talk in the beauty way". When someone says something negative it is treated as a self-curse, so they are rebuked with, "Don't talk that way!" as though this will counter the curse. English has the similar superstitious rebuke "Don't say that!". Talking about death and disease are taboo to many people, as though this somehow invokes the misfortune. To some Navajo people, talking about a potential negative event can cause it to come to pass. To illustrate this thinking, a Navajo woman described what happened when a surgeon explained to her father the risks of cardiac surgery.

> The surgeon told him he may or may not wake up, that this is the risk of every surgery. For the surgeon it was very routine, but the way that my Dad received it, it was almost like a death sentence, and he never consented to the surgery.
>
> (Carrese and Rhodes, 1995)

Dr Andrew Weil (2000) believes that the pessimistic prognoses of medical doctors constitute a kind of medical hexing. Phrases such as, "There is nothing more we can do for you", and "you will just have to live with it" are seen as shamanistic curses to patients. Weil claims that these incite a negative placebo response, causing a failure to thrive in patients. He says, "Although it is easy to identify this phenomenon in exotic cultures, we rarely perceive that something very familiar goes on every day in our own culture, in hospitals, clinics and doctors' offices."

In some Australian Aboriginal communities, the curse of "pointing the bone" can cause a negative placebo effect. This practice involves taking a human, kangaroo, or emu bone and attaching it to a rope braided from human hair. This is pointed towards the victim while a curse is sung. Medicine men and women believe that the victim's soul or blood is drawn down the rope towards the sorcerer. Alternatively, some believe that a magical disease-causing object is sent through the rope to embed itself in the victim (Byard, 1988). This is a potent curse, if you believe in it. Former Prime Minister John Howard had the bone pointed at him for cutting funding to an Aboriginal government program, but nothing happened. However, for many Aboriginal people, the terrified victims resign themselves to their fate. They co-operate with the curse, refusing to eat and drink, and allowing the curse to become a self-fulfilling prophecy.

Curses!

Curses can also backfire. The Necronomicon is a mythical magical text known as a "grimoire" that is mentioned in several H. P. Lovecraft stories. To capitalize on this fame, several hoax books have appeared, all professing to be the "real Necronomicon". The popular Simon version, written by an anonymous author, includes curses and black magic spells translated from Sumerian into English. As "words of power", some Sumerian words have been retained, as their power is said to be contained in the pronunciation. However, there is much disagreement about how the words are supposed to be pronounced. According to legend, if the incantations are mispronounced, the curse will be turned onto the practitioner. This is unlikely, since many of the Babylonian words are misspelled, or simply made up.

Wishes can backfire too. In *The Monkey's Paw*, a horror story by W. W. Jacobs, three wishes are granted to whoever possesses the monkey's paw talisman. The owner, Mr White, wishes for a windfall to pay off his house. This wish is duly granted, but it comes at a price. The money is received as a life insurance payment when his son dies in a freak accident. Each of the three wishes have unintended negative consequences because the owner has interfered with fate. Therefore, the blessed has somehow become the cursed.

Curses are often in the interpretation. According to the doctrine of prosperity churches, if you experience poverty, lose your job, fall sick, or have a car accident, then you are under a curse. Earthquakes, tsunamis, hurricanes, and other natural disasters are also explained as punishment from God according to fundamentalist Christians. The prosperity gospel blames misfortune on negative language, unconfessed sins, and a lack of faith and tithing. God will bless those who tithe, but curse those who don't. In a form of godly gambling, the "health and wealth" gospel teaches that faith, positive speech, and donations to the church will increase health and material wealth, and avoid bad luck and curses (Jenkins, 2006).

The symptoms or signs that someone has been afflicted by a curse differ across cultures, beliefs, and time. Most often, the "curse" may be that the victim suffers some inexplicable misfortune, or just a run of bad luck. When it has been established that there is a curse, the victim needs to undo the curse, reverse the curse, turn it back onto the curser, or onto some unlucky scapegoat. In the Bible, Christ casts out evil spirits from humans and transfers them to pigs (Matthew 8:28–33). From Catholicism to Voodoo, exorcisms are performed to drive Satan, demons, or other negative forces out of a person's body, or to remove a curse. Most curse removals or cleansings aren't as dramatic as those featured in *The Exorcist*. They might involve amulets, holy water, crosses, or burning sage, but language is the essential tool. Exorcisms always involve the recitation of prayers, psalms, chants, and incantations.

A present-day psychic scam is to convince clients they've been cursed, and then offer to remove the evil influences, for a fee. Unsurprisingly, the curse proves to be stronger than first believed, and the psychic must perform additional rituals, at ever-increasing costs. There are many cases of people being bilked of their entire life savings by unscrupulous psychics. Psychic Janet Adams cheated an 85-year-old woman out of $80,330. The psychic became the curser when she told the woman that "her husband would die of a heart attack if she didn't immediately pay $13,000 for 'special prayers'" (Lee, 2008). Curse removal removes money, not curses.

Curses show us that whether we're living in ancient Rome or modern America, humans have similar life experiences. We all face relationship problems with strangers, colleagues, friends, family, and partners. We experience similar emotions, such as jealousy and fear, and we seek justice and vengeance against those who mistreat us. If we can't find an immediate solution, some people take desperate measures. Curses are a kind of linguistic vigilante justice where the victim tries to take back the power. When someone curses us, we may not grow horns or turn into a newt, but we do know that someone wishes us great harm. Ultimately, saying something doesn't make it so.

Forbidden words

A taboo is a cultural prohibition and there are many kinds of words that become tabooed in society. Common categories of taboo language include cannibalism, death, illness, food, sex, body parts, and ethnicity.

Swear words and racial epithets are today's biggest word bombs, but these days, where uttering "bomb" in an airport is its own word bomb, language is full of words we "shouldn't" say. In every society there are words that are proscribed. Of course, offensiveness is dependent on context, intention, and interpretation, and perceptions change across cultures and time. But some words are believed to transgress offensiveness and endanger us mortally and magically, and maybe even invoke the penalty of divine retribution.

Sacred cows

Blasphemy is behavior or language considered to be contemptuous towards a sacred word, object or concept. These acts are branded with archaic adjectives such as sacrilegious, sinful, impious, heretical, and profane. Blasphemous language is a kind of verbal desecration of hallowed words, achieved by merely speaking them. This small inventory of words is mostly comprised of divine names, and usually spoken as exclamations, such as "Jesus!", "Christ!", and "God!". It is as though invoking these important names will magically invoke the power of the deity. Blasphemy can also be seen as a kind of religious defamation, where someone verbally expresses irreverence towards something deemed holy.

When we think of blasphemy today, irreligious profanity is lower on the list than offensive depictions of deities. We would more commonly think of the Mohammad cartoons that appeared in a Dutch newspaper, or artist Andres Serrano's "crucifix in a jar of urine" piece, entitled "Piss Christ". We don't tend to think of "taking the Lord's name into vain" as much of a crime anymore, but blasphemy was once a strong social taboo in the Western world. Until the seventeenth century this transgression was punishable by death in Britain, and usually execution by burning, as recommended by the Bible.

> And he that blasphemeth the name of the LORD, he shall surely be put to death, and all the congregation shall certainly stone him: as well the stranger, as he that is born in the land, when he blasphemeth the name of the LORD, shall be put to death.
>
> (Leviticus 24:16)

In 1697, 20-year-old Scottish student Thomas Aikenhead was the last victim of this law. He was executed by hanging on the charge of blasphemy for denying the Old Testament and Christ's miracles. Rather than being seen as blasphemy, this act might be called apostasy today.

The censorship of blasphemous words and behaviors was intended to guard against moral harm. And because it was more taboo back then, blasphemy was more common several centuries ago. The popularity of forbidden words seems commensurate with how taboo the words are. For that reason, there were more blasphemous terms in usage, and also more euphemisms to blaspheme safely. Elizabeth I favored the phrase "God's wounds", referring to the injuries suffered by Christ during the crucifixion. During her reign many minced oaths appeared, including 'swounds and zounds from that same phrase, 'sblood from "God's blood", 'sbody from "God's body" and 'sfoot, you guessed it, from "God's foot" (Allan and Burridge, 2006). Our modern equivalents include golly and gosh from "God", crikey and cripes from "Christ", and gee, jeez, and jeepers creepers from "Jesus". Without the threat of the stake these aren't used specifically as euphemisms anymore, and most people wouldn't equate these with religious names anyway.

As we can see, blasphemous terms have lost their punch. However, there are still blasphemy laws in some Western countries such as Ireland and New Zealand, whether they are exercised or not, but many are in the process of being repealed. Blasphemy laws are still common in many Islamic countries. In Saudi Arabia, Afghanistan, and Iran, blasphemy is a crime under sharia law that prescribes punishments up to the death penalty.

In heaven's name

YHWH is a four-letter word of a different kind. It is avoided, not out of fear, but out of deference. As represented in the Roman alphabet, YHWH (also YHVH or JHVH) is the name of God used in the Hebrew Bible. It is known as the Tetragrammaton, or *shem hameforash* in Hebrew. In Exodus, God reveals three names to Moses, "I am that I am", "I am", and "YHWH". The origins of YHWH are complex, but Y means "he", and HWY is connected with "being" or "becoming".

The belief that names are powerful is common in many cultures. A name is often seen as a natural connection between the word and the referent. In Christianity and Islam the name of God is invoked for the purpose of praise and prayer. To say "God" is to address God Himself. In Judaism, YHWH is believed to be the personal name of God, and for many it is a sacred word not to be spoken. Instead, titles are used that are similar to the epithets we have in English, such as *Adonai* "my Lord" and *Avinu* "our Father". In some ways, YHWH is avoided because no one is really sure how to say it! The biblical Hebrew alphabet is consonantal, that is, it is used without vowels. Diacritics known as *niqqud* are used to represent vowel sounds but appear only in modern Hebrew. The original pronunciation of YHWH has been lost, although the transliteration Yahweh is favored as a probable pronunciation of the word. This has also been anglicized to Jehovah.

YHWH is often avoided in writing too. When it must be written, abbreviations such as YH or YW are used, or two *Yods* (the tenth letter of the Hebrew alphabet). Some Jewish people afford the same respect and reverence to the English version too, and favor G-d or G'd over "God". According to Jewish belief, once written, God's name cannot be deleted or destroyed. Therefore, Jewish scribes follow a special ritual when they write divine names, and they cannot be disturbed during this procedure. When writing Torah scrolls or *tefillin* prayer boxes the author must mentally sanctify the name of God before writing it. Mistakes can't be erased. Instead, a line must be drawn around the name to cancel the error, and a new page is started. The tainted page is then stored in a *genizah*, along with worn out books containing the word God, where they all await a ritualistic cemetery burial.

You name it

The names of God, and in some cultures, the names of monarchs, VIPs, and relatives, are often avoided out of respect. However, the name of Satan is often avoided out of fear. To say the devil's name aloud is feared to somehow call upon him, draw attention to the speaker, and unleash malevolent powers. Modern language contains relics that serve as reminders of former superstitions. The proverb "Talk of the devil and he will appear" arose in the sixteenth century and was a literal warning against the apparent dangers of invoking the name of Satan, and therefore invoking Satan himself. By the eighteenth century the phrase was also used figuratively, while "Speak of the devil" is the shortened form still in common usage. There are equivalent idioms in many other languages, such as the Italian equivalent, "Talk of the Devil and the horns will appear" and the Dutch idiom, "If you speak of the devil, you step on his tail".

There is also a belief that no one knows Satan's true name, or that the true name of the devil is the name of God spelled backwards (Blake, 2010). But of course, God has many different names. Equally, the Bible refers to Satan by many names, including Beelzebub and Lucifer. The need to say "Satan" without actually saying "Satan" has led to the creation of alternative titles, such as the Prince of Darkness, Father of Lies,

Wicked One, and The Evil One. This has also led to the creation of many song titles and lyrics for rock bands! Some nicknames are more light-hearted, such as Old Nick, Old Harry, and Old Scratch. In J. K. Rowling's *Harry Potter* series, the character Voldemort is so feared that his name is tabooed. Instead, he is referred to as "You Know Who", "He who must not be named", and "the Dark Lord".

Another theory is that to know someone's real name and to speak that name is to be able to exert influence or control over them. The Egyptian Book of the Dead scrolls list the mystical names of beings we will encounter in the afterlife, as a way of giving us power over them. In some cultures, a fear of this has led to the practice of bestowing two different names to a baby: a real birth name that is kept secret, and a substitute name that is known publically. This theory is common in fiction and folklore. When gods, demons, or genies reveal their names to someone they become enslaved, and are forced to submit to the will of that person.

The best-known example is the fairy tale Rumpelstiltskin by the Brothers Grimm. In this story, a greedy king imprisons a girl because he believes she can spin straw into gold. He plans to hold her hostage until she performs this feat for him. In her despair, an imp appears and performs the trick several times in exchange for various gifts. He agrees to do it again to help free the girl, in the promise that he will receive the ultimate gift: her first-born child. The king is so impressed by the girl's apparent skill that he marries her. In due course, the couple has their first child, and the imp returns to claim his dues. The queen begs him to reconsider, and he concedes, but only if she can guess his name. He is confident that she won't be able to do so. Fortunately, one of her maidservants tracks down the imp, and overhears him singing a ditty. Here is one of the many versions.

> Today I brew, tomorrow I bake;
> And then the Prince child I will take;
> For no one knows my little game
> That Rumpelstiltskin is my name!

When the queen utters his magical name, Rumpelstiltskin is rendered powerless and he loses the bargain. There are many variants of this story, including the French imp Ricdin-Ricdon and the English version, Tom Tit Tot. Both names use the magical-sounding repetitions that we spoke about earlier.

To some, names must be kept secret because they can be used to curse or harm. On some of the curse tablets mentioned above, names would be scrambled or written backwards to produce an analogous effect on the victim (Gager, 1999). In more sympathetic magic, a name can be used as an effigy. To stab, scramble, or damage a name is to have a parallel effect on the owner of that name. In ancient Egypt, the names of gods, traitors, and usurped leaders would be erased from monuments, in an attempt to remove them from not only the historical record, but also the afterlife. The Pharaoh Tutankhamun doesn't appear on any royal lists because his successors erased his name for proscribing Egypt's traditional gods. In one Egyptian ritual, pharaohs inscribed the names of enemies on pottery bowls and smashed them (Frankfort et al., 1949). This was more than symbolic. They truly believed that to destroy the name was to destroy the actual person.

In name only

Names have also been used as cures. In a practice known as *shinnuy hashem*, a critically ill Jewish person would be given another name in an attempt to cure the illness (Jacobs, 1906). By this belief, the name represented a destiny for its owner. Bestowing someone with a new name was hoped to effectively turn them into a different person, thereby granting them a different destiny. Often, the new name would be selected randomly from the Bible, in a practice known as bibliomancy. Alternatively, an additional name was given, especially one with a meaning that would signify recovery, such as *Shalom* "peace", *Hayyim* "life", or *Raphael* "God heals" (Blake, 2010).

You can't choose your family, but you can choose a new name. Modern Wiccans and other pagans adopt a second name to separate their spiritual self from their everyday lives. This magickal or craft name is often used for ceremonies, so "Mary" only becomes "Lady Morgana" during rituals. Sometimes they use several different names, including a public name, an anonymous online name, and a secret name only shared with the gods and members of the person's coven. They choose their names based on favorite folkloric characters, or the names of herbs, stones, and animals. Sometimes they consult numerology, or claim that a spirit bestowed the name upon them in a vision or dream. The name should be selected carefully; as a chosen rather than given name it is believed to be a "true name". It is also considered acceptable to change this name as the practitioner evolves spiritually. Adopting new names is a fad for the wannabe Wiccan who watches too much television, and Sabrina becomes Willow, then Moonwoman, and so on.

In some Aboriginal Australian communities the name is such an intrinsic part of the person that it is almost considered a body part. When someone dies their name becomes taboo, and any community members with that same name will adopt a new one. This is a mark of respect, to avoid offending the spirits. It is also a fear of the possible contagious powers of the name. However, many names are common and due to the regularity of having to change their names some Aboriginal people choose unique names such as "Gerry Can", "Billy Cart", or "Vegemite".

Taboos are not only placed on names for people, deities, and entities, but also the names of animals, and especially dangerous ones like bears, wolves, and other predatory animals that pose threats to humans, livestock, and pets. These taboos reflect their origins. Fisherman in Papua New Guinea avoid talking about sharks and crocodiles, while in the northern hemisphere people fear bears, wolves, and foxes (Blake, 2010). Euphemisms are used to avoid naming these creatures. The bear is referred to as "grandfather" or "old man", while in Africa the lion is "the owner of the land", or "the great beast". Like summoning Satan accidentally, to name these feared creatures is somehow an invitation. In other languages there are "Speak of the devil"-like idioms for dangerous animals. A Croatian saying can be translated as, "When we talk about the wolf, he stands behind the door", and a Korean idiom is, "If you talk about a tiger, it will appear".

Taboos also exist for numbers considered to be unlucky. Superstitions of the number 13 still exist in the Western world, to the extent that hotels skip a 13th floor. My mother moved forward my cesarean birth to Thursday, August 12...just in case. Yet saying "thirteen" isn't a taboo, unlike saying the number four in Mandarin, Cantonese, or Japanese. In these languages, the number four and the word for death sound almost identical and are avoided. Product lines for phones skip the number four and many hotels don't label the fourth floor. Many words become tabooed by contagion, because they bear a phonetic similarity to tabooed words. This often occurs out of political correctness. "Rooster" is preferred over "cock", and "ass" for donkey has fallen out of usage. "Niggardly", "snigger" and "denigrate" have pejorated because they sound like "nigger" even though there are no etymological connections at all.

Watch your mouth!

Some words are the verbal equivalent of opening the umbrella indoors, or walking under a ladder. It's considered bad luck to change the name of a boat once it's been christened, and some athletes won't utter the name of the competing team. But the most superstitious profession seems to be the theatre. A famous theatrical taboo is to avoid saying "Macbeth", so "The Scottish Play" or "The Bard's play" are used instead. Quoting the play before a performance must likewise be avoided. If "Macbeth" is indeed said, the speaker must perform an obsessive compulsive ritual to counter the bad luck that usually involves leaving the building, spitting and cursing, then spinning around three times before going back inside the building (Garber, 1997). Alternatively, the person should recite lines from another Shakespearean play.

It is customary for actors to leave a light burning in an empty theatre and close the theatre one night each week "for the ghosts". It is also bad luck to wish someone good luck. As you probably know already, it's best to tell them to "break a leg" although that outwardly sounds like bad luck. However, many of these practices are more about preserving tradition than giving into genuine fears or beliefs. In fact, some practices have genuine practical value. It is considered bad luck to whistle in a theater but for good reason, as whistles are used as cues. An innocent whistle could accidentally initiate a curtain close or set change.

Language superstitions are not only for thespians and flakey actors, but also medical doctors. In hospitals some phrases are dirty words. Merely remarking, "things have been quiet" in emergency rooms is believed to cause or precipitate activity. If a surgeon brags, "I have never performed an unsuccessful operation" it is feared that the opposite will ensue. Uttering the magic words "knock on wood", accompanied by the gesture of physically tapping something wooden is hoped to counteract bad luck. Emergency wards are stressful environments with a random and uncontrollable workload. Researchers have found that the frequency of superstitious behavior increases under conditions of stress (Keinan, 2002). Stress reduces our sense of control, so people tend to engage in magical rituals and superstitious thinking in an attempt to regain that control.

Superstitions arise from mistaken causal connections. Even still, they can have powerful psychological effects that can affect our health. Phillips et al. (2001) found that mortality is higher on days considered to be "unlucky" among Chinese and Japanese American patients; especially those that have a "four" in them. The researchers call this the "Baskerville Effect", after Conan Doyle's *The Hound of the Baskervilles*. In this book the superstitious protagonist fears the hellhound of a legendary curse and suffers a heart attack when he believes he has encountered the monster.

Gloomy Sunday

Music stirs deep emotions in people. Rousing melodies lead people into war and bring people to tears, but some believe one song leads people to commit suicide. We're not talking about goth, emo, or death metal music, we're talking about a song written by an Hungarian poet in the 1930s. "Gloomy Sunday", which became widely known as "the Hungarian suicide song," is believed to be cursed and its melancholic lyrics are widely blamed for creating a suicide epidemic.

The suicide song

Inspired by a recent break-up with his girlfriend, László Jávor wrote the poem "Szomorú Vasárnap", meaning "sad Sunday" in Hungarian. In the story, the author mourns the death of his lover, and promises to reunite with her in the afterlife. Composer Rezso Seress wrote a haunting melody to accompany the words. It is commonly believed that the lyrics are so depressing they triggered a series of over 200 suicides worldwide during the 1930s and 1940s (Stack et al., 2008).

According to legend, suicide victims were found beside turntables playing "Gloomy Sunday", tortured people jumped into the Danube river clutching copies of the sheet music, and the lyrics were frequently quoted in suicide notes. The song affected the creators too. Jávor's ex-girlfriend poisoned herself, while Seress leaped out of the window of a building to his death. To stop the spate of suicides, radio stations across the globe banned the song. Here is an English translation of the infamous "Gloomy Sunday".

> Gloomy Sunday with a hundred white flowers
> I was waiting for you my dearest with a prayer
> A Sunday morning, chasing after my dreams
> The carriage of my sorrow returned to me without you
> It is since then that my Sundays have been forever sad
> Tears my only drink, the sorrow my bread...
> Gloomy Sunday.
>
> This last Sunday, my darling please come to me
> There'll be a priest, a coffin, a catafalque and
>   a winding-sheet
> There'll be flowers for you, flowers and a coffin

Under the blossoming trees it will be my last journey
My eyes will be open, so that I could see you for a last time
Don't be afraid of my eyes, I'm blessing you even in my death...
The last Sunday.

(Gloomy Sunday)

Surprisingly, the BBC *did* ban the song in the 1940s. These were the years before, during, and after World War II, and the song's gloomy lyrics were simply not good for morale. This ban stayed in place until 2002. No other major radio stations banned the tune. In 1941 Billie Holliday recorded "Gloomy Sunday" with different lyrics penned by Sam M. Lewis (1936), and this became the most popular version. Ironically, the original lyrics don't even mention suicide, but the rewritten version alludes to it.

Angels have no thought of ever returning you.
Would they be angry if I thought of joining you?
Sunday is gloomy, with shadows I spend it all
My heart and I have decided to end it all.

In the end

It is also true that there were many suicides in Hungary during the 1930s, but not because of the song. Statistically, Hungary has had the highest suicide rates in the world (Stack et al., 2008). Moreover, the song was released in 1933 during the years of the Great Depression, a time marked by unemployment, poverty, political unrest, famine, and depression.

Seress did indeed commit suicide, but not until 1968 when he was 69. This was some 40 years after he composed the melody. His obituary in the *New York Times* reported that he jumped out of a window in his Budapest apartment. Seress survived the incident, only to choke himself to death with a wire while in hospital. Urban legend has it that he killed himself because he thought he would never write another song to match the fame of "Gloomy Sunday". Even Ozzy Osbourne's "Suicide Solution" and the Blue Oyster Cult's "Don't Fear the Reaper" never quite achieved the fame of "Gloomy Sunday" as a suicidogenic song.

"Gloomy Sunday" could conceivably contribute to suicides among people already at risk, although there is no clear link between the song and suicide. Despite the coincidental suicide of the composer, other people associated with the song didn't commit suicide. Lou Rawls, Ray Charles, Elvis Costello, and Marianne Faithful are among the many artists who have recorded versions of "Gloomy Sunday", while millions of people have bought the song or listened to it on the radio and in movie soundtracks; all of whom have escaped its suicidal curse.

2
Divination

Many consider the magic eight-ball to be a toy, but there are still people who use it as a form of divination. Divination is an attempt to answer a question about the unknown using some kind of tool. Just about anything can and has been consulted as a device to tell the future. Some divination involves the "casting of lots", where sticks, stones, bones, beans, coins, shells, or other objects are thrown and the way they fall is interpreted as a prophetic message. Like Rorschach tests, this is about pattern interpretation, like reading candle wax or animal entrails. Some practices may be more familiar to us, such as reading coffee grounds, tea leaves, crystal balls, and other forms of scrying. The body can also be a tool for divination. Iridology is the practice of reading the eyes, and palmistry is reading lines on the hands, while graphology interprets personality through handwriting. Some people even claim to be able to read toes and bottoms.

Divination was once considered to be divine and is mentioned in the Bible, while ancient history tells us of seers and oracles. However, divination is perceived as the occult by modern religious people, and is associated with Satan. To others, divination is as innocuous as the "He loves me, he loves me not" game played with a daisy (which appears in dozens of languages). Alternatively, tarot cards and similar forms of divination are seen as spiritual, and are popularly used by psychics and other metaphysical practitioners.

While all divination involves language in the interpretation, this chapter focuses on forms that involve language as the tool, including the divination of books, speech, randomly overheard conversation, names, letters, and symbols.

The I Ching

Most people think of the I Ching as a system of divination, but the book from which it comes is an ancient Chinese philosophical text. Westerners usually know this as the Book of Changes. It is a complex and confusing system of divination. To consult the I Ching as an oracle, a burning question is asked aloud or meditated on while three coins are thrown six times to generate a number. Historically, sticks from the sacred yarrow plant were used instead of coins. The number generated corresponds to a symbol that provides a short divination text, which is interpreted as an answer to the question. This method of divination is similar to geomancy, the African Ifá, and runes.

There were eight original symbols, known as trigrams (*ba gua*), which are comprised of three horizontal broken or unbroken lines. These trigrams were developed by a man named Fu His around 3000 BCE. They represent heaven, earth, thunder, water, mountains, wind, fire, and lakes. Each has multiple meanings, denoting direction, body part, animal, and other categories. For example, *qian* features three unbroken lines and represents heaven, northwest, father, head, strong, creative, and horse. These trigrams appear a lot in modern symbolism. The South Korean flag features the heaven, water, earth, and fire trigrams, and the Vietnamese flag displays the fire trigram.

When trigrams are paired they are known as hexagrams. The complete I Ching consists of 64 hexagrams. This set of symbols show the total number of possible pairs of trigrams. Each symbol features six stacked horizontal lines of broken and/or unbroken lines. The broken lines represent *yin* (dark), and the unbroken lines represent *yang* (light), the fundamental principles in Taoist philosophy. Each symbol is numbered and has a corresponding commentary that explains its meanings.

Changes

The I Ching readings were influenced by Confucius, and indeed, they are Confucian in style. For example, "Perseverance brings good fortune" and "Undertakings bring misfortune" (Wilhelm, 1979). Confucius respected the I Ching for its philosophical value, rather than as a divination tool. In its day peasants used the I Ching for fortune telling and today it's still a popular form of divination not only in the East but also in the West.

The answers provided by the I Ching are general, allowing for multiple and ambiguous interpretations. Each symbol offers many different meanings and each line has significance. Users create their own significance and make their own personal meaning from these vague statements that can apply to anyone. However, some of the advice is obscure, and ancient Chinese idioms don't translate well to contemporary English. Some examples include, "Deliver yourself from your great toe. Then the companion comes, and him you can trust"; "A shoal of fishes. Favor comes through the court ladies", and "The companion bites his way through the wrappings. If one goes to him, how could it be a mistake?"

The I Ching is perceived as an exotic text full of wisdom. It is indeed an ancient text, but it is more an ancient version of a fortune cookie.

Rune readings

Rune readings are actually based on the I Ching, although runes themselves aren't based on hexagrams. Runes are not only a system of divination but also a writing system. There are many different runic alphabets and from the original Elder Futhark to the Cirth runes created by J. R. R. Tolkien, they are all related. Like a kind of *qwerty*, runes are traditionally known as *futhark*, named after the first six letters of the alphabet. And no, "six letters" is not a typo as *th* used to be represented by the single symbol þ, known as *thorn*.

Ruined

Runes date back to the first century CE and were the first writing system introduced to the Germanic people. In Old English *rune* means "letter". Their exact origin is disputed, although they bear a resemblance to the Roman alphabet as well as the Greek alphabet. The letters are composed mostly of straight lines and the direction of writing was once flexible so it could be written from left to right or vice versa. Word divisions aren't recognized, although dots were sometimes used to separate words. There are many extant examples of rune inscriptions related to trade and politics, grave stone carvings, love letters, and even offensive messages, like a type of ancient graffiti.

Runes also had an important role in magic and religion and in Old Germanic languages the word also means "mystery" or "secret". The letters were not created specifically for the purposes of magic, although they have the reputation today of being inherently magical. Runes were used to write prayers, chants, charms, and curses, just as people use English today to write spells or prayers.

Stories of runes used in magic are common in Old Norse literature, notably in a book called *Egil's Saga* (Svanhildur Ed. Oskarsdottir, 2004). In one story, the Viking warrior Egil Skallagrimmson arrives at the home of Helga, a Swedish peasant girl who is bedridden with a mysterious illness. Egil discovers that she has been bewitched by a misapplied runic spell that a boy carved on whalebone and placed in her bed. Egil burns the bone and writes a counter spell and the girl recovers quickly.

Runic charms and curses were written on sticks, stones, and animal bones. There are many existing examples of runic love charms: spells to attract a lover, keep a lover, bring back a lover, break up a relationship, or punish an unrequited love. In the Eddic poem "Skírnismál" if a woman rejects her suitor she is cursed with "sexual perversion, frenzy and intolerable (desire)", and to "not be able to sit still or to sleep" (MacLeod and Mees, 2006). Many love charms were as threatening and sinister as they were loving. A spell in the Icelandic spell book *Galdrabók* (Flowers, 1989) calls on Odin to afflict the victim with a range of ill-effects, from burning to rotting to freezing, "unless you love me with all your heart". There are even stories of illicit love. "Arni the priest wants to have Inga" was found on a rune-stick in a Norway church.

Runic curses called upon Thor, elves, trolls, ogres, dwarves, and valkyries to prevent theft, discover the name of a thief, or avenge a theft. There are runic curses to confine the dead to their place of burial and requests were left in tombs in the hope that the dead would enact curses on the living. There are runic curses to infect crops and livestock with disease and even to spoil someone's cooking. For those who like to look up swear words in the dictionary, a seventeenth-century Icelandic book of magic provides a curse entitled "Fart Runes". This calls for "eight As-runes, nine need-runes and thirteen ogre-runes" to plague its victim's stomach with "crapulence and wind" and "great flatulence" so that "farting may never stop, neither by day nor by night" (*Galdrabók*).

Healing charms and cure-runes were popular for exorcisms, to prevent illness, banish disease, cure infertility, offer protection from sorcery, and to trace missing people. The very act of writing was thought to cure afflictions, as shown by an inscription found on a Viking-age sheep bone, "by writing heals the crazy woman" (MacLeod and Mees, 2006). To boost their potency, charms were augmented by poetry, foreign words, and magical-sounding words.

Runic charm words were inscribed on stones and slate and worn on medals and brooches as amulets. They also appear on other objects including combs, urns, arrows, and axes. The most common individual runic charm word is *alu* although its meaning is contentious. Many commentators believe it means "ale" but it is more likely the word meant "dedication" (MacLeod and Mees, 2006). The charm words *lafru* "invocation" and *laukaz* "leek" were common too, the latter being a vegetable associated with penises, lust, and fertility in Germanic tradition.

Ruination

By the Middle Ages the runic alphabets were replaced by the Roman alphabet, although the symbols were still used for ornamental purposes. However, runes have experienced a modern revival. Far from the early runic magic of charms scratched onto sticks, runes are instead used as a system of divination known as runecasting. In their day, runes were mostly used for writing, including magical texts, but they weren't used for the purposes of divination until quite recently.

Nowadays, runes are sold as a game. The runes are carved onto wooden, metal, or plastic tiles, and kept in a pouch. The traditional futhark runes are used, in keeping with the common belief that an original form is somehow more pure, correct, or true. In modern runecasting, a question is formulated for the runes. The bag is shaken and the tiles are cast onto a cloth or on the ground, while tiles that fall face down are ignored. Alternatively, a set of tiles may be selected individually from the bag at random, like a raffle. In an early variant of this game, chickens or pre-literate children would be used to select the tiles randomly (Flint, 1991).

To read the runes a handbook is consulted. Runic letters represent sounds but they also have a symbolic value. For example, in Anglo-Saxon Futhorc, /s/ *sigel* means "sun" and /f/ *feoh* means "cattle" or "wealth". Like the I Ching hexagrams, prophetic messages are ascribed to each rune and the many guidebooks offer their own interpretations of each symbol. Often these interpretations are conflicting. Blum (1983) says that the *laguz* symbol means "flow, water, that which conducts", while Peschel (1989) states it means "intuitive knowledge", "psychic abilities", and "intelligence". For Blum, the *aggiz* symbol means "protection", while for Peschel, that's the meaning of the *eihwaz* symbol.

Like every other divination system, any reading can be made to fit any situation. Of course, the runes are never wrong. Blum talks of "runic override". That is, if it seems the reading doesn't pertain to your life, it really still does. You see, the runes are addressing a more significant issue you're avoiding, or an issue of which you're not yet aware. In truth, there are many different runic alphabets, many different runic symbols, many different meanings, and many different interpretations. Anything goes. From tea leaves to ancient alphabets, the divination tool doesn't matter. Magic is in the meaning made by us. The runic alphabets aren't any more magical than the Cyrillic, Greek, or Latin alphabets we use today.

Bibliomancy

When I was a teenager, a pastor told me that God still communicates with us today, and gave me a copy of Jack Deere's *Surprised by the Voice of God*. He told me that the book is also useful for prophecy and instructed me to, "Open the book at any page and it will answer any questions you have." Then and there I opened the book and pointed to a random paragraph. The passage read:

> When my children began to speak German, they made many grammatical errors. But they weren't embarrassed by them. They were so uninhibited, compared to me. I was so afraid to look foolish that I actually avoided conversations in German, the very thing I needed to do to learn conversational German!
>
> (Deere, 1998)

Ironically, I was learning Indonesian at the time, and I was too embarrassed to practice the language with my Indonesian-speaking friends!

Doing it by the book

Using books as crystal balls is another form of divination. The suffix -mancy means "divination" and just about anything can be divined. Hyomancy is divination of wild hogs, tiromancy is reading the coagulation of cheese, and bibliomancy is divination using books. Other names for the practice include stichomancy, *sortes sacrae* (drawing the "Holy Lots"), dipping, random reading, bible roulette, or fleecing the Bible when using the Bible to find divine answers to mortal questions. It is a kind of water-witching for written language.

Sacred texts are most often used, including scriptures from the Bible, Torah, or Qur'an. A word, phrase, or passage is chosen at random, and interpreted to predict the future, answer questions, and provide inspiration or guidance. The message is selected randomly, but the message isn't interpreted as random. It is seen as a personalized message meant for that person at that moment. It can also be interpreted as divine communication and is also known as "receiving a word from God".

Most famously, St Augustine converted to Christianity using bibliomancy. Augustine was known for living a life of wine and women, so his mother Monica and his friend Alypius encouraged him to become a good Christian boy. To appease his mom he tried reading the book. According to his autobiographical *Confessions* (Book VIII), one day he heard a mysterious voice that began chanting "Take up and read!". Well, it was in Latin so it was actually "Tolle, lege!". At first he assumed the voice came from neighboring children, but he chose to interpret the words as a command from God to read the Bible right now. He opened the copy of Paul's Epistles that he had been reading.

> I seized, opened, and in silence read that section on which my eyes first fell: Not in rioting and drunkenness, not in chambering and wantonness, not in strife and envying; but put ye on the Lord Jesus Christ, and make not provision for the flesh, in concupiscence. No further would I read; nor needed I: for instantly at the end of this sentence, by a light as it were of serenity infused into my heart, all the darkness of doubt vanished away.

Augustine had stumbled across Romans 13:13–14 which ordered the rejection of the debauchery of which he was so fond. He took this as a revelation from God and it inspired him to become a Christian. He eventually became the bishop of Hippo and even acquired sainthood. Ironically, St Augustine later condemned bibliomancy, as Leviticus (19:26) warns, "You must not practice either divination or soothsaying". Elsewhere the Bible condones bibliomancy, but makes it known who's the boss, "The lot is cast into the lap, but its every decision is from the Lord" (Proverbs 16:33).

Every trick in the book

The Bible also encourages divination of another kind. Fortuitous messages often came from invisible voices, like the revelation on Mount Sinai, "Ye heard the voice of the words, but saw no similitude; only ye heard a voice" (Deuteronomy 4:12). Some Jews believe in *Bat Kol*, "a voice from heaven". These messages allegedly came from the Holy Spirit but were usually chance words and phrases accidentally overheard from anyone speaking or reading aloud. An early Christian practice was for parishioners to listen to whatever hymn lyrics were being sung when they entered the church. These words were then interpreted as prophetic or God's will. Similarly, if a verse of scripture simply popped into the minds of the faithful, this would be considered as being presented with a revelation.

John Wesley the founder of Methodism, was a lifelong bibliomancer. He picked up the habit from the Protestant Moravian Church where the drawing of lots for decision-making was a popular tradition. Welsey became obsessive about this religious fortune telling, to the point where he couldn't decide what to eat for breakfast without consulting something. He even designed his own draw cards marked with hymn verses and was known to draw pieces of paper out of a hat to make decisions. If he didn't like the answer he chose randomly, he'd simply try again.

Scripture and hymns aren't the only texts used for bibliomancy. Historically, pagans used the *Aeneid* by the Roman poet Virgil, or the works of the Greek poet Homer, especially the *Iliad* and the *Odyssey*. Today, bibliomancy is also practiced for spiritual, occult, or artistic reasons. Theoretically, any book can be used, from dictionaries to phone books. There is a certain power about books for many and the written word seems to hold magical truths. Some people trust anything that is written. If it's in print, then it must be gospel.

Alternatively, a specific text may be used, especially one viewed as relevant to the cause. An atlas may be consulted to decide where to travel. The book may "choose" the person, if it has fallen from its bookcase. Or a book may be chosen randomly, but this may have mixed results. The English poet Robert Browning used bibliomancy to seek advice about his courtship with fellow poet Elizabeth Barrett. He was initially disappointed when he blindly selected *Cerutti's Italian Grammar* from the shelf. With his eyes closed, Browning randomly chose a page. Amazingly, his eyes fell on the sentence, "If we love in the other world as we do in this, I shall love thee to eternity" (Browning, 2010). Browning took this as prophetic and decided to marry Barrett, although the quote was just a translation exercise.

Thomas Hardy's *Far From The Maddening Crowd* mentions the English custom of bibliomancy using a Bible and a key. The Bible would be opened at random and the key dangled over a Bible like a pendulum. In the book the heroine Bathsheba tries to divine the identity of her future husband, with disastrous results. This method was also used to find out the names of wrong doers. For example, a key was dangled over a Bible while reciting the names of suspected thieves and would move when the correct person was named. Rather than being a divine answer, this is an unconscious muscular reaction known as the ideomotor effect.

There are many different techniques for bibliomancy. Typically, a book is opened to a random page and the first passage read is interpreted in a prophetic manner. Sometimes the book is placed on its spine and allowed to fall open at a random page, and then a passage is picked. But the procedure isn't always random. Books tend to fall open where they've been opened frequently in the past. Many people like to close their eyes during the process and then be guided by the first words they see. Some people jab the book with their finger, or allow a finger to rifle through the pages and lines until they "sense" that it's time to stop. Sometimes the page is determined by rolling dice or using another type of randomizer.

An "accurate" reading is all in the interpretation. As in my own experiences above, coincidence is at play. Every time I divined that book I was able to relate each random reading to my life, either directly or indirectly. Many of us have had the experience of breaking up with a partner, then hearing lovelorn ballads on every radio station. Relevance can be drawn from any situation, and any word, phrase, or passage can be forced to fit. But our decision-making should be done with intelligence. Life is a "choose your own adventure", whereas bibliomancy allows an arbitrary process to do the choosing for you.

3
Prediction

Divination always requires a tool, such as runes or a copy of the Bible, but prediction doesn't always require a prop. Prediction can be all in the mind. In this same way, accuracy is in the eye of the beholder and some psychics tend to predict things that are already known. This chapter looks at the prophecies attributed to Mother Shipton, the postdictions of Nostradamus, and the story of Edgar Cayce, the "sleeping prophet" who was believed to have the ability to fall asleep on a book and absorb its contents.

Mother Shipton

Ursula Southeil, better known as Mother Shipton, is England's answer to Nostradamus. Like the humble birth of Jesus born in a manger, Mother Shipton was born in a cave in 1488. Known as Mother Shipton's Cave, in Knaresborough, North Yorkshire, the cave and a nearby petrifying well are popular tourist attractions to this day.

The mother of all seers

The stereotype of the old crone, Mother Shipton was said to be hideously ugly. The Mother Shipton moth (*Callistege mi*) is named after her, for the Rorschach-like witch shape that appears on each wing. However, she was comely enough to entice carpenter Toby Shipton, who became her husband. Mother Shipton led the life of a wise woman, selling spells and herbal remedies, but she was best known for her ability to predict the future. She is believed to have predicted many major events, including the Great Fire of London in 1666, the English defeat of the Spanish Armada, and the invention of cars and airplanes.

Mother Shipton's prophecies were filled with confusing riddles and rhymes, apparently to protect her from the stake. However, these visions were not published until 1641, some 80 years after her death. Instead of predicting the future she was predicting the past, or rather, other people were predicting it for her. Modern events were forced to fit her predictions retroactively. These were not predictions, but postdictions, made after the fact. The following passage taken from "Mother Shipton's Prophecy" is said to predict cars, modern ships, hot air balloons, telephones, satellites, and the internet.

> Carriages without horses shall go,
> And accidents fill the world with woe.
> Around the world thoughts shall fly
> In the twinkling of an eye.
> The world upside down shall be
> And gold be found at the root of a tree.
> Through hills man shall ride,
> And no horse be at his side.
> Under water men shall walk,
> Shall ride, shall sleep, shall talk.
> In the air men shall be seen,
> In white, in black, in green;
> Iron in the water shall float,
> As easily as a wooden boat.

> (Bogg, 1894)

Mother Shipton is also known as a doomsday prophetess. Here is the most famous couplet attributed to her:

> The world to an end shall come,
> In eighteen hundred and eighty one.

> (Charles Hindley, *Notes and Queries*, 1873)

Searing insight?

That was another Armageddon prediction that didn't happen. However, in taking a closer look at the writing style, it reads suspiciously like mock medieval English rather than Tudor English. It turns out that Mother Shipton's famous predictions were not her predictions at all. These prophecies were said to be "Published in 1448, republished in 1641".

In reality, they first appeared in 1873. Mother Shipton didn't pen these words, they were fabricated by Victorian writer Charles Hindley.

The story of Mother Shipton's life and times is reconstructed from a book written by Richard Head in 1677 with the catchy title, *The life and death of Mother Shipton being not only a true account of her strange birth and most important passages of her life, but also all her prophesies.* According to Head, the seer was born to a woman named Agnes Shipton (who strangely had the same last name as Mother Shipton's future husband). Mother Shipton's father was Satan. But Satan didn't want to live in sin, so he married Agnes and promised her great powers and riches, on one condition. She must utter the magical words: *Raziel ellimiham irammish zirigai Psonthonphanchia Raphael elhaveruna tapinotambecaz mitzphecat jarid cuman hapheah Gabriel Heydonturris dungeonis philonomostarkes sophecord hankim.* The story becomes even more psychedelic from here, so we can't really take this as an accurate account.

Over the centuries, almanacs, pamphlets, and books have fabricated the history and predictions of Mother Shipton. Many books have then repeated these legends, so no one knows what is fact and what is fiction anymore. Mother Shipton's life is folklore, and like King Arthur and Robin Hood, no one even knows if she ever existed.

Nostradamus

French seer Michel de Nostradamus (1503–66) lived in the sixteenth century although he is today's most famous prophet. In the time of the Protestant Reformation, the expansion of the Ottoman Empire, and the exploration of the New World, Nostradamus allegedly predicted major contemporary events, including the rise of Adolf Hitler, the Apollo moon landing, both world wars, and the September 11, 2001 terrorist attacks.

Despite what my spellcheck thinks, Nostradamus began his life as "Nostredame", before Latinizing his name. He worked as an apothecary, although he was a frustrated physician, not that there was much of a difference between the two in those days. He wrote *Traité des fardemens et confitures*, a book of remedies and recipes that includes instructions on how to prepare jam, tooth cleaning powders, a beauty cream (that contained mercury), and a cure for plague. Clearly, Nostradamus had no success in treating plague, because he lost both his wife and child to the scourge.

He wrote an almanac of predictions for 1550 that was so well received that he penned annual versions until his death. However, his posthumous bestseller is the 1555 *Les Prophecies de M. Nostradamus*, a book of almost 1,000 predictions. These are all structured as four-line rhyming verses known as quatrains. Even though he preferred not to present himself as a prophet, for fear of the Inquisition, he enjoyed great success as a seer. He even secured the support of Catherine de Medici when he predicted a glorious future for her husband, Henri II of France. However, his predictions had to be reinterpreted to account for the king's untimely death in 1559. Nostradamus's predictions have been reinterpreted selectively ever since.

Turning a prophet

One of the most persistent claims is that Nostradamus predicted the rise of Adolf Hitler and the Third Reich. This appears to have begun when Nazi propaganda minister Joseph Goebbels developed an interest in Nostradamus's prophecies. Astrology was outlawed at that time, but Goebbels had an agenda. In what sounds like a plot for a spy movie, Swiss astrologer Karl Ernst Krafft was enlisted to decipher the prophecies with a pro-German bias. Cleverly, he unearthed the following quatrain.

> Bêtes farouches de faim fleuves tranner;
> Plus part du champ encore Hister sera,
> En caige de fer le grand sera treisner,
> Quand rien enfant de Germain observa.

> (II.24)

Krafft translated *"Hister"* as a code word for "Hitler", and *"Germain"* as "Germany". Propaganda pamphlets quoted this passage and others as predictions of the emergence of Hitler, and the success of the German army. However, this translation is inaccurate. *"Hister"* refers to the Lower Danube, a geographical region, rather than a person, while *"Germain"* refers to a person, "brother (in God)", but not a country. Randi (1995) provides a more accurate translation.

> Beasts mad with hunger will swim across rivers,
> Most of the army will be against the Lower Danube.
> The great one shall be dragged in an iron cage
> When the child brother will observe nothing.

These deliberate mistranslations have left a long legacy of belief. Both the modern fascination with Nostradamus, and claims of the accuracy of his predictions, can be attributed to this World War II propaganda tactic.

In a strange postscript of counter clairvoyance, Hungarian-born astrologer Louis de Wohl was recruited by the British army for their Special Operations Executive. This was a sabotage section typically known for assisting resistance groups and blowing up bridges. As a tool of psychological warfare and in an effort to boost public morale, "Captain" de Wohl invented a series of Nostradamus quatrains that prophesized an Allied victory (Winter, 2006). De Wohl's predictions were far more accurate. He compared Hitler's strategies to the errors made by Napoleon and foretold that Hitler would ultimately fail too.

Nostradamus' quatrains have also been interpreted as predicting the life and times of the French Emperor. It is said they reference Napoleon as the first of three warmongering Antichrists. Hitler is considered to be the second. This leaves room for a third (unless you believe the current Antichrist is Johnny Rotten, as sung in the Sex Pistols' "Anarchy in the UK"). The title of "third Antichrist" has been awarded to Saddam Hussein, Osama Bin Laden, Vladimir Putin, and Kim Jong-il, or whichever foreign political figure is the current enemy of the United States.

The end of the world as we know it

Nostradamus is also considered a doomsday prophet. Quatrain 72 is unique in that it names a specific month and year. Therefore, this was taken to be the date of Armageddon.

> The year 1999, seventh month,
> from the sky will come a great King of Terror
> To bring back to life the Great King of the Mongols.
> Before and after Mars to reign by good luck.

> (Nostradamus, 1555)

The year 1999 was feared to herald the end of the world, even though the quatrains make predications up to the year 3797. Doomsayers believed that an asteroid, alien invasion, nuclear weapon, or natural disaster would destroy the earth in 1999. They sat out the seventh month living in fear, in accordance with the Julian and Hebrew calendars, just in case. When the world didn't end, the passage was reinterpreted to predict retrospectively the death of John F. Kennedy Jr in a plane crash in July 18, 1999.

Following the September 11, 2001, terrorist attacks on the World Trade Center, quatrains were "discovered" that allegedly foretold the events.

> In the year of the new century and nine months,
> From the sky will come a great King of Terror...
> The sky will burn at forty-five degrees.
> Fire approaches the great new city...
> In the city of York there will be a great collapse,
> 2 twin brothers torn apart by chaos
> While the fortress falls the great leader will succumb
> Third big war will begin when the big city is burning.

> (Hitchcock, 2002)

This was a hoax, but only one of many versions of a chain email that circulated the internet. The verses were written in the style of Nostradamus but there were a few clues that it was a prank. The year is suspicious because the only time Nostradamus named a month and year was in the "King of Terror" quatrain, and this phrase was clearly stolen for the hoax. It seems the prank was created to make meaning of the chaos of 9/11, as though there was a sign or omen all along. Interestingly, the verse didn't begin as a hoax. It was written by student Neil Marshall as part of an essay to illustrate how Nostradamus's quatrains are so cryptic they can be taken to mean anything (Wilson, 2003).

The prophecies of historical oracles, soothsayers, seers, shamen, and other fortune tellers are typically cryptic. The Delphic Oracle uttered prophecies in a kind of speaking in tongues while we have seen that Mother Shipton's prophecies were written in riddles and rhymes. These techniques gave the prophecies an air of magic and mystery, while explicit prophecy runs the risk of being disproved. Nostradamus's predictions are so vague they are nearly impossible to falsify. He had a plausible excuse for this ambiguity, to avoid persecution by the Inquisition and the French government. However, for someone avoiding persecution he had a very public profile as consultant to the queen.

Nostradamus's quatrains are so stylistic their value today is only as poetry. They are encoded in cryptic rhymes written in a mishmash of sixteenth-century French, sixteenth-century French dialect Provençal, and classical Latin and Greek. They are further obscured by abbreviations, anagrams, and metaphor. There is evidence that his book plagiarizes and paraphrases the Bible, historical texts including works by Livy and Plutarch, and various books of astrology (Lemesurier, 2010). Of course, these were the days before plagiarism laws, and authors often copied material without acknowledgement. Scholars now believe that Nostradamus also used bibliomancy to select these borrowed verses for his prophecies.

Nostradamus' original work no longer exists, and due to printing conventions of the time, no two editions were identical. Over the centuries there have been hundreds of editions and thousands of commentaries, with wide variances in his biography and prophecies. The hodgepodge of languages, sources, and stylistic quirks are further scrambled by translations of translations, mistranslations, and the subjective interpretations of contemporary writers and readers who twist and contort the verses to force-fit them to the modern world. There are heated debates and disagreement over the analyses, and fanatics use numerical codes to decipher and further distort his writings. The prophecies are the very worst example of the telephone game.

Prophet or profit?

Nostradamus' prophecies have been attributed to predict every significant historical event since his death. For nineteenth-century people, Nostradamus predicted the assassination of Abraham Lincoln, and for twentieth-century people, the same passage predicted the assassination of John F. Kennedy. Like Mother Shipton's prophecies, the predictions are really postdictions – prophecies that are attributed to past events retroactively. These retroactive prophecies don't tell the future, they tell the past. The future is as uncertain as it's always been, but one thing is certain, this medieval prophet still turns a profit today.

Edgar Cayce

Many people fall asleep reading and can't remember what they just read, but some believe they can fall asleep on a book and absorb the book's contents while they sleep. It's like subliminal learning without the learning. Edgar Cayce was a psychic who was best known for being a medical intuitive, that is, having the alleged ability to diagnose disease using psychic powers. Cayce's technique was unique in that he performed his psychic readings in a trance state. For this reason he was known as the sleeping prophet. Cayce's channeling is discussed in Chapter 9, but here we look at another talent he had in his sleep. It was believed that Cayce could fall asleep on a book and when he awoke, he would knew what it said inside.

Sleeping on the job

The story began one day when Cayce misspelled "cabin" in class and was forced to write the word 500 times on the blackboard as punishment.

> That night, even more than usual, he seemed unable to concentrate on his lessons. There was an invisible barrier between him and his book. But his father had told him he would have to stay up until he had his lesson. At eleven o'clock, long past his bedtime, as his head nodded drowsily, he heard a voice within himself, as in a dream. It was the voice of the previous afternoon. It kept repeating, "Sleep, and we may help you."
>
> He fell asleep for a few minutes. And when he awakened, as absurd as it may seem, he knew every word by rote in that particular spelling book. He had slept on it.
>
> (Stearn, 1989)

The belief that people can sleep speed read has been around for awhile. An old theatrical superstition is that sleeping with a script under their pillow will help actors learn their lines faster. This is also known as "learning by diffusion", the ability to absorb information magically or subliminally. Subliminal learning is the claim that we can learn, stop smoking, or lose weight by listening to tapes as we sleep. Cayce's sleep-reading differs in that there is no communication of the information on any level. As we saw in Chapter 1, a common cure for headaches was to use a copy of the Gospel of St John as a pillow. There is also the hundredth monkey effect. Scientists in Koshima, Japan, observed a group of macaques monkeys learn to wash sweet potatoes. They believed that once a critical number of monkeys had learned the behavior, the so-called hundredth monkey, the behavior instantly spread across all monkeys (Watson, 1979).

There are many legends surrounding Cayce, including the claims that he was illiterate and uneducated. The *New York Times* (1910) is greatly responsible for the illiteracy myth with their profile of Cayce entitled, "Illiterate Man Becomes a Doctor when Hypnotized". However, there is no evidence that Cayce could fall asleep on a book and awaken knowing its contents. Johnson (1998) reveals that the story doesn't appear in

Cayce's own memoirs, it is only told by Cayce's biographers. It seems that this is yet another myth designed to maintain the mystique of the sleeping prophet.

Almanacs

Before the days of modern meteorology, people relied on almanacs for long-range weather forecasts. Various versions have been in existence since Babylonian times, when astronomers produced tables to predict planetary phenomena. As we saw above, Nostradamus also wrote a series of almanacs featuring his prophecies. In recent modern history, almanacs were as common a sight as the Bible in the homes of farmers, whose livelihoods depended on the seasons. They were also popular as a sort of *Reader's Digest*, as they contained calendars, handy hints, recipes, puzzles, poems, and serialized stories.

Adopting the pseudonym "Richard Saunders", Benjamin Franklin published *Poor Richard's Almanack* from 1732 until 1758. This pseudonym was taken from the author of the *Apollo Anglicanus*, which had been a popular London almanac the century before. The almanac was a bestseller of its day and was famous for Franklin's aphorisms and proverbs. Since they were captured in print, much of this folk wisdom lives on in contemporary English, including, "Early to bed and early to rise, makes a man healthy, wealthy and wise" and "He that lies down with Dogs, shall rise up with fleas" (Franklin, 1999).

Today, almanacs are still published worldwide although most are encyclopedic rather than books of prediction. However, two weather almanacs have survived into modern times in the United States. The *Old Farmer's Almanac* has been produced out of Dublin, New Hampshire, since 1792, and its rival *The Farmers' Almanac* has been published in Lewiston, Maine, since 1818. It's difficult enough to predict the weather for the week ahead, but these two almanacs claim amazingly accurate long-range weather predictions for the year ahead. Both publications still sell millions of copies annually, although they are more likely to be used to plan a vacation than to sow a crop of radishes.

Meteorology is naturally about prediction, but some kinds of prediction are more accurate than others. Modern scientists use super computers and advanced weather modeling, while almanacs put the paranormal back in the phrase "weather prediction". The *Old Farmer's Almanac* uses a "secret method" to generate its forecasts, devised by the publication's first editor, Robert Thomas.

Based on his observations, Thomas used a complex series of natural cycles to devise a secret weather forecasting formula, which brought uncannily accurate results, traditionally said to be 80 percent accurate. (Even today, his formula is kept safely tucked away in a black tin box at the Almanac offices in Dublin, New Hampshire).

(*Old Farmer's Almanac*)

The *Farmers' Almanac* forecaster, who is only known by the pseudonym Caleb Weatherbee, uses a "top secret mathematical and astronomical formula, that relies on sunspot activity, tidal action, planetary position and many other factors". These mysterious methods seem to be the 11 herbs and spices of weather forecasting.

Almanacs offer an awkward mix of science and superstition. They provide factual astronomical information about moon phases alongside spurious astrological claims. They still offer gardening tips, recipes for comfort food, and teach you how to clean the toilet with Coca-Cola and keep fleas away from your dog naturally. Sticking to their roots of prediction, they provide the "best days" to cut hair to increase growth, to quit smoking, apply for a loan, or shop for clothes. They're also full of curious classifieds: advertisements for charms, blessed holy water, and love potions; while Sister Sally and Mother Thompson will "remove evil influences", "reunite lovers", and "solve all problems" (*Old Farmer's Almanac*, 2012).

Unforeseen circumstances

The almanacs claim to have made some amazing predictions in the past. The *Old Farmer's Almanac* says it made a "near-perfect prediction" of Florida's Hurricane Andrew in 1992. They did indeed predict a "possible hurricane south" for August 30–31, although the destructive hurricane struck on August 24. At any rate, southern Florida is hit by hurricanes most years, which occur in August or September (Sherden, 1998). The same publication brags, "Skeptics can laugh, but there have been several miraculous predictions, including the July snow of 1816, which was forecast in a few errant copies." However, this most astonishing prediction was an unforeseen circumstance. The absurd forecast for New England on July 13, 1816 predicted, "rain, hail and snow". This was a prank pulled by a copy boy when editor Thomas fell ill. Upon his recovery, he destroyed most of the copies in horror. Ironically, the 1815 eruption of Mount Tambora in the East Indies brought about an episode of freak weather. A cooling dust cloud caused a "Little Ice Age" in New England that summer, during which ponds and lakes froze over and never thawed. When the unlikely "forecast" came true, Thomas reclaimed the prediction and announced, "I told you so!" (Sherden, 1998). A wag might joke that almanacs are so accurate they can even "change" the weather.

Both almanacs report an accuracy rate of 75–80 per cent. In fact, they have a dubious track record and in relying on historical norms they fare no better than chance at predicting weather. When they're too specific they run the risk of exposure. The *Old Farmer's Almanac*'s forecast of a particularly perilous winter for 1994 led to a panic that drove up the sales of snow blowers, snow shovels, four-wheel drives, and rock salt for use on highways. When it arrived, the winter of 1994 was especially warm (Sherden, 1998). Short-term weather predictions are always more accurate and right now the weather can't be predicted a year ahead. However, there are worse methods. Some still swear by the accuracy of onion calendars and reading pig spleens to predict the weather.

The *Old Farmer's Almanac* and *The Farmers' Almanac* have been predicting the weather inaccurately for over 200 years, but that hasn't dampened their popularity. There is plenty of anecdotal evidence that almanacs are accurate, from those who swear they provide the best times to catch fish, plant potatoes, or select a wedding date. Almanac readers are nostalgic for this piece of Americana from its colonial days. People also have a fondness for the mystery and secrecy surrounding the weather predictions of almanacs. They like the story of the simple man who outperforms the snotty scientists with their fancy equipment and degrees, while meteorology is subject to stereotypes that the TV weatherperson is always wrong. In the end, almanacs perform no better than chance in predicting the weather. It is safe to say that weather almanacs are indeed accurate...weather permitting.

4
Prayer

A prayer is a request made to an object of worship. The word comes from the fourteenth-century French *priere*, "to obtain by entreaty", although the modern meaning doesn't imply that the petition has been granted. Any expression of hope, desire, or intention made in thought, speech, singing, or writing can loosely be called a prayer, even if a divine entity isn't invoked. But in its most salient sense, praying presupposes belief in a higher power that exerts influence over the external world, and that by way of prayer, we can effect change magically in our own lives.

Prayer has pagan roots. Pagan charms were precursors to prayer, and as we saw in Chapter 1, there was a lot of overlapping between pagan and Christian rituals. When Christianity spread throughout Europe, pagan charms were gradually replaced in popularity by Christian prayers (Blake, 2010). Nowadays, most people don't think of prayers as spells, but they are. Prayers are simply spells that aren't sacrilegious.

Today, there are lots of different ways to say your prayers. They're not just said in church or kneeling by the bedside. This chapter explores traditional prayer and not-so-traditional prayer, including prayer online, prayer by mail, prayer by classifieds, and affirmations – the prayers you pray when you think you're not praying.

Intercessory prayer

Prayer can be petitionary, when people pray for themselves as the hopeful beneficiary, or intercessory, when they pray for others. People pray for the health, wealth, protection, and salvation of themselves, family, and friends. As a kind of spiritual intervention they also pray for strangers – missing people, soldiers at war, victims of natural disasters, firefighters, police, presidents, and countries. Prayer can be urgent, to receive rain during drought, or frivolous, for the local football team to win. Whatever the petitioner prays for, they always think their God is on their side. Prayers don't invariably ask for something; sometimes they give thanks, praise, or daily blessings, such as grace said before tucking into your meat and three veg, or the vespers and vigils of Catholicism.

Billions of people pray to many different deities under the flag of many diverse religions. Praying seems to be a universal practice across belief systems. It is the primary form of communication between the deity and the devout. Presumably, Christian prayers are equally as effective as Buddhist or Islamic prayers. Whether God, Allah, Odin, the universal life force, or the flying spaghetti monster, the name of a higher power is usually invoked to address the prayer to, and empower the intent. Everyone prays in their own way but some believe that the prayer should not be mechanical. For the prayer to be truly effective the act must be full of fervor and preferably spoken aloud. Alternatively, the prayer can be internal and reflective, like a moment of silence.

Prayer is an internal or external one-way conversation although the person praying believes that someone is listening. They also expect an answer. Higher powers are believed to "reply" to prayer by getting us that job, or making that late mortgage payment. Some believe that God speaks in a metaphorical sense via His creations of nature. Others believe that God literally talks back, through dreams, visions, and prophecies.

Testing God

Are prayers answered or not? Some maintain that prayer can't be tested because God can't be tested. The Bible warns, "You shall not put the Lord your God to the test" (Deuteronomy 6:16). If God can intervene then He can choose to accept or reject prayers without accountability. After all, it would be impossible to double-blind an all-seeing, all-powerful God. However, one of the most common prayers is for healing. In fact, prayer is the most popular complementary medicine. Beyond the whims of a capricious God, some of the alleged therapeutic benefits of prayer *are* testable. We can measure the effects of healing prayer, or lack thereof.

Francis Galton was the first person to research the effects of prayer in 1872. In a partly satirical study, Galton hypothesized that the British royal family would live longer than other members of the population, given that their well-being was prayed for by millions of people in church every Sunday. In comparing the longevity of sovereigns to clergy, lawyers, scientists, doctors, aristocracy, and gentry, Galton concludes,

The sovereigns are literally the shortest lived of all who have the advantage of affluence. The prayer has therefore no efficacy, unless the very questionable hypothesis be raised, that the conditions of royal life may naturally be yet more fatal, and that their influence is partly, though incompletely, neutralised by the effects of public prayers.

A number of well-known modern studies support the beneficial effects of prayer. That is, at first glance. Randolph Byrd (1988) measured the effects of healing prayer on 192 patients with heart disease. A team of born-again Christians were assigned to a prayer group, and "each inter-cessor was asked to pray daily for a rapid recovery and for prevention of complications and death". In six different categories, the prayer group showed a small improvement over the control group. They needed fewer antibiotics and fewer developed heart failure and pneumonia. So, the study concluded, "intercessory prayer to the Judeo-Christian God has a beneficial therapeutic effect in patients admitted to a coronary care unit".

But the researchers were living on a prayer. There were positive differences in six categories, but these were the results of chance. However, in the other 20 categories there were no significant differences, including mortality, despite the explicit prayers for the prevention of death (Posner, 1990). In this study about prayer, prayer itself was not controlled for, "It was assumed that some of the patients in both groups would be prayed for by people not associated with the study; this was not controlled for... Therefore, 'pure' groups were not attained in this study."

Say your prayers

A study lead by Fred Sicher and Elisabeth Targ (1998) included only 40 subjects, but became "widely acknowledged as the most scientifically rigorous attempt ever to discover if prayer can heal" (Bronson, 2002). Twenty patients with AIDS received prayers from Christian, Jewish, Buddhist, Native American, and Hindu healers who were instructed to "direct an intention for health and well-being" towards the subjects. Incredibly, the results revealed that, after a six-month period, those who were prayed for had significantly fewer AIDS-related illnesses, less frequent hospitalizations, and fewer visits to the doctor.

On the basis of the sensational-sounding results, Targ received a grant for additional studies, including the effects of distant healing on *glioblastoma multiforme*, the most common and aggressive type of malignant brain tumor. Ironically, during the study, Targ was diagnosed with this very condition. As a pro-prayer researcher she became the patron saint of prayer. Her many followers prayed for her recovery, convinced that if anyone could be healed through prayer, it would be her. Despite being the most prayed for person on earth Targ died less than four months later.

Her research was discredited posthumously. The original goal of her famous study was to measure mortality rates following distant healing. During the testing, triple-drug anti-retroviral therapy began increasing the longevity of AIDs sufferers, but instead of reporting this fact, the researchers did some data mining. On a wing and a prayer, they found another seemingly statistically significant result and reported on that instead. This is known as the Texas sharpshooter fallacy – to draw spurious correlation after the fact. The name comes from the story of a shooter who sprays bullets randomly, then draws a bulls-eye around them.

Another infamous study discovered that women who were prayed for when undergoing in vitro fertilization treatments experienced a double success rate of pregnancy (50 per cent) (Cha et al., 2001). However, the study soon turned into a scandal. Author Kwang Cha had an ulterior motive – he was revealed to operate fertility clinics around Korea. Co-author Daniel Worth was a parapsychologist, not a medical doctor, who was later arrested by the FBI and pled guilty to mail fraud and theft. Finally, the study's apparent leader, Dr Rogerio Lobo, denied participating in the study and withdrew his name from the published findings (Flamm, 2005).

Sloan et al. (1999) reveals that prayer studies are marred by flawed methodologies, bad statistics, no controls, replication problems, data mining, selection bias, and test groups too small to draw conclusions. Prayer researchers often don't account for variables such as the participant's age, sex, ethnicity, socioeconomic situation, and health status. For example, one study claims that people who attend church are healthier, but the researchers didn't realize that sick people are less likely to attend church anyway (Comstock and Tonascia, 1977).

When the studies are conducted under properly controlled conditions, the claims haven't got a prayer. In 2006, Benson et al. undertook the "Great Prayer Experiment". After undergoing coronary bypass graft surgery, 1,800 patients across six different hospitals were involved in an experiment to test the effects of intercessory prayer. The patients were assigned to one of three different groups: an experimental or a control group who were told they may or may not receive prayer, and a group who received prayer after being informed that they would receive prayer.

Starting the night before surgery, daily prayer was provided for two weeks by parishioners from three different Christian churches. Only the first names and last initials of the patients were supplied, without photographs. Those doing the praying were allowed to pray in their own way using their own words, but were instructed to include the following phrase in their prayers: "for a successful surgery with a quick, healthy recovery and no complications". The patients were monitored for 30 days after the surgery.

The results showed that major events and mortality were the same across groups, and that prayer did not ensure complication-free recovery from surgery. There was no evidence to indicate the healing effects of prayer. However, something strange happened in the group who knew they were receiving prayer. These people suffered a higher incidence of complications, such as abnormal heart rhythms. They seemed to experience additional stress in knowing they were being prayed for, in what the researchers called prayer "performance anxiety". People usually say "I'll pray for you" and "You'll be in my prayers" when the situation is hopeless.

Knowing you are being prayed for often helps, if you're a believer. Prayer can have a placebo effect, that is, psychosomatic benefits that aren't any different to sugar pills. Prayer can be psychologically beneficial. It can be comforting, empowering, and can function as a coping mechanism. As for those who pray for relationships to heal or wars to end, prayer helps those who help themselves. We can only make changes in the external world through doing, not hoping. As the Dalai Lama (1999) said, "Change only takes place through action, not through meditation and prayer."

These arguments probably won't convince those who believe in the power of prayer. Perhaps believers and non-believers will never meet eye to eye, because they don't meet brain to brain. Studies have shown that religious and atheist brains exhibit differences. Religious brains exhibit higher levels of dopamine, and people who've had "born again" experiences exhibit a smaller hippocampus than atheists, but larger frontal lobes. Researchers are unsure if these physiological factors cause people to be religious or if being religious triggers these changes (Newburg, 2012). In magnetic resonance imaging tests of religious people, thinking about God, or prayer, activates the same parts of the brain as thinking about an airplane, a friend, or a lamp post. Perhaps prayer is just about perception. In the brain of the religious person, God is as real as an object or a person.

Online prayer

The internet offers unique ways to communicate with deities in the digital age. Prayer requests were once deposited into prayer boxes at church and stuck to cork boards. Now they're posted online as e-prayers. Prayer boards are a way to email God. The prayer box was a confidential way to submit prayers to a family-like congregation. Submissions to electronic prayer boards are anonymous but they are public, and prayer requests are often syndicated on Twitter and Facebook to increase their audience.

Emailing God

Whether they are made in writing or speech, or they're just thoughts, prayers are believed to cause changes in the external world. However, people believe that written and spoken prayer makes the thought real and concrete, making for a powerful combination. This power is intensified when other people, especially pious strangers in the virtual congregation of millions, also pray for the petitions. Requesting the prayer online is considered the prayer itself. The faithful send their hopes out into the ether by clicking "enter", like making a wish and throwing a coin into a well, or blowing out the candles on a birthday cake.

Personal prayers are free but there are thousands of free prayer boards and some people are preyed on for prayer. The Christian Prayer Center has turned prayer into a business and makes their flock pay for prayer.

> Local churches and small group prayer lists have been a wonderful way to share the blessings of prayer, but these methods are limited in their ability to rally the true power of thousands of voices all praying in agreement for a single request. The Internet has enabled us to build a massive congregation to lift your prayer requests to a whole new level.
>
> (Christian Prayer Center)

To request prayer, the person is asked, "Do you believe in what the Bible tells us about prayer?" and, "Do you have faith in God to answer this prayer request?". Of course, they are expected to click "yes" in response. They are then asked to rate the level of importance of their request. Finally, they are asked how much they will give to the Center in exchange for the posting of their prayer request. This begging is bolstered with scripture and guilt.

> Give, and it will be given to you. For with the measure you give, it will be measured to you in God's gifts.
>
> (Luke 6:38)

The Bible tells us repeatedly that the most important way to have our prayers answered is to have faith, and give with overwhelming generosity. Give when times are tough, give when it does not seem that giving is possible, and God will reward your faith with His generosity in answering your important prayers quickly.

Terms like "gift", "offer", and "donation" imply that it's something given without payment in return, rather than a service. Although for some people, paying probably increases the perceived value of the prayer, especially since the company claims that for a fee, "thousands" will provide the "strongest prayer". But they don't pay those who actually do the praying.

If you don't elect to donate, you won't receive prayer, and the following prompt appears: "I'm sorry, but we cannot post your request without an offering. There are too many in need of powerful prayer at this time, so we can only broadcast requests that have made a seed offering." This is known as a "seed-faith" ministry, where donations are considered "seeds" that grow in return for the donor, who is promised blessings, healing, miracles, and wealth. This is another kind of prosperity church. To prove that their prayers are effective they offer testimonials from satisfied customers. These are all stories of unspecified fortune:

> Our lives went from awful to wonderful in so many ways thanks to your powerful prayers for us. Thanks for your continued blessings!

These are businesses, not churches. They are operated out of garages and laptops, not places of worship. The websites display stock photos of churches and congregations. The virtual congregation is made up of those who request the prayers and those who do the praying. But what *is* real are the prayer requests: Betty has stage IV cancer. Nancy was hospitalized for suicidal thoughts. Brett is addicted to cocaine, and Tom can't pay his mortgage. If the prayer doesn't work, the person is blamed. Clearly, they didn't "believe in what the Bible tells us about prayer", or they didn't "have faith in God to answer" their prayer request. Paid prayer preys on the vulnerable.

Direct mail prayer

One day I was visiting Mission San Miguel, one of the churches set up by the Spanish Franciscan Catholics in California. Parked outside the dilapidated building, I noticed a small tithing box, presumably to collect donations for a restoration fund. The small box was painted black with a white cross and sealed with a padlock. Soon, a man appeared on the lonely road. He sauntered up to the box, stuck his hand into the opening and pulled out the small amount of cash inside. He quickly thrust the money into his pocket and went on his way.

Whether for the steeple fund or donations for the poor, churches raise funds by passing around the collection tray on Sundays and hoping no one burglarizes the donation box. Just as the prayer box has evolved into the online prayer board, the donation box has gone electronic with PayPal donations.

False prophets

Direct mail donation is still common too but not all campaigns are legitimate. Mail order churches send letters that address us intimately yet distantly as "Resident", "Friend", or "Occupant". They contain crosses, rosaries, statues, medallions, and blessed oil. These items have allegedly touched the relics of saints or been prayed over, despite the fact that they are plastic, mass-produced trinkets. To dodge the illegality of asking for money for nothing, donations are solicited in exchange for these unsolicited "gifts".

One such campaign is the "Jesus eyes prayer rug" that St Matthew's Churches "loans" to millions of people who never asked to borrow it in the first place. The "rug" is just a sheet of paper, featuring a Shroud-like depiction of Jesus with closed eyes. A tear falls from his right eye, and a crown of thorns sits on his head. The letter instructs you to:

> Look into Jesus' Eyes (and) you will see they are closed. But as you continue to look you will see His eyes opening and looking back into your eyes. Then go and be alone and kneel on this Rug of Faith or touch it to both knees. Then please check your needs on our letter to you. Please return this Prayer Rug. Do not keep it.

Like a pious magic eye puzzle, it is an optical illusion for the eyes to "look" back at you. But this isn't a typical church that will pray for your spiritual welfare. St Matthew's Churches will pray for your riches, if you make them rich in return. Testimonials written by J. B., A. R. F., and other anonymous people claim that faithful donors have won a heavenly lottery of money, houses, cars, and healing.

St Matthew's Churches doesn't need donations for a church organ. Formerly known as St Matthew's Publishing Inc., this is a business. This seed-faith ministry was founded in the 1970s by the Reverend James Eugene Ewing, although the church claims to be 60 years old. They rent churches for photo shoots because God's "House" is a mailbox in Tulsa.

This Shroud of Tulsa scam exploits desperate and devout people, using census information to target the poorest zip codes. Ewing went from a tent revival ministry in the 1970s to Beverly Hills, while St Matthew's Churches went from prayer rugs to riches, raising six million dollars per month for the owner, not for God (Bransterrer, 2007).

Known as "God's ghost writer", Ewing also writes these letters for other evangelists, including Robert Tilton and Oral Roberts. These letters use scripture references, testimonials, and magical language to convince the public to submit their prayer requests with a donation. However, the responses are opened, the cash removed, and the addresses collected for mailing lists, while the prayer requests are dumped in the trash.

St Jude novenas

As a young girl in Australia I used to read the classified advertisements in the local newspaper. Between the psychics and escorts were ads including a prayer and giving thanks to St Jude. They promised that if you recited the prayer over nine consecutive days, your prayers would be answered too. In thanks to St Jude, the ad must be republished.

From accountants to virgins, everyone has a patron saint. Whatever your career, cause, or complaint, there's a specific saint dedicated to that. As go-betweens to God, their names are invoked against misfortune, and they are petitioned to perform miracles. For example, St Peregrine (1260–1345) developed a cancerous sore on his foot, which was to be amputated. He spent many hours in prayer, and eventually had a vision of Christ touching his impaired limb. Allegedly, this cured his cancer miraculously, and he became the patron saint of cancer patients. St Jude's causes are broader. He is known as "the Patron of Hopeless Cases and Matters Despaired of", and "the Saint of the Impossible" (Orsi, 1998). St Jude's role is to make the impossible possible.

Hey Jude

In the days when he was a man rather than a saint, Jude was one of the many disciples of Jesus. As one of the 12 apostles he was somewhat a celebrity, and a possible cousin or even brother of Jesus. Jude is often represented with the name *Thaddeus*, meaning "meek" and "amiable", but this name may have referred to another Jude, as this was a popular name amongst early Jews and Christians. *Yehudhah*, meaning "Praised by the Lord" or "I will praise the Lord" was the single Hebrew name for the translations Judah and Juda, and the nickname Jude (Trotta, 2005). And no, the Beatles' "Hey Jude" wasn't in honor of St Jude. Initially titled "Hey Julian", then "Hey Jules", the song was written by Paul McCartney about John Lennon's son, Julian (Miles, 1997).

Given the similarity in name, Jude is often confused with Judas Iscariot. The *Oxford Dictionary of Saints* jokes that Jude's hopeless cause "is said to have originated because nobody invoked him for anything since his name so closely resembled that of Judas, who betrayed the Lord". In the Gospel of John he is called "Jude, not the Iscariot," probably to distinguish him from the traitor (Orsi, 1998). For this reason, the name Jude pejorated, and St Jude became known as the "Forgotten Saint". But Jude was about to comeback with a vengeance.

Jude lived during the first century AD, but as a saint, Jude is a modern American hero. He was born again in 1929 when the Claretian Fathers, a Spanish order of missionaries, dedicated a national shrine to him in Chicago. During his life, Jude preached to the faithful that they should persevere in the environment of harsh, difficult circumstances, just as their forbearers had done before them. This sentiment appealed to people in the years of the Great Depression and World War II, especially new immigrants from Europe to the United States.

St Jude is alive and well today as the namesake of numerous hospitals, and in the advertisements that still appear in the classified ads of newspapers around the world. Jude is the saint of the last resort, and modern devotees continue to petition Jude to heal terminal illnesses, make mortgage payments, or pass that exam they didn't study for. Praying to St Jude is not Catholic dogma, but it has become tradition and superstition. St Jude seems to be the Catholic saint for non-Catholics.

There are many different prayers to St Jude. Some will also instruct the reader to say Our Fathers, Hail Marys, or Gloria prayers, and usually in multiples of three. But the formula for the advertisement remains the same. The reader is provided with a prayer and instructed to recite it nine times a day for nine consecutive days. The ad must be republished when the prayers are answered, and they will be answered because they "never fail".

Most advertisements resemble the following found in the "Religious Announcements" section of the *Los Angeles Times*. They are always signed anonymously with only the publisher's initials.

> SAINT JUDE NOVENA. May the Sacred Heart of Jesus be adored, glorified, loved and preserved throughout the world now & forever. Sacred Heart of Jesus, pray for us. St. Jude, Worker of Miracles, pray for us. St. Jude, Helper of the Hopeless, pray for us. Say this prayer 9x a day for 9 days, then publish & your prayers will be answered. It has never been known to fail. R.P.
>
> (VanArsdale, 2014)

According to the Catholic Church a novena is a nine-day-long private or public devotion said to obtain special graces. The word comes from the Latin *novem*, meaning "nine". This number marks the nine days between the ascension of Jesus on a Thursday, and the coming of the Holy Spirit on Pentecost Sunday (Acts 1:14). Novena devotions are said in remembrance of those nine days. The number nine is commonly used in early Eastern and European magic and folklore. Charms frequently required nine ingredients, or specify that a ritual must be performed nine times (MacLeod and Mees, 2006).

The St Jude novena has developed its own formula. The prayer becomes a spell that must be said in a heartfelt way, or it won't work. The prayer must be republished, or it won't work (this probably comes from Roman times when vows were made to God in exchange for favors, and these vows were kept and passed around). Many St Jude websites publish anonymous testimonials of success, for a fee. But we'll never know how many times the prayers failed, or how often a coincidental result was attributed to St Jude. Today, St Jude notices and emails constitute another kind of chain letter.

In the end, Jude never escaped his own hopeless cause. In about 65 CE, Jude suffered martyrdom in Beirut when he was beaten and his head shattered with an axe.

Affirmations

Affirmations are a form of positive self-talk. Proponents believe in the power of positive language – that positive thinking, speaking, and writing will effect change in the external world. Affirmations are New Age prayers that are said to oneself, or to the universe. Prayers are requests for things we want, and while affirmations also express things we want, they are stated as things we already have, to act as a magical magnet to attract those desires.

Paranormal prayer

Affirmations are used to attract all the things that prayer is used to achieve; health, wealth, and happiness. With a self-help slant they are also used to achieve success, weight loss, and to stop smoking and treat depression and anxiety. With a spiritual slant they are also used to achieve consciousness, mindfulness, wholeness, and oneness. Affirmations are conversations with the universe. To get what you want, you need to tell the universe what you want, like writing a note, placing it into a bottle and tossing it into the sea.

Affirmations are a form of enchanted goal-setting popularized by self-help gurus. The Law of Attraction theory and Rhonda Byrne's *The Secret* claim that we can manifest our desires with positive thinking and language. This gimmick has been done before. The forerunners to these books were Napoleon Hills' *The Law of Success* and *Think and Grow Rich*, and Wallace Wattles (1910) *The Science of Getting Rich*. But there is no science to it, and many different ways to do it. However, all proponents agree that the affirmation must be positive, said in the present tense, and said until it works.

Advocates believe that all thoughts are affirmations, either positive or negative. However, they claim that our inner dialogue is mostly pessimistic rather than optimistic, and 90 per cent of thoughts are negative. Like a belief in jinxes, these negative thoughts sabotage our success. Negative thoughts are like poison, but positive thoughts act like medicine. Therefore, affirmations must always be positive to counter negative self-talk.

In what is known as "talking to our minds", affirmations are suggestions people make to themselves, in the form of statements. They may be single words such as "relax", "patience", "understanding", or "forgiveness". They may also be sound bites, such as "I like myself", "People like me", and "I bring out the best in others". These statements should never invoke negatives. If you want to lose weight and say to yourself, "I am not fat", the mind allegedly only hears "I am fat", and ignores the negative. The theory that the mind can't process negation is popular in Neuro-Linguistic Programming and the Law of Attraction.

These hopes for the future should be expressed in the present tense. If we use the future tense "I will be rich someday", the desire will forever be in the future. You have to speak as though the desire is already achieved, "I am rich" or "I choose to be rich". Prayers address a higher power and make appeals. Asking God for good health can sound like a letter, "Dear God, please give me good health". As an affirmation this translates to, "I am healthy", but means, "I want to be healthy". Like invoking the name of God or other deities, some New Age gurus with messiah complexes suggest you call out their name. For example, John Payne (2001) channels the spiritual guide "Omni", and recommends you call out this name before making your affirmations to help "energize" your goals.

Repetition is also an important part of the process. Like litanies and novenas, the affirmation must be repeated. But instead of being repeated for nine days, the affirmation must be repeated until it works. Like the timed prayer services of Catholicism and Islam, affirmations are to be repeated at various times throughout the day. Some believe you should repeat them ten times every morning and ten times at night. Others recommend you take any opportunity to reinforce them – sing them in the shower, say them while you're working or shopping, listen to recorded affirmations in the car, while you meditate, or sleep, and recite them with a musical soundtrack. Some use affirmations in conjunction with meditation or visualization techniques. To increase the potency of the affirmations, tell them to yourself in front of the mirror. This is supposed to metaphorically magnify the importance of the message.

Like a mantra or chant, these scripts should be uttered again and again and again. This is a form of self-hypnosis, but the intonation and rhythm shouldn't be hypnotic. How you say them is equally important. Getting what you want seems to be contingent upon how much you want it, so it must be said emphatically, with conviction and passion. The person should have focused intent, and avoid mechanical or dry repetition of the affirmations. To that end, the words in your affirmation should be carefully chosen by the speaker and personalized. They should also use your favorite words and be in the style of your personal speech, as the subconscious mind doesn't understand the speaking styles of others.

Some believe in the additional power of the written word to amplify the affirmation. They suggest that you write down your affirmation as a way of thinking out loud, and to impress the desire on the subconscious mind. The affirmation should be written down again and again and again in list form, like a naughty school child who has to write on a blackboard 20 times. Like charms and amulets, some suggest you write down the affirmations on cards and keep them in your pocket, or store them in a Bible to further enhance the magical properties. Like a Hoodoo spell, writing down negative thoughts and trashing or burning the paper is believed to banish negative thinking.

Sympathetic magic is the basis for affirmations and the belief that desires can be transformed into reality merely because we think, write, or say them. The reality is that as much as we think, write, or say something, it won't happen until we do it.

5
Chain Letters

Chain letters go by many different names and forms. What links them as chain letters is that they are all unsolicited communication; that which we call spam. They usually address us by name, and are sent to multiple recipients. They are received from family, friends, colleagues, and strangers with connections to these people. These messages all contain some sort of information and instructions, and are sent with the explicit request that they be forwarded on to others. Most of all, these letters appeal to superstition and often greed. Rewards are promised for complying with the request, while punishment is threatened for those who dare to "break the chain".

The weakest link

I once broke the chain, and it made me deeply unpopular back in kindergarten class. I received a mysterious letter addressed to me personally, but curiously with no name or return address. The long letter was handwritten. The writer explained that the message had been sent to thousands of people, all around the globe. They were trying to "break the record" for the world's longest-running chain letter. My role in this scheme was to duplicate the lengthy letter ten times, by hand, and mail these to an additional ten people. Fulfilling this task would result in undisclosed good fortune for me and ensure the perpetuation of the chain. Then came the threat. To that date, no one had ever "broken the chain". To do so would incur grievous yet nonspecific bad luck for all eternity and beyond. All my school friends received the letter and followed the instructions diligently, but I didn't. Feeling lazy at the prospect of such an administrative effort, the chain letter died with me.

The average chain letter doesn't break any world records, but amazingly, the practice itself has been around in one form or another for over 1,000 years. The predecessors to modern chain letters are ancient prayers, poems, and spells. The earliest versions appear in pyramid texts that decorate the tombs of the pharaohs in Egypt.

> The man who shall make a picture of these things which are to the north of the hidden house of the Tuat shall find it of great benefit to him both in heaven and on earth; and he who knows it shall be among the spirits near Ra, and he who recites the words of Isis and Ser shall repulse Apep in Amentet, and he shall have a place on the boat of Ra both in heaven and upon earth. The man who knows not this picture shall never be able to repulse the serpent Neha-hra.
>
> (Budge, 1904)

Eighth-century Buddhist magical incantations called *dharani* promised good fortune and spiritual merit for their reproduction and distribution.

> A total of over one million copies of four different dharani from the Great Dharani Sutra of the Spotless and Pure Light...were printed to be placed in...[one million pagodas] built at the command of [Empress] Shotoku. In this sutra it is stated that if a person were to build several million small pagodas and place copies of dharani in them, that person's life would be lengthened, evil karma would be expunged, and rebels and enemies would be vanquished.
>
> (Mizuno, 1982)

Early religious books printed using wood block reliefs also had features of today's chain letters. A Buddhist manual called the *Surangama Sutra* urged people to "observe and study this Scripture, explain it to others and circulate it widely" to ensure good luck.

> Ananda, should any sentient beings in any of the kingdoms of existence, copy down this Dharani on birch-bark or palm-leaves or paper made of papyrus or of white felt, and keep it safely in some scented wrapping, this man no matter how faint-hearted or unable to remember the words for reciting it, but who copies it in his room and keeps it by him, this man in all his life will remain unharmed by any poison of the Maras.
>
> (Goddard, 1938)

Heavenly letters

Other predecessors to chain letters are letters claiming divine author-ship. "letters from heaven", commonly known by the German name *Himmelsbrief*, were believed to be copies of letters written by God, Jesus, or some other divine agent. The original letters were said to be written in gold, or with the blood of Jesus. They fell from the heavens, were found near the crucifixion site, or the Virgin Mary appeared and delivered the letter to a mere mortal (Van Arsdale, 2007).

Letters from heaven contained commandments, Biblical narratives, prayers, and threats. If the owner should copy and distribute the letter, the author promises forgiveness of sins and magical protection from misfortune. In this way, letters from heaven were like amulets, and were often carried by the owner for good luck and protection. However, should readers doubt the letter and fail to pass it on, they are threatened with disease, death, and destruction. These letters seem to be a lesson in having blind faith.

Letters from heaven are found in Islam, Hinduism, and other pre-Christian religions. Examples can be found across cultures, reflecting beliefs and practices; Indian versions preach cow protection and con-demn the breeding of pigs and consumption of alcohol. They are found across languages, including Greek, Latin, Arabic, and Ethiopic. These letters circulated throughout Europe for centuries and copies were dis-tributed by the flagellant movement during the Black Death pandemic. Letters from heaven made a resurgence when they were carried by American soldiers during both world wars.

Early chain letters

No one is certain who created the very first chain letter or when. The earliest example of a chain letter as we know them today dates back to 1888. The letter solicits dimes for the education of "the poor whites in the region of the Cumberlands", and instructs the recipient to send the letter on to four others to receive the following reward, "the blessing of Him who was ready to die for us" (Van Arsdale, 2007).

The start of the twentieth century saw improved literacy rates, the rise of international mail, and the popularity of postcards – all factors that increased the spreading of chain letters. But the themes had changed. Along with changing attitudes to religion and miracles, claims of divine authorship and magical protection were removed (Van Arsdale, 2007). Instead, these versions of letters from heaven exploited superstitions, begging the recipient to replicate the letters with promises of good luck and threats of bad luck. Here is one of the oldest of this kind that is dated January 6, 1905.

> Oh, Lord Jesus Christ, we implore Thee, O Eternal God, to have mercy upon mankind. Keep us from all sin and take us to be with Thee eternally. Amen

> This prayer was sent by Bishop Lawrence, recommending it to be rewritten and sent to nine other persons. He who will not say it will be afflicted with some great misfortune. One person who failed to pay attention to it met with a dreadful accident. He who will rewrite it to nine other persons commencing on the day it is received – and sending only one each day will on or after the ninth day experience great joy. Please do not break the chain.

> (Van Arsdale, 2007)

Over the next few decades, chain letters evolved into a more recognizable format. These letters included copy quotas and deadlines. The following chain letter is dated August 6, 1922.

> Copy this and send to nine people you wish good luck. The chain was started by an American officer and should go three times around the world. Don't break the chain for whoever does will have bad luck. But do it in 24 hours and count nine days and you will have good fortune.

> (Lardner, 1946)

Pushing your luck

By 1935, prosperity letters began appearing. These included managed lists; a list of names and instructions to copy the list, omit the first name, and add the receiver's name to the end.

> We trust in God. He supplies our needs.
> Mrs. F. Streuzel ... Mich.
> Mrs. A. Ford, Chicago ... Ill.
> Mrs. K. Adkins, Chicago ... Ill.
> Mrs. R. Arlington ... Ill.
> Mrs ... *Quincy* ... *Ill.*
> Mrs ... Quincy ... Ill.

> Copy the above names, omitting the first. Add your name last.
> Mail it to five persons who you wish prosperity to. The chain was

started by an American Colonel and must be mailed 24 hours after receiving it. This will bring prosperity within 9 days after mailing it.

Mrs. Sanford won $3,000.

Mrs. Andres won $1,000.

Mrs. Howe who broke the chain lost everything she possessed. The chain grows a definite power over the expected word.

DO NOT BREAK THE CHAIN.

See what happens on the 9th day.

Hoping it brings you luck. J.E.K.

(Hyatt, 1935)

Soon the chain letters began requesting that the recipient send get-well cards, stamps, prayers, recipes, or postcards to one of the names on the list.

Money for nothing

On March 19, 1935, an article in the *Denver Post* reported that a group called the "Prosperity Club" was responsible for "floods of send-a-dime chain letters threatened to swamp the Denver mails." Despite threats of prosecution, on April 28 alone the Denver post office handled an estimated 165,000 chain letters. Interesting, the letter is referred to as a "charm". Van Arsdale (2007) suggests that chain was an early miscopy of charm and an advantageous copying error.

Hope, Faith, Charity

This charm was started in the hope of bringing prosperity to you. Within three days, make six copies of this letter, leaving off the top name and address, and adding your name and address at the bottom of the list, and mail the six copies to six of your friends to whom you wish prosperity to come.

In omitting the top name send that person 10 cents wrapped in paper as a charity donation. In turn, as your name leaves the top, you will receive 15,625 letters, with donations amounting to $1,652.50.

Now, is this worth a dime to you? Have the faith your friend had, and this charm will not be broken.

(Denver Post, 1935)

The authorities searched for the author to prosecute him or her but they were unsuccessful in their hunt. Within a few months, the letter was copied over a billion times worldwide. The promise of such riches, especially during the times of economic hardship in the 1930s, encouraged many people to continue the chain letter campaign. For a brief period of time the schemes worked! Of course, they never work for long, or for everyone.

Money chain letters

Money chain letters are managed lists of names and addresses. The recipient sends money to the name at the top of a list, then strikes out that name and adds his or her own name to the bottom of the list. This is then copied and mailed to acquaintances, in the hopes that the cycle will be repeated and the recipient will reap the rewards in due turn. But it only works out this way for the initial few and most will spend more money mailing these chain letters than receiving any returns. These schemes are also susceptible to dishonesty, where people add their name to the top of the list, or to receive multiple returns the same person lists themselves under different names and addresses.

It is mathematically impossible that all will be winners. These schemes only work for a few people, just like multi-level marketing and pyramid schemes. Money chain letters and other get-rich-quick schemes are simply bad investments, but they are also illegal if they request money or promise a return. Sending them via mail, computer, or in person violates Title 18, US Code, Section 1302, the Postal Lottery Statute, and they are regarded as a form of gambling.

Advance fee fraud

We've all received emails from kings, princes, bishops, presidents, dictators, rich widows, and CEOs of corporations. These strangers have confided in us about their unfortunate personal situations, but significant wealth, and promised us a share of their fortune if we assist them. These "Nigerian letters" are the most dangerous relative of the chain letter.

Jerusalem letters

Also known as advance fee fraud or 419 scams, this is a type of confidence trick perpetrated by deceptive letters, faxes, or emails. The scheme first appeared in the eighteenth century with the "letter from Jerusalem", a handwritten plea from a wealthy person imprisoned in a

Jerusalem jail. The recipient was promised a share of these vast riches in exchange for funds to secure the prisoner's release. Of course, when the victims contributed money they never saw the reward (Vidocq, 1834). This evolved into the "Spanish prisoner letter" scam in the nineteenth century. The author claimed to know the location of hidden treasure but he was locked away in prison. If the recipient would just send money to bribe his guards he could be released to hunt down and share the treasure.

Nigerian letters

As reflected in the name, the modern scam originated in Nigeria. "419" refers to the section of the Nigerian criminal code for obtaining property through fraud. Nigerian letters began appearing in the mid-1980s, as the country's oil-based economy declined and the scam developed to entice foreigners into suspicious oil deals. This local scam ended up becoming one of Nigeria's biggest industries, with millions of letters and millions of dollars extorted annually (US Secret Service, 2002). The scam was copied worldwide, throughout West Africa and beyond, in Korea, Switzerland, Russia, Australia, the United Kingdom, and the United States. The advent of the internet made this a prolific scam. Unlike the handwritten "letters from Jerusalem" and "Spanish prisoner letters", " 'Nigerian letters' " evolved from snail mail to email.

While the details differ, there are some common features across these emails. Here is an example of a Nigerian letter/email:

FROM THE DESK OF MR. EGOMAH FELIX, LAGOS, NIGERIA, an account officer to late Mark Jones an Immigrant, who was a Businessman and Building Contractor in my Country. On the 21st of April 2001, this customer was involved in a Car accident along Lagos-Shagamu express road. All occupants of the Vehicle unfortunately lost their lives. The deceased has an account valued at USD$15.5 million, I have be in contact with his lawyer prior to locate any of his relatives for over 2 years that seems abortive.

Now, I seek your consent, to present you as the Next of kin of the Deceased, you could not be of same name and Nationality with the deceased, this grants you opportunity to be presented. 35% will be given to you for your involvement/assistance to the successful accomplishment of this transaction, 10% will be mapped out for any Internal and External expenses that we will run in the course of this transaction execution and 55% will be invested on my behalf under your management.

(Carroll, 2010)

The missive can range from a few lines to several pages of text, and presents a stereotypical story. The author is beset by personal misfortune – death, natural disaster, a political situation, or a complicated business investment. This has left them with a large but inaccessible amount of money, gold, diamonds, or other asset. They require your assistance to manage the booty, and you'll receive a generous percentage as compensation. What begins as being something for nothing soon develops catches: processing fees, stamp duty costs, and other vague charges that escalate into thousands of dollars, and must be paid via irreversible, untraceable wire transfers. The victims are willing to advance money in the hope of a significantly larger gain that they never quite reach.

There are economized versions, for the grifter on the go, like the one below that I received at the time of writing.

I am Mr. C.Y. Ling, Executive Vice President of CITIC Bank International, China. I have a proposal for you in tune of 105 Million Euro, Please reply to this email (ling.5648@yahoo.com.hk) for specific DETAILS.

Warmest,
Mr. C.Y. Ling

The authors adopt a fake identity or impersonate an individual, but the author is always a stranger to the recipient. Sometimes the author signs off with only initials, like Mr C. Y. Ling. A convoluted email handle is usually used, via a free web-based email account. Often the return email will be conflict with the sender account, as in the above email where the "from" address is ling@epm.br. Despite the semi-anonymous nature of these messages, they are not automated and there is always a real, human perpetrator.

The victims are acquired from public forums, bulletin boards, and email harvesting programs. Nonspecific salutations are often used, such as sir or madam, or they may be personalized. The author may hedge his or her bets with honorifics. A friend was once addressed as "Dear Dr Mr Mrs Ffred Thornett". The letters give the appearance of being sent to select individuals, but they are actually sent to many different people and identical messages may come from different names.

French letters

Nigerian letters aren't only written in English, and examples exist in French, German, and other languages. The English versions are often characterized by unusual syntax and missing parts of grammar. For example, "I have proposal for you" and "I bought you a good news" (Dyrud, 2005). There are misspellings, capitalization of nouns, and the use of caps lock for emphasis, especially in subject titles, such as "URGENT" and "REPLY ASAP". Alternatively, formal language is used. There is a lack of slang and contractions, for example "cannot" instead of "can't", and the use of archaic phrasing that we might interpret as quaint, "I am contacting you in anticipation of a cordial business relationship" (Dyrud, 2005). Politeness is an important feature of Nigerian letters. The author apologizes for the rude intrusion, "I strongly apologize for this unsolicited mail", and preempts suspicion, "Pardon me if I have offended you by contacting you for such a big transaction through an ordinary letter which makes it suspicious considering the type of fraud proposals moving around the world today" (Kienpointner, 2006).

   This way of speaking is seemingly indicative of nonnative speakers, suggesting that English is not the mother tongue of the author. However, this may be a cunning plan. The majority of Nigerians speak African languages, especially in rural areas, but English is the official language of Nigeria and is widely used for education and business. The use of "corrupt" or foreign-sounding English may be a deliberate ploy to add authenticity to the plea and to present the sender as naïve and easily cheated by the "smarter" Westerner.

   The promises seem too good to be true but Nigerian letters manipulate the recipient's greed. Pirates and prisoners appeal to the sense of adventure of people past, while missives from VIPs appeal to the modern ego. The language is also persuasive – the authors are presented as honest and flatter the recipients as trustworthy people who will keep the deal a secret. The authors evoke sympathy with tragic stories and altruistic plans to donate a large sum of money to charity before they die. They offer emotional petitions with subject titles like "Cry for help" and "Fulfill my last wish, please" (Dyrud, 2005). Some claim to have a divine purpose, "after my fervent prayer over it, you were nominated to me through divine revelation from God" (Kienpointner, 2006). And like the chain letters above, they appeal to magical thinking and religious compassion with blessings and prayers.

Finally, Nigerian letters are persuasive with their use of official-sounding language and the supporting documentation they supply to the victims, such as fund management agreements, fund release orders, power of attorney forms, and affidavits of fund ownership (Dyrud, 2005). As proof of their sincerity, some provide links to natural disasters and other evidence of their stories. They construct fake online personas, and even set up sham bank sites for the victims to view their fraudulent transactions.

A dead letter

Nigerian letters are clearly deceptive and the stories implausible, and most of us just hit the delete button. However, despite the prevalence of the emails and the warnings issued by various government agencies, some people have taken the bait. In movie-worthy stories, credulous victims have lost their assets and life savings, or even their lives. Some have even traveled to Nigeria, supposedly to secure the deal, but have instead been blackmailed, taken hostage, held for ransom, beaten, tortured, or even murdered.

Chain letters

There are many different types of chain letters but they all follow a formula. They tell an apocryphal tale, but there may be a kernel of truth buried within the story. The letter explains its origins, the name of the person who started the letter, and where it came from; but chain letters never begin in Wisconsin; they always begin somewhere exotic. The letter brags about its circumnavigations and ensures you that its continuation will earn an entry in the *Guinness Book of World Records*.

They instruct you to spread the chain letter, promising good luck in return. The luck is nonspecific, but they offer testimonials of successes for compliance: Betty won the lotto, Jim got a new job, and Bob recovered from herpes. As a warning to the skeptics they threaten bad luck if you fail to do the email's bidding, and present anecdotal evidence of misfortune: Betty won the lotto, then died, Jim lost his job, and Bob died of herpes. The chain letter provides instructions for its replication, telling you how many copies to send and giving a deadline. They try to deter people from discarding the letter and from a delay in responding.

Dolan Fairchild received the chain and not believing threw the letter away. Nine days later, he died.

(Van Arsdale, 2007)

Chain emails

The net has also changed the face of the chain letter and chain emails have been popular since the early 1990s. Receiving one used to be an infrequent event. Now, it is a weekly, if not daily affair. Rather than painstakingly reproducing copy after copy by hand, the sender simply hits "'forward", at no cost. The letter sent to thousands is replaced by the email forwarded to millions. It isn't sent from some puzzling anonymous source, it's received from colleagues, acquaintances, friends, family, and that annoying stranger who somehow got your email address.

The structure of chain letters by email tends to stay the same. Emails can be reproduced exactly and most readers don't bother modifying them. Their traditional text makes them vulnerable to automated detection and deletion by junk mail screening programs. However, like the telephone game, with repeated copying, the names, dates, places, promises, and threats all reveal subtle variations across chain letters.

Yanking our chains

Chain emails have adapted to the modern environment. Today's chain letters are not mere digitizations of the paper versions, there are many different themes. Like the horror movie that claims to be a "true story" (which is a good indication it isn't), chain letters try to avoid their stigma by insisting, "This is *not* a chain letter!". Instead, they masquerade as jokes, stories, religious parables, urban legends, rumors, consumer warnings, political commentary, seasonal themes such as Christmas and Halloween, admonitions of safe sex and sobriety, personality tests, petitions, prayer requests, false quotations, hoaxes about viruses, special offers and advertisements, email tag, chain letter parodies, and anti-chain letters (Van Arsdale, 2007).

Chain letters have an enduring popularity, despite the fact that they are widely condemned and don't work. Even as beliefs and attitudes change, they reflect our cultural customs, values, and morals. Recipients are motivated to comply with the demands of chain letters for a number of reasons. They appeal to our hopes and fears, our charity and greed, and our desire to receive good luck and avoid bad luck. Senders often have good intentions, to share the good luck, or to warn or inform us. The sender may be driven by curiosity, or a sense of duty to maintain the chain. What kind of fiend would spoil a chain that had been running around the globe for years and was going to win a world record? As in my kindergarten story above, even though the chain had probably been broken many times before, I was the one seen to break the rules of the game. But the primary motivation for perpetuating chain letters is superstition. Like Pascal's wager, the charms, curses, predictions, prayers, and chain letters might just work, and it's better to be safe than sorry.

References

Allan, Keith and Burridge, Kate. 2006. *Forbidden Words. Taboo and the Censoring of Language*. Cambridge University Press.

Austin, J. L. 1962. *How to Do Things with Words*. Harvard University Press.

Benson, H., Dusek, J. A., Sherwood, J. B. et al. 2006. "Study of the therapeutic effects of intercessory prayer (STEP) in cardiac bypass patients: a multicenter randomized trial of uncertainty and certainty of receiving intercessory prayer". *American Heart Journal*. Vol. 151, No. 4, pp. 934–42.

Blake, Barry. 2010. *Secret Language: Codes, Tricks, Spies, Thieves, and Symbols*. Oxford University Press.

Blum, Ralph. H. 1983. *The Book of Runes*. St. Martin's Press.

Bogg, Edmund. 1894. *From Edenvale to the Plains of New York*, Forgotten Books.

Branstetter, Ziva. 2007. "Watchdog: monthly take is $6 million". *Tulsa World*.

Bransterrer, Ziva. 2007. *Prayers, Cash Flow into Tulsa*. Trinity Foundation, http://www.trinityfi.org/

Brosnon. 2002. "A prayer before dying". *Wired Magazine*. December.

Browning, Robert. 2010. (1899). *The Letters of Robert Browning and Elizabeth Barrett Barrett 1845–1846*. Vol. I (of 2), Qontro Classic Books.

Budge, E. A. Wallis. 1904. *The Gods of the Egyptians*. Vol. I & II. Dover.

Burridge, Kate. 1999. *Ma's Out, Pa's Out, Let's Talk Rude: Pee – Po – Belly – Bum – Drawers!* Ozwords, Australian National Dictionary Centre.

Byrd, R. C. 1988. "Positive therapeutic effects of intercessory prayer in a coronary care unit population". *Southern Medical Journal*. Vol. 81, No. 7, pp. 826–29.

Byard, R. 1998. "Traditional medicine of aborigial Australia". *Canadian Medical Association Journal*. Vol. 139, No. 8. 792–94.

Byrne, Rhonda. 2006. *The Secret*. Atria Books.

Carrese, J. A. and Rhodes, L. A. 1995. "Western bioethics on the Navajo Reservation. Benefit or harm?" *Journal of the American Medical Association*. Vol. 274, pp. 826–29.

Carroll, Robert. T. 2010. "Advance fee fraud". Available at: http://www.skepdic.com/nigerianscam.html

Cavendish, Richard. 1967. *The Black Arts. A Concise History of Witchcraft, Demonology, Astrology, and other Mystical Practices Throughout The Ages*. Perigee.

Cha, K. Y., Wirth, D. P. and Lobo, R. A. 2001. "Does prayer influence the success of in vitro fertilization – embryo transfer? report of a masked, randomized trial". *Journal of Reproductive Medicine.* Vol. 46, No. 9, pp. 781–87.

Comstock, G. W. and Tonascia, J. A. 1977. "Education and mortality in Washington County, Maryland". *Journal of Health Society and Behavior.* Vol. 18, pp. 54–61.

Deere, Jack. 1998. *Surprised by the Voice of God. How God Speaks Today Through Prophecies, Dreams, and Visions.* Zondervan.

Denver Post. 1935. "Headline story about Send-a-Dime. 'Here's a sample of one of the letters, turned over to Nelson by Stevic Friday.' " April 19 (Friday), pp. 1&4

Dossey, Larry. 2011. *Be Careful What You Pray For, You Might Just Get It.* Harper Collins.

Dyrud, Marilyn. 2005. "I Brought You A Good News": An Analysis of Nigerian 419 Letters'. Proceedings of the 2005 Association for Business Communication Annual Convention.

Egils Saga. 2004. By Svanhildur Ed. Oskarsdottir. Penguin Classics.

El Mahdy, Christine. 1989. *Mummies, Myth and Magic.* Thames & Hudson.

Flamm, B. L. 2005. "Prayer and the success of IVF." *Journal of Reproductive Medicine.* Vol. 50, No. 1, p. 71.

Flint, V. 1991. *The Rise of Magic in Early Medieval Europe.* Princeton University Press.

Flowers, Stephen. 1989. *The Galdrabók: An Icelandic Grimoire.*

Frankfort, Henri. 1949. *Before Philosophy. The Intellectual Adventure of Ancient Man.* Penguin Books.

Franklin, Benjamin. 1999. *Wit and Wisdom from Poor Richard's Almanack.* Courier Dover Publications.

Gager, John. G. 1999. *Curse Tablets and Binding Spells from the Ancient World.* Oxford University Press.

Galton, Francis. 1872. "Statistical inquires into the efficacy of prayer". *The Fortnightly Review.* No. 68.

Garber, Marjorie. B. 1997. *Shakespeare's Ghost Writers: Literature as Uncanny Causality.* Methuen.

Gloomy Sunday, http://lyricstranslate.com/en/Szomoru-Vasarnap-Gloomy-Sunday.html

Goddard, Dwight (Ed.). 1938. *A Buddhist Bible.* Beacon Press.

Grimm, Jacob and Grimm, Wilhelm. 1812. *Grimm's Fairy Tales.*

Harrison, William Henry. 1881. *Mother Shipton Investigated. The Result of Critical Examination in the British Museum Library, of the Literature Relating to the Yorkshire Sibyl.*

Head, Richard. 1677. *The Life and Death of Mother Shipton Being Not Only a True Account of Her Strange Birth and Most Important Passages of Her Life, But Also All Her Prophesies*, EEBO editions.

Hill, Napoleon. 1953. *Think and Grow Rich.* The Ralston Publishing Co.

Hill, Napoleon. 2013. *The Law of Success. Create Space.* E-artnow Books 2013.

Hitchcock, Mark. 2002. *What on Earth is Going On?* Random House.

Hyatt, Harry Middleton. 1935. *Folk-Lore From Adams County Illinois.* Memoirs of the Alma Egan Hyatt Foundation.

Jacobs, Joseph. 1906. *The Jewish Encyclopedia. A Guide to Its Contents, an Aid to Its Use.* Funk & Wagnalls Company.

Jacobs, W.W. 1997. *The Monkey's Paw: And other Tales of Mystery and the Macabre.* Academy Chicago Publishers.

Jenkins, Philip. 2006. *The New Faces of Christianity: Believing the Bible in the Global South.* Oxford University Press.

Johnson, K. Paul. 1998. *Edgar Cayce in Context: The Readings, Truth and Fiction.* State University of New York Press (SUNY).

Keinan, Giora. 2002. "The effects of stress and desire for control on superstitious behavior". *Personality and Social Psychology Bulletin.* Vol. 28, No. 1, pp. 102–08.

Kienpointner, Manfred. 2006. "How to present fallacious messages persuasively. The case of 'the Nigerian spam letters'". In Van Eemeren, F. H., Houtlosser, Peter, van Rees, Agnes, and Haft-van Rees, M. A. (eds) *Considering Pragma-Dialectics.* Psychology Press.

Lama, Dalai. 1999. "Dalai Lama says prayer alone won't bring world peace". *Asia Daily.*

Lardner, Ring. 1946. "On chain letters." *The Portable Ring Lardner.* Viking.

Lee, Henry. 2008. "Psychic jailed, charged with bilking woman, 85". *The San Francisco Chronicle.* December, 20.

Lemesurier, Peter. 2010. *Nostradamus, Bibliomancer: The Man, The Myth, The Truth.* New Page Books.

MacLeod, M. and Mees, B. 2006. *Runic Amulets and Magic Objects.* Boydell Press.

Miles, Barry. 1997. *Paul McCartney: Many Years From Now.* Henry Holt and Company.

Mizuno, Kogen. 1982. *Buddhist Sutras: Origin, Development, Transmission.* Kosei Publishing Co.

New York Times. 1910. "Illiterate man becomes a doctor when hypnotized". *Sunday Magazine Section.* October 9.

New York Times. 1968. "Rezsoe Seres commits suicide: Composer of gloomy Sunday". *Obituaries.* January 14.

Newburg, Andrew. 2012. *Scientific American Mind.* January/February issue.

Nostradamus, Michel. 1555. *The Complete Prophecies of Nostradamus.* Wilder Publications.

Old Farmer's Almanac, http://www.almanac.co./content/history-old-farmers-almanac

Olsan, Lea. 1992. "Latin charms of medieval England: Verbal healing in a Christian oral tradition". *Oral Tradition.* Vol. 7, No. 1, pp. 116–42.

Orsi, Robert. 1998. *Thank You, Saint Jude. Women's Devotion to the Patron Saint of Hopeless Causes.* Yale University Press.

Payne, John. 2001. *Omni Reveals the Four Principles of Creation.* Findhorn Press.

Peschel, Lisa. 1989. *A Practical Guide to the Runes.* Llewellyn.

Phillips, D. et al. 2001. "The Hound of the Bskervilles Effect. Natural experiment on the influence of psychological stress on the timing of death". *British Medical Journal.* 323, 7327.

Posner. 1990. "God in the CCU? A Critique of the San Francsico Study on Intercessory Prayer". *Free Inquiry.* Spring.

Posner, Gary. 1999. "God in the CCU? A critique of the San Francisco hospital study on intercessory prayer and healing". *Free Inquiry.* Spring Issue.

Pradelli, Chad. 2009. "Animal sacrifice?" *Philadelphia News Leader.* February, 17.

Randi, James. 1995. *An Encyclopedia of Claims, Frauds, and Hoaxes of the Occult and Supernatural.* St. Martin's Press.

Segal, Robert. A. 2006. *The Blackwell Companion to the Study of Religion.* Wiley Blackwell.

Sherden, William. 1998. *The Fortune Sellers: The Big Business of Buying and Selling Predictions.* John Wiley and Sons.

Sicher, F., Targ, E., Moore, D., 2nd and Smith, H. S. 1998. "A randomized double-blind study of the effect of distant healing in a population with advanced AIDS. Report of a small scale study." *The Western Journal of Medicine.* Vol. 169, No. 6, pp. 356–63.

Simon. 1977. *Necronomicon.* Anon Books.

Skemer, Don. 2006. *Binding Words: Textual Amulets in the Middle Ages.* The Pennsylvania State University.

Sloan, R., Bagiella, E. and Powell, T. 1999. "Religion, spirituality, and medicine". *The Lancet.* February 20, Vol. 353. pp. 664–67.

Stack, S.S., Krysinska, K. and Lester, D. 2008. "Gloomy Sunday: Did the 'Hungarian suicide song' really create a suicide epidemic?". *Omega: Journal of Death & Dying.* Vol. 56, No. 4, pp. 349–58.

Stearn, J. 1989. *Edgar Cayce: The Sleeping Prophet.* Bantam.

The Confessions of St. Augustine. 1907. Translated by E.B. Pusey. J. M. Dent & Sons.

Trotta, Liz. 2005. *Jude: A Pilgrimage to the Saint of the Last Resort.* HarperCollins.

US Secret Service. 2002. *Public Awareness Advisory Regarding "4-1-9" and "Advance Fee Fraud" schemes.* Available at: http://secretservice.gov/alert419.shmtl

VanArsdal, Daniel W. 2014. Chain Letter Evolution. http://www.silcom.com/~barnowl/chain-letter/evolution.html

Vidocq, Eugène François. 1834. *Memoirs of Vidocq, Principal Agent to the French Police Until 1827.* Google Books.

Watson, Lyall. 1979. *Lifetide: A Biology of the Unconscious.* Hodder & Stoughton Ltd.

Wattles, Wallace. 2013 (1910). *The Science of Getting Rich.* Start Publishing.

Weil, Andrew. 2000. *Spontaneous Healing: How to Discover and Embrace Your Body's Natural Ability to Maintain and Heal Itself.* Random House.

Wilhelm, Richard. 1979. *The I Ching or Book of Changes.* Trans. from the Chinese by Richard Wilhelm. Trans. from the German by Cary F. Baynes. Princeton University Press.

Wilson, Ian. 2003. *Nostradamus: The Man Behind the Prophecies.* Macmillan.

Winter, P. R. J. 2006. "Libra rising: Hitler, astrology and British intelligence, 1940–43." *Intelligence and National Security.* Vol. 21, No. 3 (June) pp. 394–415.

Part II
Possessed Language

Introduction

We often hear bizarre stories about language. The news tells us about the woman who went to bed with a headache, and awoke to find that she suddenly spoke with a different accent. We hear about the man who suffered a bump on his head and became spontaneously fluent in a language he'd never learned. We read about people who speak in foreign languages under hypnosis, telling detailed stories of former lives they've lived. These cases are often presented as evidence for reincarnation and life after death.

Unusual language is a part of religion and spirituality too. Spirits, gods, and other entities are channeled for the purposes of worship, healing, prophecy, and to receive messages from beyond the grave. Pentecostal churches practice glossolalia, where the Holy Spirit communicates through the congregation. Modern prophets claim to be a voice for God. Exorcists believe that demons and the devil talk through possessed victims. Psychic mediums seem to be hosts for spirits that speak during séances.

These chapters explore real-life cases where people appear to be possessed by something that talks or writes through them. We look at strange, spontaneous accents, the sudden ability to speak foreign languages, speaking in tongues, past-life regression, mediumship, and spirit writing, as we search for possible explanations for these phenomena.

6
Foreign Accent Syndrome

January 4, 2010, started out as just another day for Kay Russell of Gloucestershire, England. The 49-year-old grandmother suffered from severe migraines and later that evening, she went to bed with a debilitating attack. She awoke the next day to discover that she had a French accent (*Guardian*, 2010).

There are dozens of similar stories of people who developed a new accent suddenly, but this isn't "National Talk Like a Pirate Day". Karen Butler of Oregon was sedated for routine dental surgery, and awoke with an Irish accent (*Irish Central*, 2010). After a neck adjustment from her chiropractor, California-born CindyLou Romberg developed an accent that sounds alternatively Russian, German, or French (*Seattle Times*, 2010). Robin Jenks Vanderlip of Virginia speaks English with a Russian accent, although she has never learned Russian (*Washington Post*, 2010). Mary Gashaw of West Michigan awoke one morning with neck pain, and a Norwegian accent (*WWMT*, 2010). Linda Walker suffered a stroke in her sleep and woke up to discover that her Geordie accent had transformed into a Jamaican one (BBC, 2006).

This amazing phenomenon has been documented in cases around the world. There have been accent changes from Japanese to Korean, British English to French, American English to British English, Scottish English to South African English, and Spanish to Hungarian. Is this paranormal, psychological, or physiological?

In a manner of speaking

These people aren't possessed by demons or pulling a prank. This is a speech motor disorder caused by neurological damage that affects a speaker's pronunciation. However, it is an extremely contentious

79

condition because there is no consistent cause or effect. The only connection across cases is that the patient sounds like they are speaking with a foreign accent. For this reason, the phenomenon is called "foreign accent syndrome" (FAS), "pseudo-accent" or "unlearned foreign accent". However, these are misnomers in that these patients haven't acquired a true foreign accent. These names tend to sensationalize an already stigmatized and misunderstood condition.

FAS is a type of language disorder known as aphasia. Some forms of aphasia are particularly well documented. Broca's aphasia is caused by damage to the frontal lobe of the brain. Speakers with this condition tend to omit grammatical words such as "the" and "we". They can say short sentences that are grammatically accurate, but this is done with great difficulty. Wernicke's aphasia is another well-known disorder that is caused by damage to the temporal lobe of the brain. These speakers speak nonsensical words and sentences in what is called a "Word Salad". There are several different types of aphasia and over a million sufferers in the United States alone. In contrast, FAS is extremely rare. There are only about 60 alleged cases, with even fewer reported in academic journals. Science still has a lot to learn about the disorder. Still, it's not all Greek to us, even though it may sound like it at times.

FAS is an impairment in language ability resulting from damage to portions of the brain responsible for language. This typically occurs in the left hemisphere of the brain, affecting the primary motor cortex and either its cortico-cortical connections or its cortico-subcortical projections (Kurowski and Blumstein, 2006). The cause of FAS is little understood, but it is usually brought on by a stroke. There are many other potential causes, including brain tumors, hematoma, brain injuries, dementia, cancer metastasis to the brain, or infections, such as encephalitis. There have also been cases where FAS has been caused by multiple sclerosis lesions, migraine attacks, or anesthesia.

The condition may occur suddenly, following a bump on the head. The patient might remain mute for a few days before the symptoms present. When caused by brain tumors or degenerative disease the condition has a gradual onset. Overall, the prognosis of FAS is unpredictable. The condition may be temporary. There are cases of patients recovering in days or making a spontaneous remission. For others, the condition may be long term or permanent. The outlook is generally better for younger patients because their nerve cells heal themselves faster.

The symptoms are the biggest clue towards diagnosing FAS, but these are not consistent. Each case is unique. Generally, changes take place in the speaker's pronunciation, pitch, pause, emphasis, and intonation. This is known as dysprosody. Speakers are unable to make certain sounds or sound combinations, and may delete, substitute, or add alternative sounds to compensate for this deficit. An English woman suffered a stroke and afterwards she sounded Scottish. This is because she lost the ability to make a regular English /r/ sound and instead could only make a trill, which is that rolling r-sound for which Scottish English is famous. Basically, FAS is a speech impediment.

An accidental accent

It also helps to know what FAS isn't. Speech motor disorders can affect speech production and comprehension, and even the ability to read and write. However, in FAS, other language faculties, such as grammar and vocabulary, are generally left intact. In some speech disorders, patients make errors in their grammar, yet they are unaware of this. However, in FAS, the condition doesn't affect understanding. Patients are painfully aware of the changes in their voices. Their speech remains comprehensible but their accent becomes unrecognizable. When the changes are significant it sounds as though the person is speaking with a foreign accent. This is when an "accent" is an accident.

A person's accent is like a linguistic fingerprint. The accent can be a clue revealing the places where we've lived. National and regional accents are identifiable by their distinctive features. For example, standard American English is known for its pronunciation of /r/. This is especially clear when the "r" is at the end of a word following a vowel sound, like "car" and "computer". Alternatively, some regional accents are distinctive for not pronouncing these "r's", like the accents found in Boston, Massachusetts. Similarly, Australian English is characterized by dropping this /r/ in some contexts, and replacing it with a double-vowel sound called a diphthong. This makes the /r/ sound like "uh" at the ends of words. However, if the "r" is followed by a vowel sound in a following word, it *is* pronounced. For example, the /r/ in "beer addict" would be pronounced. These features make the speaker sound like they are from Boston, or Australia, depending on other aspects of the accent.

Accents are also recognizable by the sound combinations in a language. For example, Japanese doesn't allow clusters of consonants, but instead repeats a consonant-vowel pattern. Therefore, "Yoko Ono" sounds Japanese. English allows consonant to go together, but not like the set you'd find in the Polish name "Krzysztof". In Middle English, the /kn/ in "knife" and "knight" were pronounced, but this sound combination isn't found in Modern English, so the /k/ has become silent. These permissible and restricted sound patterns give a language its distinctive sound.

Turning Japanese

As we have seen, the FAS patient loses the ability to produce certain sounds. Instead, they pronounce different sounds that are characteristic of other accents. They may even transpose similar sounds. This often occurs when people learn a foreign language. Speakers of some Asian languages have difficulty distinguishing /r/ from /l/ when they learn English, so they often switch these two sounds without even knowing it. When I used to work in a post office in Sydney, Australia, I once handled a letter from Japan that was addressed to the suburb of Collaroy, but was spelled "Corraloy". Following a series of migraines possibly caused by a stroke, Sarah Colwill of England had difficulty in differentiating /r/ from /l/ (*Guardian*, 2010). This is a salient feature of Chinese languages, so to listeners, Colwill suddenly "sounded Chinese".

These people haven't suddenly developed a different national accent, like those common to German or French people. Nor is it a regional accent, like a Texan or Yorkshire accent. They haven't developed a genuine foreign accent. Their new accent resembles sounds found in natural languages, but they don't characterize any particular language. They have lost features distinctive to their personal accents. These have been replaced with features that make them sound like they are speaking in another accent. This is what it sounds like, not what it is.

Sufferers are sometimes accused of faking their accent. However, the features of each case are too specific and systematic to be fraudulent. Mimicry is intentional and voluntary, while FAS is unintentional and involuntary. We can put on an accent, but FAS sufferers can't even imitate their native accent. They are simply unable to say these sounds, although speech therapy offers the possibility of relearning their accent.

Some speculate that the sufferer has simply recalled the accent of a language they learned in school. However, FAS creates an unlearned accent. Developing a genuine foreign accent is not a spontaneous or speedy process. I have spent almost a decade in the United States and while I can hear gradual signs of American English in my accent, Americans hear the obvious traits of my Australian English and overall, perceive me as "Australian" or "English".

Now you're talking

FAS isn't only about how the sufferer sounds. It is also about how we hear them. Only some aspects of their speech are affected and they still retain features of their native accent. However, hearers tend to only notice what is different, rather than what is the same. In the case of FAS, hearers recognize foreign-like sounds and incorrectly identify a foreign accent. Which foreign accent do people hear? Listeners categorize FAS speech as "foreign", but there is a general lack of agreement as to which accent they are hearing. The same sufferer might be variously described as sounding "Dutch", "Russian", or "French". This is because the identification is subjective and foreignness is an illusion. This is reminiscent of a passage from Edgar Allen Poe's *Murders in the Rue Morgue*.

But in regard to the shrill voice, the peculiarity is not that they disagreed – but that, while an Italian, an Englishman, a Spaniard, a Hollander, and a Frenchman attempted to describe it, each one spoke of it as that of a foreigner. Each is sure that it was not the voice of one of his own countrymen. Each likens it – not to the voice of an individual of any nation with whose language he is conversant – but the converse. The Frenchman supposes it the voice of a Spaniard, and "might have distinguished some words had he been acquainted with the Spanish." The Dutchman maintains it to have been that of a Frenchman; but we find it stated that "not understanding French this witness was examined through an interpreter." The Englishman thinks it the voice of a German, and "does not understand German." The Spaniard "is sure" that it was that of an Englishman, but "judges by the intonation" altogether, "as he has no knowledge of the English." The Italian believes it the voice of a Russian, but "has never conversed with a native of Russia." A second Frenchman differs, moreover, with the first, and is positive that the voice was that of an Italian; but, not being cognizant of that tongue, is, like the Spaniard, "convinced by the intonation." Now, how strangely unusual must that voice have really been, about which such testimony as this could have been elicited! – in whose tones, even, denizens of the five great divisions of Europe could recognize nothing familiar! (Poe, 1841)

Speaking my language

Unfortunately, the media sensationalizes the condition. News items are full of exaggerations, and medical and linguistic inaccuracies. "Woman wakes up with a foreign accent" is a headline editor's dream. We need to be suspicious of some cases. There are many unverified stories of this condition with no evidence but the anecdotal kind. Mel Blanc, the voice behind Daffy Duck and Porky Pig, once fell into a coma following a car accident. When he regained consciousness three weeks later, it was said that he was temporarily unable to speak in anything but his Bugs Bunny voice (Blanc and Bashe, 1989).

Some believe that developing a "new accent" is a paranormal ability but this condition is a type of brain damage and a loss of ability, not a gain. It is a serious physiological condition, and not a psychological or paranormal phenomenon. But this isn't just about losing an accent. People form assumptions and have stereotypes about us based on our accents. FAS sufferers have reported frustration, anxiety, and isolation as a result of their condition. Many feel like immigrants in their own country and experience prejudice from fellow country people who see them as foreigners. According to one account, this had serious consequences. During an air raid in World War II, a Norwegian woman known as Astrid sustained a head injury that caused her to sound like she had a German accent (Monrad-Krohn, 1947). The anti-German sentiment of the time resulted in her ostracism from society.

Intelligence and personality are not affected by this condition, but losing an accent affects the person's sense of identity. They aren't speaking a foreign accent, but it sounds foreign to the sufferers, and their friends and families. CindyLou mourns the loss of her accent, "It's the voice I said 'I do' with". Kay is now unable to say her grandchildren's names. Linda laments, "I don't sound like me anymore". For people with this condition, in losing their accents they have lost a part of themselves.

7
Xenoglossia

Xenoglossia is the spontaneous acquisition of a foreign language. These are existing human languages, unlike the alien and Bigfoot languages we encounter in Part IV of this book. However, they didn't learn this language though Berlitz or Rosetta Stone. These languages are said to be previously unknown to the speakers. In claims of xenoglossia, the person speaks the foreign language suddenly, without taking classes, watching *Banzai!* or having any exposure at all.

It's all Greek to me

On April 12, 2010, a 13-year-old girl from the Croatian town of Knin fell into a coma. When she awoke a day later, she could no longer speak or understand her native tongue. Instead, she was suddenly fluent in German (*Daily Mail*, 2010). Was this teenager possessed by a German spirit, was she not speaking German, or could she speak German all along?

In this case, the foreign language was not entirely unlearned and the girl had had previous exposure to the German language. She was learning it in school and had taken up the task enthusiastically, watching TV shows in German and reading books in the language. Therefore, this was not an example of xenoglossia, the spontaneous speaking of an unknown, unlearned language. Instead, it appears to be a case of bilingual aphasia.

Bilingual aphasia

Second languages (any languages learned after the first language) are stored in different parts of the brain to the native tongue. Therefore, brain injuries can affect bilingual speakers differently to monolingual people. As we read in the section above, aphasia is a general name for speech impairments caused by damage to the language-producing parts of the brain. Bilingual aphasia is damage caused to the fronto-subcortical loop. This can lead to switching between the first and second language and cause attrition of the language that is more automatic to the speaker. For example, J. Z. is bilingual in Basque and Spanish. He suffered a blood clot in the brain and this resulted in impaired abilities in Basque, his first language (Adrover-Roig et al., 2011).

The Croatian girl likely suffered a swelling of the brain that caused a selective deficit in her native language. This doesn't mean that she lost all of her abilities, or that she suddenly acquired more of her second language than she had before the illness. The coma gave her less fluency in Croatian, but didn't magically give her more fluency in German. These are embellishments by the media. The girl was barely bilingual, but having access to some German enabled her to communicate. As a young girl, it is likely that her condition is temporary. With recovery and rehabilitation she should regain her language skills in Croatian, and be able to continue learning German.

Rosemary

Not all claims of xenoglossia are examples of bilingual aphasia. Some cases can be explained as scams, while others involve a complex series of factors that lead a person to think they have an ability they don't really have. The "Rosemary" story is considered the best case of xenoglossia. Like most other cases, this story is big on sensationalism, but short on facts. Ivy Carter Beaumont of Blackpool, England, became better known as "Rosemary". In a trance state it was said she channeled spirits and could speak and write in an ancient Egyptian dialect (Wood, 1939). Rosemary channeled a few colorful characters. These included "Vola", a young temple dancer during the reign of the eighteenth dynasty pharaoh Amenhotep III, and "Nona", a Babylonian princess and member of the pharaoh's harem.

Rosemary had been channeling in English, until Egyptologist Alfred Hulme came on the scene to investigate her claims. Suddenly, Rosemary began receiving messages in "ancient Egyptian". Hulme spent five years translating her readings and concluded that they revealed authentic examples of an early Egyptian language. Subsequently, several scholars examined the data independently and concluded that Hulme's analyses were grossly inaccurate. Hulme had confused Middle Egyptian and Late Egyptian, which is tantamount to confusing classical Latin and contemporary Italian. They also found evidence that he had falsified many results (Fenwick and Fenwick, 1999). Interestingly, a gramophone recording of Rosemary's utterances still exists today, but the sample doesn't reveal any kind of Egyptian language. Instead, it suggests that she was speaking was gibberish, like a kind of speaking in tongues.

Rajesh

The *Times of India* reported the story of "Rajesh", a Hindi-speaking boy from the Bilaspur village of Saharanpur in Uttar Pradesh, India. According to this version, Rajesh witnessed his mentally disabled father being struck by a brick to the head. This traumatized the 14-year-old so much that he refused to talk for three months. When he resumed speaking he could no longer speak Hindi but instead could only speak in English. However, Rajesh had never learned English and had never traveled out of his hometown. Remarkably, he spoke English with a perfect American accent.

Rajesh may be a real person but the story appears to be an urban legend as there are few details, but many variations. If it were true, it could be a case of bilingual aphasia. However, we're not presented with any physical cause, and there is no evidence to suggest that Rajesh was deficient in Hindi. English is also commonly spoken in India. It is used for education, in the government, and by the media. As a relic of British colonial rule, English remains an official language in India. There are a quarter of a million speakers of English as a first language, and over one billion people who speak English as a second language. It would be no surprise if Rajesh had some exposure to English, and especially American English, which is the world's fastest growing variety.

There is a strange twist to this story. It was reported that Rajesh also acquired an expert knowledge of physics and chemistry. Coupled with his sudden acquisition of fluent American English, he developed graphic memories of a past life. Rajesh was obviously the reincarnation of an American scientist! Of course, there is no evidence that this is true. Reincarnation is a central tenet of Hinduism and the story of Rajesh supports this popular belief.

Sharada

Stories of xenoglossia are often hyped as evidence of reincarnation. Psychiatrist and parapsychologist Ian Stevenson (1966, 1974, 1984) analyzed several such cases and concluded that each one validated the theories of both past lives and xenoglossia. However, it appears that his reports of the linguistic competency of these people were greatly exaggerated.

One example was the case of Uttara Hudder, a Marathi-speaking Indian woman who was a resident patient in a psychiatric hospital (Stevenson, 1984). Under hypnosis, Hudder became possessed by Sharada, a nineteenth-century native speaker of Bengali. When Sharada manifested, Hudder could suddenly speak long and complex sentences in Bengali. It was clear that Sharada was not of this time, as she was unfamiliar with modern inventions like trains and fountain pens.

Amazingly, many of Sharada's claims were verified and traced back to a family in Bengal. However, the claims weren't so amazing after all. By Stevenson's own admission, Hudder had previous exposure to the Bengali language, people, and culture in early life rather than an earlier life. As a girl, Hudder had taken lessons in Bengali. Her native tongue Marathi uses a related writing system, and she had also learned Sanskrit, the parent language to both Marathi and Bengali (Thomason, 1996). Moreover, Hudder's Bengali was not regarded as natural or fluent by experts and her accent was clearly nonnative. It seems that, in a suggestible state, Hudder regained access to her forgotten second language in which she only had limited skills. Stevenson insisted that Sharada wasn't a charade. He argued that Sharada's abilities were limited because she had to use Hudder as a mouthpiece!

Past-life regression

In other cases of xenoglossia the subjects have had exposure to the language in question, but not always consciously. Past-life regression therapy has generated many claims of xenoglossia. These therapists believe that regressing patients to past lives can reveal and heal the traumas in the present lives. They also believe that our past lives explain our personality, interests, careers, and talents in our present life. By this theory, if we spoke a different language in a former life, we could tap into that language via the subconscious. Some therapists claim to be able to induce xenoglossia by placing their patients under hypnosis.

Past-life regression therapy was popularized by one such case. In 1952, Virginia Tighe was hypnotized by Morey Bernstein. In a trance, the woman from Pueblo, Colorado, became Bridey Murphy, a nineteenth-century Irish woman. Under hypnosis, Tighe took on her former personality. She sang Irish songs, told stories, and provided a remarkably detailed account about her childhood in Cork. She recounted memories of her parents Duncan and Kathleen, her marriage to Sean Brian McCarthy, her move to Belfast, the accident that caused her death, and how she witnessed her own funeral. Tighe even spoke with an Irish English accent. She also became bilingual and could speak fluent Irish Gaelic. Here was seemingly amazing evidence for the existence of past lives, and this was seized as proof by the burgeoning reincarnation movement.

Tighe revealed startlingly vivid information about her former life, although she'd never been to Ireland. But one woman had: Bridie Murphy Corkell, an Irish immigrant who lived across the street from Tighe's childhood home. Bridey did indeed exist, but as a real woman who lived during the twentieth century, not as a past life. Tighe's memories of this "previous life" were memories of stories told by her childhood neighbor. She was recounting someone else's memories, embellished by memories from her own childhood and her imagination.

When she was under hypnosis, Tighe didn't develop an Irish English accent. She affected an accent that sounded Irish to her. As for the claim that she was fluent in Gaelic, her vocabulary was unimpressively small. Transcripts of Tighe's hypnosis with Bernstein reveal the limited extent of her bilingualism. She incorrectly states that *banshees* are Irish ghosts, and that a *lough* is a "river" (Glubok and Smith, 1956).

Past-life regression therapy, repressed memory therapy, and other related therapies are dangerous. These practices have lead to the creation of false memories of sexual molestation, satanic ritual abuse, and alien abductions (Loftus and Ketcham, 1994).

Xenoglossia also has ties to occult theory and demonology. According to the Catholic Church, speaking an unknown foreign language can be a symptom of demonic possession. As exorcist Father Jeremy Davies says, "Occasionally there may be preternatural knowledge, as of a spiritual reality or a foreign language or a future event (e.g., *Acts* 16:16–18)" (Davies, 2008). In this biblical passage, Paul witnesses a slave girl who is possessed by a spirit. He exorcises her with the words, "In the name of Jesus Christ I command you to come out of her!". At that moment, the spirit left her body.

The sudden utterance of Latin phrases might just require an exorcism. Indeed, the exorcism itself might cause the demon to speak through the person's mouth in a foreign language, or the demon's voice. In popular culture, a demon alerts its presence by speaking in a (typically classical) language unknown to the host. In the movie *The Exorcist*, Regan MacNeil is possessed by a polyglot demon that speaks Latin, Greek, and French.

Braco the Gazer

According to some religions, xenoglossia means you're more holy, rather than less. In the Bible, Acts 2 describes the Day of Pentecost where the apostles speak in their native language but are heard and understood in terms of the listeners' languages. I encountered a form of this alleged xenoglossia when I attended a session by the spiritual healer Braco.

Braco is a "Gazer", that is, he stands on a podium and simply gazes at his audience. Testimonials report that his gaze is healing, brings good luck, and performs miracles. He and his staff assert that they don't make any claims about his abilities; his devotees do. It is also said that the sound of his voice is healing, but paradoxically, he refuses to speak in public. Instead, recordings of his voice are played during his sessions.

I attended one of his gazing sessions in Denver, Colorado. During the performance, Braco stood on stage before an audience of hundreds as his eyes scanned across the room for ten minutes. This was followed by a pre-recorded speech by Braco, spoken in his native Croatian. Amazingly, some people in the audience claimed they could understand him! His website says:

> It was very amazing to see, that even in Germany or other countries, where people cannot understand what Braco is speaking, the reactions of the visitors during the session with his voice are exactly the same as with those people who understand Braco's words.
>
> (Stollznow, 2011)

There are several possible explanations for this. People may simply guess the spiritual-related themes in Braco's speech. His followers attend in the hopes of receiving healing, luck, and miracles, so in this context, they may believe they hear him talking about these and other New Age topics.

As for claims that people can "understand" Croatian, they are probably hearing cognates. These are words from different languages that share common origins. They still have the same or similar meanings, and still resemble each other in spelling and pronunciation. For example, "antique" means the same in French and English, while "horror" is the same in Spanish and English. Other cognates don't have the exact same form, but they still look and sound similar, for example, English "milk" and Croatian *mlijeko*.

There are also false cognates where two forms are misleadingly similar but have entirely different meanings. For example, German *Nutte* looks like English "nut" but it means "prostitute", while "nut" is *Nuss*. There

are many Croatian words that sound familiar because they are historically related to words in English. Some are still recognizable even when
they are not related. We're dealing with different languages but similar
human sounds from natural languages. The familiar words may even
be English words borrowed into Croatian, or vice versa. These phenomena may all give listeners the false impression that they can understand
Braco, or by extension, comprehend Croatian.

Pareidolia may also be at play. This is when we search for recognizable patterns in unrecognizable ones. In this case, the English-speaker
searches the unfamiliar Croatian speech for familiar sound patterns. Like
seeing Jesus on a tortilla, people may hear English words where there
aren't any. Alternatively, Braco's followers may hear and understand him
because they're supposed to do so. There is also a certain amount of hypnosis, influence, and paranormal peer pressure in an environment like
this. The attendees are primed to follow directions and suggestions in
this susceptible state. Therefore, when they are told upfront that the
faithful can understand Braco's speech, and that they will understand it
too, they will convince themselves that they can make sense of a foreign
language.

8
Speaking in Tongues

During a faith healing session at a Charismatic church in Sydney, I was not healed. The parishioners encircled me, laid their hands upon me, and ordered me to stop thinking "impure thoughts". The female minister signed a cross on my forehead with sweet-scented oil, and prayed. The group joined her in prayer, but after awhile the language of their prayers turned from English into a strange language like they were possessed. They were speaking in tongues.

The minister pressed her hand firmly against my forehead. Slipping back into English easily, she declared, "The holy spirit flows through you...now!". But nothing happened. In disbelief, the parishioners suddenly stopped their performance. Take two. The minister's prayers resumed, and then the speaking in tongues grew more fervent. "The holy spirit flows through you...NOW!"

This time I fell over backwards...filled with the holy spirit of the minister's fist.

Slip of the tongue

In biblical times, God spoke directly to people, including Adam, Noah, and Moses. God also spoke to Joseph Smith, the founder of the Church of Jesus Christ of Latter-day Saints. And if we believe them, He continues to talk to the Mormon "modern prophets". But nowadays, it seems God prefers to talk through people, rather than to people.

Speaking in tongues is the belief that gods, angels, spirits, or the Holy Spirit can talk through a living person. In practice, the entities emerge during a religious ceremony conducted for the purposes of healing and worship. Similar to xenoglossia, speaking in tongues is said to be language previously unknown to the speaker. Xenoglossia differs in that the spoken languages are unlearned human languages. In speaking in tongues, the languages spoken are believed to be divine.

Speaking in tongues is usually associated with the feast of Pentecost, but the practice pre-dates the Bible. Prophets and mystics in ancient Egypt, Assyria, and Greece also practiced this ritual. Most famously, the Oracle of Delphi was a mouthpiece for the god Apollo. Known as the "Pythia", the priestess would reveal Apollo's prophecies in a frenzied gibberish. Fortunately, the priests could translate these messages into poetry or prose (that was still ambiguous).

Speaking in tongues is described in the New Testament in Mark (16:17), 1 Corinthians (14:2), and most significantly in Acts (2:1–13, 10:44–48; 19:1–7). The Acts account describes the day of Pentecost during which the apostles spoke in tongues. But in the Bible, speaking in tongues was something very different.

> When the day of Pentecost came, they were all together in one place. Suddenly a sound like the blowing of a violent wind came from heaven and filled the whole house where they were sitting. They saw what seemed to be tongues of fire that separated and came to rest on each of them. All of them were filled with the Holy Spirit and began to speak in other tongues as the Spirit enabled them.
>
> Now there were staying in Jerusalem God-fearing Jews from every nation under heaven. When they heard this sound, a crowd came together in bewilderment, because each one heard their own language being spoken. Utterly amazed, they asked: "Aren't all these who are speaking Galileans? Then how is it that each of us hears them in our native language? Parthians, Medes and Elamites; residents of Mesopotamia, Judea and Cappadocia, Pontus and Asia, Phrygia and Pamphylia, Egypt and the parts of Libya near Cyrene; visitors from Rome (both Jews and converts to Judaism); Cretans and Arabs – we hear them declaring the wonders of God in our own tongues!"
>
> (The Bible, The Book of Acts)

Therefore, biblical speaking in tongues was really a kind of xenoglossia. The 12 apostles addressed the crowd in Galilean, their own language, but the languages heard were the native tongues of each person in the audience. This was like an inverse Tower of Babel, where a single language was made comprehensible to a multilingual crowd.

Holy Spirit, hoax, or hysteria?

Charles Parham and his Bethel Bible school initiated the Pentecostal movement in 1901 when one of his students, Agnes Ozman, began speaking in tongues. It was believed that Ozman was speaking a real foreign language that was previously unknown to her. It was said that she sounded like she was speaking Chinese. Since that time, speaking in tongues has changed, and the languages spoken are said to be spiritual languages rather than natural human languages. Outside of its religious context speaking in tongues is known as glossolalia.

Glossolalia has been practiced globally, in the United States, Japan, Indonesia, Korea, Mexico, and Russia. Historically, it has been a feature of a range of traditional denominations, including Presbyterians, Lutherans, Baptists, and Roman Catholics. It has also been practiced by non-Christian religions, including Voodoo, Santeria, and shamanism. As shown by my experience described above, glossolalia is still commonly practiced. In fact, it seems to be on the increase. This modern trend seems to be based on a belief in the Second Coming of Christ, and that salvation is contingent upon acquiring the gift of this spiritual language.

Despite its popularity, glossolalia is marginal and not a feature of all modern Christian denominations. It is a particular ritual of Pentecostal churches and some Charismatic churches. It is also becoming a New Age practice where it is seen as a spiritual experience to expand consciousness. To some traditional Christians, glossolalia is attributed to Satan rather than God.

In the Pentecostal Church, glossolalia is known as "the gift of tongues" and is believed to be a gift from God. This is when "giving a tongue" to the congregation is conveying a message from God. There are two purposes of glossolalia. It can be directed *to* God, in praise or prayer. It is also believed to be *from* God, as prophecy or for miraculous healing, especially when used in conjunction with the "laying on of hands". During the ceremony, devout followers believe they are possessed by the Holy Spirit and have become a mouthpiece through which the Holy Spirit speaks. However, it appears that glossolalia is not so much a gift from God as learned behavior.

Tongue in cheek

Glossolalia is language-like, but it is not language. The less kind might call it gibberish. Glossolalia bears only superficial similarities to language. During the ritual, participants spontaneously speak a stream of speech-like sounds that appear to form distinct words and are uttered with enough fluidity to appear language-like. In trying to unscramble the noise, it sounds like the speaker has switched into a foreign language but glossolalia is incomprehensible. It is only like a language superficially, in that the sounds come from existing human languages. Examples of glossolalia conform to the sounds, sound sequences, stress, and intonation found in the speaker's native language, or other languages to which they have had exposure.

Glossolalia is devoid of other linguistic elements that would classify it as a language. Glossolalia imitates language in its phonology, but it has no grammatical structure or internal organization. It has no consistent or shared meaning, other than the meaning given to it by the faithful. Linguist William Samarin (1972) sums it up as, "a meaningless but phonetically structured human utterance believed by the speaker to be a real language but bearing no systematic resemblance to any natural language, living or dead". Some argue that spiritual languages are not subject to the rules of human language.

It's all in the interpretation

In what is known as the "gift of interpretation", some people claim to be able to understand glossolalia. They argue that the language is simply not yet understood. Others maintain that only the faithful can understand this sacred language. As of yet, no one has provided any analyses of speaking in tongues. This isn't to say that they are being deceptive (although some may be) but this is evidence that glossolalia is fabricated. It can't be described or codified as natural languages are because each example of glossolalia is unique. No two instances will ever be the same. Translating "divine messages" is open to abuse and the subjective interpretation may be one that suits the beliefs and agendas of the congregation and its leaders.

Glossolalia has even been turned into song. This is a worship practice known as "singing in the spirit". I once had the opportunity to examine an example of this. I was approached by Mike, the vocalist of the Christian punk band, The Knights of the New Crusade. Mike sent me a copy of their album *A Challenge to the Cowards of Christendom*, and asked me to analyze the song, "Knight Beat: Speaking in the Holy Spirit". In Mike's own words, this is an "end of session jam where I started speaking in tongues (or scatting, in secular terminology)" (Stollznow, 2007).

This is a loud, fast-paced punk song, with rapid-fire vocals. The glossolalia initially appears to resemble words and speech, but this is an illusion. Hearing language in glossolalia is a form of pareidolia. In Mike's song some of the lyrics sounded like "mosquito", "Bora Bora", and "Boutros Boutros-Ghali". This is subjective interpretation, so others could hear something different. In one study of glossolalia the subjects all heard different words (Kildahl, 1972). Alternatively, they might hear what other people hear if they were primed by being told what words to listen for.

Mike had stumbled across his own explanation when he compared his speaking in tongues to "scatting". We can think of speaking in tongues as inspirational improvisation. Like beat boxing, drum talk, and free jazz, glossolalia imitates speech, but with a lot less rhythm. The more you do it, the more natural and convincing it sounds. Glossolalia is more stylized singing than speech. "Knight Beat: Speaking in the Holy Spirit" is just a jam session that is great for crowd surfing and moshing, but the song is as much a message from the Holy Spirit as Cab Calloway's "Hi-de-hi-de-hi-di-hi".

Fa-la-la-la-la la-la-la-la

This highlights some interesting sound combinations found in glossolalia. It typically exhibits permissible groups of sounds as found in the languages spoken by or familiar to the speaker. Like a Lewis Carroll nonsense word, speaking in tongues produces word-like units that are nonsensical but phonologically possible. For example, *gomble* is a possible English word, but *tngsch* isn't. However, glossolaliacs can't be as creative as Carroll and his "slithy toves". Glossolalia is too rapid-paced to allow for the creation of clever would-be words. Instead, it tends to involve repetition, and combined with its rhythmic qualities, glossolalia resembles chanting.

Glossolalia also has parallels to baby babbling. This is a stage in first language acquisition during which babies learn to navigate their speech organs and mimic the sounds used in their native language. Late in the first year of age, babies begin making formative sounds, such as /b/ and /d/, usually following a consonant vowel pattern, such as *babababa* or *dididiidi*. Babbling uses more vowels than are found in language.

Glossolalia also has a higher frequency of vowels and recurring sound patterns. As far as real words are concerned, this phenomenon is found in many of the world's languages and usually indicates plurality or emphasis. In Indonesian, *orang* means "a person", while *orang orang* means "people". The process is less common in English, and is mostly found in baby talk such as *choo choo* for "train". However, in glossolalia, recurring sequences are random and meaningless, and made simply because they are sounds that are easy to pronounce and replicate rapidly.

That's the spirit!

We shouldn't only consider the language side of glossolalia, we should also consider the behavior. In some ways, the ritual of being filled with the Holy Spirit is a form of hypnosis, and the minister acts as a hypnotist of the congregation. The minister guides the process and the congregation follows suit in a kind of role-playing. It's a very theatrical procedure. The participants may enter into trance states or a kind of hysterical religious ecstasy where they laugh, cry, fall to the ground, roll about, and even go into convulsions. In their belief that they are overcome with the Holy Spirit they are overcome with emotion. And glossolalia is more about emotion than language.

Research bears this out. One study used neuroimaging technology to observe brain activity during glossolalia. It was discovered that when someone speaks in tongues the emotion centers of the brain show an increase in activity, while the language centers show a reduction in activity (Newburg, 2006). This supports the theory that glossolalia is not language. Subjects also showed a decrease in frontal lobe function, the part of the brain that enables reason and self-control, but increased activity in regions of the brain that process sensory information. This may explain the emotional behavior exhibited during a visit from the Holy Spirit.

Glossolalia is also used in private prayer. "Praying in the sprit" is encouraged to establish a personal connection with God. However, glossolalia is more often a social phenomenon practiced within a group to establish community and reinforce belief. Glossolalia is also an expected practice in some churches. Churchgoers are socialized into this behavior and are taught how to speak in tongues. There is a social expectation that everyone will participate in the activity. In this way, there is a kind of pious peer pressure to speak in tongues.

9
Mediums and Channelers

Psychic mediums and channelers are not common in modern traditional religions but are instead a feature of the hodgepodge doctrine of New Age, spiritual, and metaphysical beliefs. These people claim to be intermediaries for deceased people, spirits, angels, demons, and gods from the other side, or other planets and planes. These hosts are possessed by the entity in a trance, during a séance, on stage, or even spontaneously. They act as human voices for these nonhumans, bringing important teachings, personal messages, and healings. Their claims can be differentiated from xenoglossia and glossolalia by one important feature: the entity conveniently speaks in the language of the medium.

J. Z. Knight and "Ramtha"

J. Z. Knight was a housewife living an ordinary life in Tacoma, Washington, until her life became unexpectedly extraordinary. One day in 1977, in the kitchen of her trailer, Knight was suddenly possessed by Ramtha, a 35,000-year-old spirit from Atlantis. Ramtha was once human, a Lemurian warrior who led men into battle and conquered the Atlanteans. He never died as such, instead he ascended, but before he did so he vowed he would return to earth one day. Now he is an Ascended Master who channels via his chosen host. Knight established Ramtha's School of Enlightenment in Mount Rainier, Washington, to share Ramtha's teachings and philosophies. But Ramtha didn't live in limbo during those millennia in-between. According to Ramtha himself, he taught the ancient Egyptians, influenced Hinduism and Judaism, and inspired Socrates and Leonardo da Vinci. Most amazing of all, Ramtha speaks English, Knight's native tongue.

Medium rare but not well done

For an all-knowing, all-seeing Ascended Master, Ramtha has made many failed predictions. Ramtha prophesized that a world war and holocaust would start in 1985. His accounts also contain many historical inaccuracies. When Ramtha claimed to have led 2.5 million men into battle 35,000 years ago, this figure was more than twice the estimated population of the time. Then there's the spurious existence of Atlantis and Lemuria. There are also many inconsistencies in Ramtha's messages. Ramtha showed cultural ignorance with his questions such as, "What is a Safeway?" (Knight, 1987). Nevertheless, Ramtha managed to track Knight down to her Tacoma trailer, and was seemingly knowledgeable about modern science and politics. To give the appearance of having difficulty with a second language, Ramtha stumbles over modern English. However, Ramtha swears like a sailor at other times, and using profanity in a grammatically correct manner demonstrates a high proficiency in a language.

Most of all, Ramtha reveals many linguistic inaccuracies and inconsistencies. Ramtha's language is unremarkable and the differences are superficial. When Knight is "possessed" she continues to speak in contemporary English. Ramtha, though an Ascended Master, doesn't speak any other language. But Ramtha's English is spoken with an inconsistent accent that alternatively sounds like an Indian Raj accent (Sagan, 1997) or a Hollywood version of Elizabethan English (Carroll, 2014). Knight adopts a deeper pitch to sound masculine, but a deeper pitch does not a 35,000-year-old spirit make. Ramtha's language is simply how Knight imagines a 35,000-year-old spirit might sound.

We don't know what an indigenous language from the Pleistocene ice age sounds like, which gives Knight free reign to invent it. Apparently, "Ramtha" translates to "the God" in his language, but he doesn't share any more vocabulary or grammar from his language. Instead of revealing evidence for a new proto-language for linguists to examine, Ramtha speaks with a pseudo-Tudor accent. Perhaps Knight once had a summer job selling turkey legs at a Renaissance festival. Most tellingly of all, Ramtha mispronounces the same words that Knight mispronounces (Cunningham, 2001).

Knight had many pretenders to her pretend spirit. Ramtha might not know what a Safeway is, but he understands modern copyright laws as Knight once sued a woman who copied her act, and trademarked the name "Ramtha". Knight and Ramtha spawned a whole generation of channelers and spirits during the 1980s. These include "Mafu", a

32,000-year-old spirit manifested by Penny Torres. Mafu sounded a lot like Ramtha, and even displayed similar gestures. That is, until Torres became flustered by questions from skeptics on an Australian TV show and broke character.

In a study, linguist Sarah Thomason (1989) analyzed the speech of channeled entities. She examined readings by 11 channelers and her research uncovered some damning results. Channelers don't tend to do their historical and linguistic research. "Matthew" is the spirit of a sixteenth-century Scotsman channeled by Marjorie Turcott. However, he pronounces "neighbor" as a contemporary English-speaking person would, with a silent "gh". Matthew also likes the word "rapscallion", although he lived about 100 years before the word existed! Julie Winter's "Mitka" switches between American English and British English dialects. And while Mafu was reincarnated 17 times, and last in first-century Greece, he speaks with an eighth-century English accent. Overall, the channelers accents and dialects were inconsistent and implausible, suggesting that these characters are fakes.

Abraham Hicks

Since 1985, Esther Hicks has manifested "Abraham", a council of non-physical entities. Abraham avoids the stigma of "channeling" by asserting that Hicks translates or interprets "their" messages. Hicks says she receives Abraham's thoughts, like radio signals, then translates these into physical words (Hicks, 2006). Hicks' performance is in real time, so her act can definitely be categorized as channeling or mediumship.

Hicks works with her husband Jerry, a former circus performer and Amway distributor. They are best known for their book *The Law of Attraction* (2006), supposedly dictated to Hicks by Abraham. If so, then Napoleon Hill and William Walker Atkinson must have dictated it to Abraham, as Hill's (1883–1970) *Think and Grow Rich* and Atkinson's (1862–1932) *Thought Vibration and the Law of Attraction in the Thought World* (1906) all pre-date the book by Hicks.

Verbal hiccup

During her performance, Hicks begins breathing deeply, enters into a trance, and then becomes possessed by Abraham. In earlier years, Hicks spoke in Abraham's voice, even though "they" are a collective. Abraham didn't sound much different to Hicks. When she was in character, her pitch deepened slightly and her vocabulary became more formal.

Abraham is described as "group consciousness from the non-physical dimension", without reference to time or place, allowing Hicks to affect any accent that is plausible-sounding to an audience eager to believe anyway. Hicks' unimpressive act is explained by true believers as Hick's "interpretation" of Abraham. It was clearly difficult to maintain as Hicks' normal accent would return during the course of her lecture. In recent years, Abraham no longer has a different voice but uses Hicks'. We know that Hicks is channeling the "collective" Abraham when she starts using the second-person pronouns "we" and "us". We are not amused.

Followers are quick to protect Hicks and justify any accent anomalies. They argue that when she had the accent, she was still learning how to channel Abraham. Perhaps her voice was affected by the immense energy required to channel Abraham. Maybe this was Hicks' interpretation of Abraham, as "they" have no voice. Then why adopt an accent at all? Because adopting an accent distinguishes Hicks' from Abraham. Of course, the simplest explanation is that Hicks feigned the accent. When her stage act became more polished and she attempted to establish greater credibility she ceased affecting "Abraham's voice".

Talking spirit guides

Strangely, other entities have had accents just like Abraham's, including the extraterrestrial "Bashar" channeled by Darryl Anka, Carla Rueckert's "Ra", and Jane Robert's "Seth". From ancient astronauts to spirits, the speech of these paranormal beings is all characterized by nondescript, vaguely "European" sounding accents and a formal vocabulary to make them sound archaic. Like glossolalia, these feigned accents and dialects are based on natural languages to which the speakers have had exposure.

The flesh is willing but the spirit is weak

Channelers say that spirits, aliens, angels, and demons speak through them, while psychic mediums specifically claim to be able to hear, speak with, and even smell spirits of the dead. They usually don't risk exposure by feigning the voices of people's deceased loved ones, but instead relay these "messages" in their own voices. Many mediums have spirit guides, guardian angels, and totems that assist them in their readings (and take the blame for any errors). These entities act as intermediary between the medium and the deceased. Psychic medium John Edward claims to have a team of spirit guides he calls "the boys" that communicate with him via visual images (presumably these aren't the same "the boys" we speak about in Chapter 20). However, some psychics claim their spirit guides can talk through them during readings.

Sylvia Browne

Late psychic medium Sylvia Browne's spirit guides were Francine and Raheim, and she was also in communication with her psychic grandmother Ada. Browne claimed that, by special arrangement with God, her spirit guides could take control of her body so they could communicate directly with her clients (Browne, 2002). Francine was her most infamous alter ego, who apparently dictated entire books to Browne. Francine was born as "Iena" in Columbia in early 1500. She was murdered by the Spanish colonizers, and spent the time from her death until 1936, Browne's year of birth, preparing to become Browne's spirit guide.

Perhaps Francine needed longer still, because her accent wasn't very convincing. Browne rarely did trance readings, but when she did her routine varied. In one act, Browne's body jerked aggressively as Francine possessed her; her pitch dropped (if it's at all possible!) and her speech slowed down, but she continued to speak in contemporary English rather than sixteenth-century Spanish. However, during other readings she did the channeling warm-up act but there was no noticeable change in her voice. Browne claimed to suffer "psychic amnesia" during a deep trance, with no memory of what took place. In her later years, Browne claimed that Francine spoke to her, rather than through her, which must have been much easier to pull off.

James Van Praagh

Medium James Van Praagh claims to have four spirit guides that assist him with readings. Sister Theresa was a nun from the Sisters of Mercy order, Golden Feather was a Native American Indian, Harry Aldrich was an English doctor who died in the 1930s, and Master Chang was a Chinese spiritual teacher (Van Praagh, 1999). Van Praagh claims that he can manifest Harry Aldrich and Golden Feather when in a trance state and that they speak through him using their own voices. When he is Golden Feather, Van Praagh reputedly sings in a Native American language (although this language is never identified). As the doctor, Van Praagh adopts Aldrich's English accent, and he assists him in diagnosing and healing his patients during medical intuitive readings (it's debatable how knowledgeable an early twentieth-century doctor would be!).

Van Praagh maintains that these possessions were captured on tape and witnessed by others, but he's never supplied evidence of these events.

Edgar Cayce

Like Van Praagh and his alter ego Dr Harry Aldrich, Edgar Cayce (1877–1945) was believed to be a medical intuitive. That is, a psychic diagnostician. It started when Cayce began losing his voice at age 21 and doctors were unable to diagnose or cure his condition. One day a friend hypnotized him. Amazingly, under hypnosis he could speak, whereby he prescribed a treatment for himself. It worked. Cayce's fame spread and while in a trance, he began diagnosing and prescribing treatments for the public. Cayce became known as the "sleeping prophet" and he slept his way to legendary status.

It is said that he performed 30,000 readings and cured thousands of people with his natural remedies. The reality is that his cures were hearsay and his treatments were folk remedies that were useless at best and dangerous at worst. Beyerstein (1996) notes that Cayce recommended, "the raw side of a freshly skinned rabbit, still warm with blood, fur side out, placed on the breast for cancer of that area". Cayce wasn't able to cure his own cousin, or his own son who died as a baby. Many of Cayce's readings took place after the patient had already died.

Cayce also claimed to read past lives and predict the future. When his predictions weren't vague, they were wrong. He said that Armageddon would happen in 1999, that the lost city of Atlantis would be found, and that 1933 would be "a good year" – that infamous time when Adolf Hitler was appointed German chancellor, and the global economy hit rock bottom during the Great Depression.

Head case

There were also inconsistencies with Cayce's accent and his vocabulary. Cayce didn't purport to channel spirits, as such, but he claimed that he could psychically diagnose patients while under hypnosis. Cayce was a Kentucky gentleman with a southern accent, but some accounts claim he lost his accent during his readings. Others claim he went into a trance and his speech was garbled for a few minutes before he then settled back into his usual accent.

Cayce performed his readings in the presence of assistants who transcribed his instructions. Martin Gardner (1957) observed that when

Cayce's readings were done in the presence of an osteopath the diagnosis and prescriptions were phrased in the terminology of an osteopath.

> The condition in the body is quite different from what we have had before...from the head, pains along through the body from the second, fifth and sixth dorsals, and from the first and second lumbar...tie-ups here, and floating lesions, or lateral lesions, in the muscular and nerve fibers.

The language of Cayce's trance readings seems to be influenced by whoever was doing the note taking. At other times Cayce was simply prescribing popular folk remedies of the time, many of which are still popular today, and just as ineffective as they were back then.

10
Spirit Writing

There are many names and claims of spirit writing. Also known as automatic writing, trance writing, direct writing, inspired writing, autography, or psychography, some believe there is a paranormal explanation, and that this is when the ghostwriters really are ghosts. Others believe the practice has therapeutic value, or is useful as a creative tool. Whether it's to be found in the New Age or self-help section of the bookstore, does it work?

A session of spirit writing

Jade sat at a table in front of a blank pad of paper and a pen. She closed her eyes and started breathing deeply. When she opened her eyes again she stared at me vacantly. "I have a message for you from the spirits," she said enigmatically. Seemingly in a trance, she took the pen and started writing feverishly. Jade, or rather the spirits, produced many pages of writing, without a pause. Suddenly, she dropped the pen and announced, "The spirits have left."

The spirit writing session with Jade was like a psychic reading with a pad and pen. I asked her if the spirits were doing the writing and she replied, "Yes. I can't write that fast myself!" This writing was in the same style as her normal handwriting but it became more illegible the more she wrote. According to Jade, three spirit guides with the mysterious names Malai, Asti, and Morphi dictated the messages to her. Here is one of their messages.

> At this time it is a time for solitary travel within oneself. What is that you are truly seeking. Is it an insight into oneself?
>
> (Stollznow, 2004)

The language was a combination of the archaic-sounding pronouns *one* and *oneself* but mixed with contemporary idioms such as "on the cards" and "go with the flow". The spirits were sloppy spellers at times too. Either they were still learning English, or the mistakes reflected the linguistic performance of the psychic. The messages were a combination of esoteric, generalized, and mundane revelations, but these were obviously based on the information she had gathered during the consultation. This is known as a cold reading (Rowland, 2008). The spirit writing was merely a stream-of-consciousness style that is about as paranormal as James Joyce's *Finnegans Wake*.

Houdini and spirit writing

There are several different kinds of written spirit communication. One type is where a spirit, angel, demon, or other entity is believed to possess a living person. This being uses the host's physical body to write a message for a client. Following the death of his beloved mother, Cecelia Weisz, magician Harry Houdini made many attempts to see if she could contact him from beyond the grave. Due to their mutual interest in spiritualism, Houdini had a surprisingly close friendship with Sir Arthur Conan Doyle, the author of Sherlock Holmes and a fervent believer in the paranormal. Doyle arranged for Houdini to have a private séance with his mother Lady Doyle, who happened to be a spirit writer. Houdini attended the session with an open mind, hopeful that contact would be achieved. Claiming to be guided by the spirit of Mrs Weisz, Lady Doyle produced an impressive 15 pages of handwriting.

However, what she had written wasn't as impressive. There was no sign that Houdini's mother had really been contacted, although there were many messages that she could have communicated to her son to validate the contact. For example, the day before the session had been her birthday – surely she would have mentioned that. But there were some glaring inaccuracies. The message began with the sign of a cross but Houdini's mother would never have drawn this Christian symbol, she was a Jew. In fact, she had been the wife of a rabbi! Furthermore, the letter continually referred to Houdini as "Harry", but she had never called him that as he was born Erik Weisz. The letter was also written in flowery, formal English but Houdini revealed, "Although my sainted mother had been in America for almost 50 years she could not speak, read nor write English" (Houdini, 1924).

Houdini knew that he had not heard from his mother and he became skeptical of spirit writing. Soon afterwards, Houdini attempted to duplicate Lady Doyle's ability. His efforts produced the name "Powell", referring to his magician friend Frederick Eugene Powell. However, Doyle interpreted this as a message from his recently deceased friend also by the name of Powell. Ironically, this left Doyle convinced that Houdini had psychic powers.

Slate writing

In the heyday of the spiritualism movement people held séances where there were strange knocking sounds and lights, ectoplasm oozed from people's mouths, tables levitated, and unexplained messages magically appeared on slates. It was believed that the spirits wrote these messages. Shepard (1984) describes the process.

> The medium and the sitter take their seats at opposite ends of a small table, each grasping a corner of an ordinary school slate, which they thus hold firmly pressed against the underside of the table. A small fragment of slate-pencil is first enclosed between slate and table, for the use of the supposed spirit-writer. Should the séance be successful, a scratching sound, as of someone writing on a slate, is heard at the end of a few moments; three loud raps indicate the conclusion of the message, and on the withdrawal of the slate, it is found to be partly covered with writing – either a general message allegedly from the spirit world, or an answer to some question previously written down by the sitter.

These spirit writing séances occurred in the dark where the sitters couldn't see the spirit wielding the pencil or chalk. Slate writing was a simple parlor trick, often involving a double-sided chalkboard or a hidden slate upon which the "message" was already written. Many mediums were caught faking the practice, including Henry Slade, the man who discovered the phenomenon (Houdini, 1924). Slade was writing these messages from the "dead" using tiny pieces of chalk held in the fingers of either hand, the toes of either foot, or his mouth.

A write off

Medium Pierre Louie Ormand Augustus Keeler said that he was in contact with the spirit of Abraham Lincoln. Mary Todd Lincoln was a believer in spiritualism and attended séances, including one held in the White House's Red Parlor. During one séance, Keeler produced a slate in which the following message appeared, supposedly penned in

Lincoln's actual handwriting. During his life, Abraham Lincoln had been a skeptic; until now.

> We come to you Sir because we see you are spreading the truth in the right way. I understood this phenomenon while in earth life, and had I lived, should of proclaimed it to the world. Press fo[r]ward My Brother. Never let thy step stray from the path of progress and truth. Your Friend

Abraham Lincoln

Joe Nickell (2004) compared the slate writing to a known sample of Lincoln's writing and determined that the two were completely different in appearance alone. Aside from the self-serving endorsement of spiritualism, and Keeler, the style and grammar were also highly suspicious. Lincoln's alleged signature was the formal "Abraham Lincoln" although he typically signed his missives as "A. Lincoln". Nickell also points out that the archaic "thy" is used, and the phrase "should of"; "That grammatical error is unimaginable for Lincoln." While linguists don't see this as an error as such, it is nonstandard grammar that raises doubts of the authenticity of the document.

The writing's on the wall

Another type of spirit writing is phantom handwriting that appears magically, and is penned invisibly by a divine, demonic, or spiritual source. Messages appear on walls, windows, and other surfaces, and are written with ink, blood, or, as in a horror movie, drawn on a foggy bathroom mirror. The earliest documented claim is an example of God's graffiti mentioned in the Book of Daniel (5:1–31). In 539 BC, Belshazzar, the despotic King of the Babylonian empire, held a great feast with his lords, wives, and concubines. They drank wine from sacred vessels stolen from the Temple of Jerusalem, and "praised the gods of gold, and of silver, of brass, of iron, of wood, and of stone". A disembodied hand appeared suddenly and wrote the words "Mene, Mene, Tekel, Parsin" on a palace wall. But no one could understand the Hebrew symbols. Daniel, a Jewish captive of the Babylonians, was brought in to translate the message seemingly written by his God. He interprets it to mean that the Babylonian Kingdom will fall to the Medes and Persians as a result of Belshazzar's sacrilege and idolatry. As predicted by the writing, Belshazzar was slain that very night, and succeeded by King Darius the

Mede. As I'm sure you have already guessed, this story is the origin of the modern idiom "the writing is on the wall".

Borley Rectory

The infamous haunting of Borley Rectory offers another example of phantom writing. Seminal paranormal investigator Harry Price promoted Borley as the "Most Haunted House in England" (Price, 1940). This was well before the days of *Ghost Hunters*. From when it was built in 1863 until the time it burned down in 1939, Borley was the alleged scene of poltergeists, a ghostly nun, a phantom coach driven by a headless horseman, and spirit writing. As the story goes, Rector Lionel Foyster was working alone in his study one night when a pencil arose from his desk and scrawled words on the wall in front of him, although no hand was visible. His wife, Marianne Foyster, soon received strange messages that were scribbled on scraps of paper and on the walls of the rectory. These were chilling pleas for "rest", "light mass prayers", and "Marianne please get help". The rectory's residents and guests would often respond to the mysterious messages in an attempt to help the tortured spirits. The messages were written in a shaky childish hand and often ended with a dash, suggesting eerily that the spirit writer had been pulled away. However, there were two children in the house who may have been the culprits, if not Mrs Foyster and the rector himself who have since been accused of trickery. These wall writings were even more mysterious because they were scrubbed off soon after being done, yet they were described and photographed many years later (Clarke, 2005).

The exorcist

The "true story" that inspired William Peter Blatty's novel *"The Exorcist"* and the film by that name also involves occurrences of phantom writing. Unlike the fictional version, which tells the story of a little girl named Reagan MacNeil, the real-life victim was a 13-year-old boy who is variously referred to as "Roland" or "Robbie Doe". During manifestations of the demon, scratches appeared on the boy's body that spelled out words. The markings looked like they were scratched into his skin by claws. During several exorcisms, the words "SPITE", "HELL", and "DEVIL" appeared in red welts on his chest. His mother once considered sending him to school in St Louis, but the letter "N" appeared in welts on both of his legs, which she interpreted as a supernatural order of "NO". Apparently, his hands were always visible during episodes of this skin branding. However, there is only anecdotal evidence of these claims. In the movie version, welts appear on Reagan's stomach that spell out "Help me", as though the little girl is trying to communicate from within her demon-possessed body. Similarly, in the movie *The Shining*, Danny is possessed by his imaginary friend "Tony" who directs him to write the word "REDRUM" (with the "D" and second "R" reversed) on a bathroom door in red lipstick. When viewed in the bedroom mirror, the letters spell out "MURDER", which is a prophecy of the attacks that follow.

Mediumship

The most common type of spirit writing is a form of written mediumship. A psychic claims to channel a spirit, an angel, or even a living person, who communicates via the medium's handwriting. The entity may even produce paintings or drawings through the medium. Some mediums claim that the spirit dictates the messages, while others explain that the spirit operates the writing tool, sometimes possessing the medium's body to control the implement. As a form of divination, spirit writing is similar to the Ouija board, and some use a planchette to guide their pen. Spirit writing and the use of a planchette pre-dates the Ouija board, which appeared as a novelty game in the 1890s.

More theatrical mediums fall into a trance-like state. Some report sensitive or empathic abilities, that is, they claim to "feel" the emotion behind the words. For example, a spirit writing "angry" through them causes the medium to feel literal anger. While spirit writing is generally seen as an occult practice, "journaling" is viewed by some as a Christianized version, where a person receives and transcribes messages from God during prayer. Many Christians would still perceive this as an occult practice and an act of Satan rather than God. Spirit writing can also be found across cultures. It was practiced in China as a form of divination, and in the Japanese religion Shinto, where it is known as *Tenjo*, the heavenly stick, and Shinto priests received divine messages through a brush or pen.

Spirit writers typically produce many pages of messages during a reading. As we can see, some mediums claim to have poems, music, and even entire books dictated to them by chatty spirits. Not all mediums perform spirit writing. It is a contradiction worth noting that other mediums only receive vague and obvious snippets of information from the spirits during readings that don't involve spirit writing, like the first initial of a name, or stock messages like "I'm sorry" and "I love you".

Enochian

Spirit writing became fashionable during the peak of the spiritualism movement (c.1840–1920), but the practice pre-dates this period. An early example is the sixteenth-century "angelical language" popularly known as Enochian. This was a language used to communicate with angels, said to be dictated to seers John Dee (astrologer to Elizabeth I) and Edward Kelley by angels. The writing system was also revealed to them by scrying. Enochian has been used in ceremonial magic in modern times, by occultist Aleister Crowley and Anton La Vey, founder of the Church of Satan. Linguist Donald Laycock (2001) examined the writings and concluded that Enochian is an artificial language that attempts to replicate an ancient-sounding language. Apparently, angels use a grammar that is remarkably similar to the syntax of the English language. Furthermore, Enochian phonology resembles Elizabethan English and its writing system looks a lot like the Latin alphabet. Some of the texts appear to be transcribed from sessions of speaking in tongues.

Patience Worth

There have been a number of famous spirit writers. Patience Worth wrote over 5,000 works, including poetry, plays, and novels, during the twentieth century, but she died in the seventeenth century. Patience Worth was a spirit channeled by Pearl Lenore Curran (1883–1937), a St Louis housewife with little education. The two met through the Ouija board in 1912. Here is one of Worth's early messages.

> Many moons ago I lived. Again I come. Patience Worth my name. Wait, I would speak with thee. If thou shalt live, then so shall I. I make my bread at thy hearth. Good friends, let us be merrie. The time for work is past. Let the tabby drowse and blink her wisdom to the firelog.
> (www.patienceworth.org)

Worth was a seventeenth-century English ghost, but according to linguist Professor Shelling, she spoke in a mixture of pidgin Shakespeare and, strangely, the contemporary St Louis dialect spoken by Curran (Christopher, 1970). Some believe that Curran suffered from dissociative identity disorder, and that Patience Worth was another personality of Curran's. Others think that Curran was just a creative writer and that Worth was a persona.

Rosemary Brown

Rosemary Brown (1916–2001) was an English psychic who claimed that Bach, Beethoven, Brahms, and other famous, not to mention deceased, composers dictated new works to her. This began in 1924, when she was seven years of age and Hungarian composer Franz Liszt (1811–86) appeared to her, some 40 years after he died. He told her that he would soon begin to compose through her. Lazy Liszt waited until 1964 to reappear, but he brought along a few friends. Liszt controlled Brown's hands as she played the piano, Schubert sang her the notes, Chopin told her which notes to play and guided her fingers to the keys, while Beethoven and Bach dictated the notes to her. These European composers spoke to her in English, because they must have become bilingual on the other side. They also liked to discuss topics beyond music, including politics and religion. They weren't all decomposing composers; in 1987 John Lennon appeared to her and dictated a few new songs to her.

Many commentators were astounded by the compositions and remarked that they couldn't be faked without years of training. Presumably, they could be faked with years of training, but Brown claimed to have none. Other commentators remarked that these new compositions sounded like reworked classical compositions. Paranormal investigator Harry Edwards (1996) reveals that Brown originally claimed to have no musical training but she later admitted that she grew up in a musical household and was a competent musician and pianist. It seems that she was composing the music herself, in the style of the composers. Edwards also marvels that Brown was able to talk with Beethoven because he was deaf for the second half of his life!

Jane Roberts

Decades before J. Z. Knight heard from Ramtha, Jane Roberts was channeling "Seth". During experiments with an Ouija board in the early 1970s, Jane Roberts (1929–1984) began encountering a spirit named "Seth". Soon, Seth could communicate without the board and through Roberts. Her husband Robert Butts would transcribe these sessions or Roberts would write or type automatically using a typewriter. When in a trance state, Roberts also claimed to be able to channel the thoughts of artist Paul Cézanne and philosopher William James. Her channeling sessions resulted in the 1972 book *Seth Speaks*, which was followed by other "Seth" books and a set of monologues collectively known as the Seth texts or Seth material. However, much of her work was criticized for being a rip-off of Christian and Eastern philosophy. It comes as no surprise that Seth influenced such authors as Deepak Chopra and Louise Hay.

Chico Xavier

Chico Xavier (1910–2002) was a Brazilian medium who wrote over 400 books. Well, his spirit guide Emmanuel wrote them. According to Xavier, Emmanuel first lived as a senator in ancient Rome. Then he was reincarnated as a Spanish priest, and then as a professor at the Sorbonne. In a trance, Xavier channeled deceased loved ones for his clients who penned spirit letters through him. Spirit letters channeled by Xavier were accepted as valid evidence by Brazilian courts in two murder trials (Carroll, 2003). However, Xavier was revealed to be a cheat. In what is called a hot reading, Xavier's staff at his Spiritist Center in Brazil gathered personal information from clients as they lined up to see the psychic. In the letters from the dead, these details were presented back to the clients as though they had been psychic messages (Mori, 2010).

Hélène Smith

Swiss medium Hélène Smith (1861–1929), formerly known as Catherine Müller, was a spirit writer. With the help of her spirit guide Leopold, she also read past lives, and claimed she had been both a Hindu princess and Marie Antoinette in her former lives (Randi, 1997). Smith is most famous for writing an entire alphabet and language that were dictated to her by Martians (see Chapter 19). Psychologist Théodore Flournoy examined this language and discovered that people from Mars seem to be fluent in French, which also happened to be Smith's native language.

Nothing to write home about

If spirit writers don't offer a paranormal explanation, they offer a pseudoscientific one, and the practice becomes automatic writing. This has been used as a form of psychotherapy in the twentieth century, most notably by Pierre Janet, Morton Prince, and Anita Muhl. They taught that the practice taps into the subconscious mind and unlocks hidden truths. Automatic writing isn't used in mainstream therapy today but it is a popular treatment in NLP, past-life regression, and recovered memory therapy. Along with hypnosis, guided imagery, and truth serums, automatic writing is used to recover repressed memories of childhood abuse or alien abductions. However, repressed memories are really false memories implanted by disreputable therapists. There is no scientific evidence that automatic writing has any kind of therapeutic value.

In a less dangerous practice, some people use free writing as a creative tool. Surrealist artists use this technique of automatism, not only for writing poetry, music, and stories, but also for drawing and painting. Salvador Dali practiced automatic drawing and André Breton wrote books and poetry using this method. Free writing is used for improvisation, self-expression, and inspiration. As a free-flowing style of writing, the spelling, grammar, and theme can become a bit messy, so free writing often produces unusable material. However, free writers never claim that the material comes from an external source, unless they're talking about the "muses".

In all of the "best cases" of spirit writing the phenomena are shown to be natural, not supernatural, and spirit writers themselves are revealed to be deceiving others, or deceiving themselves. The ideomotor effect is behind honest cases of spirit writing, explaining the way the pen seems to move independently across the page. These subtle and involuntary muscle responses also explain the movement of dowsing rods and the planchette that slides across the Ouija board. No information is revealed to spirit writers other than what is already known to them.

To prove that they channel paranormal entities, some spirit writers claim that the appearance of their handwriting changes. However, it's not difficult to adopt a different style of writing, and our writing naturally changes when we write quickly as opposed to carefully, or when we print instead of using cursive. Not all spirits have good penmanship nowadays. Psychics went from telling fortunes in tents to telephone and email readings and, like Jane Roberts and her automatic typewriting, some mediums keep up with the times. Rather than using a pad and pen, modern spirits are technology savvy and prefer to communicate via computers and other electronic devices. These spirit writers type, they don't write, but it's still the medium speaking for a "spirit". The messages come from the mind of the medium, not a supernatural being.

References

Adrover-Roig, D., Galparsoro-Izagirre, N., Marcotte, K., Ferré, P., Wilson, M. A., and Inés Ansaldo, A. 2011. "Impaired L1 and executive control after left basal ganglia damage in a bilingual Basque-Spanish person with aphasia". *Clinical Linguistics and Phonetics*. Vol. 25, No. 6–07, pp. 480–98.

BBC. July 4, 2006. http://news.bbc.co.uk/2/hi/uk_news/england/tyne/5144 300.stm

Beyerstein, Dale. 1996. "Edgar Cayce". In Stein, Gordon (ed.) *The Encyclopedia of the Paranormal*. Prometheus Books.

Blanc, Mel and Bashe, Philip. 1989. *That's Not All Folks!* Warner Books.

Browne, Sylvia. 2002. *Conversations with the Other Side*. Hay House.

Carroll, Robert, T., 2014. http://skepdic.com/ramtha.html

Christopher, Milbourne. 1970. *ESP, Seers & Psychics*. Thomas Y. Crowell Co.

Clarke, Andrew. 2005. *The Bones of Borley*. Available at: http://www.foxearth.org.uk/BorleyRectory/index.html. Accessed September 10, 2011.

Cunningham, Glenn and McCarthy, David. 2001. *Glenn Cunningham Interview*. JZ Knight. Part 1.

Daily Mail. 2010. "Croatian teenager wakes up from a coma speaking fluent German". Available at: http://www.dailymail.co.uk/news/worldnews/article-1265433/Croatian-teenager-wakes-coma-speaking-fluent-German.html#ixzz0 lqP6D3gV Accessed September 16, 2010.

Davies, Jeremy Fr. 2008. *Exorcism. Understanding Exorcism in Scripture and Practice*. Catholic Truth Society.

Edwards, H. 1996. Rosemary Brown (1931–). *A Skeptic's Guide to the New Age*. Australian Skeptics Inc.

Fenwick, Peter and Fenwick, Elizabeth. 1999. *Past Lives – an Investigation into Reincarnation Memories*. Penguin Books.

Flournoy, Theodore. 1900. *From India to the Planet Mars*. Princeton University Press.

Gardner, Martin. 1957. *Fads and Fallacies in the Name of Science*. Dover Publications, Inc.

Glubok, Norman and Smith, Bob. 1956. "Bridey a 'burden' – so was Ruth". *Chicago American*.

Guardian. 2010. "The condition that gave me a Chinese accent". Available at: http://www.guardian.co.uk/lifeandstyle/2010/apr/20/foreign-accent-syndrome Accessed September 16, 2010.

Guardian. 2010. "Woman's Migraine Gave Her French Accent". Available at: http://www.guardian.co.uk/uk/2010/sep/14/woman-awoke-migraine-french-accent Accessed September 16, 2010.

Hicks, Esther and Hicks, Jerry. 2006. *The Law of Attraction: The Basics of the Teachings of Abraham*. Hay House.

Houdini, Harry. 1924. *A Magician among the Spirits*. Reprinted. Grosset & Dunlap, 1972.

Irish Central. 2010. Available at: http://www.irishcentral.com/news/US-Woman-visits-dentist-wakes-up-with-Irish-accent—VIDEOS-121377954.html.

Kildahl, John. 1972. *The Psychology of Speaking in Tongues*. Harper & Row.

Knight, J. Z. 1987. *A State of Mind: My Story/Ramtha: The Adventure Begins*. JZK Publishing.

Kurowski, Kathleen and Blumstein, Sheila. 2006. "The foreign accent syndrome: A perspective". *Journal of Neurolinguistics*. Vol. 19, No. 5, pp. 346–55.

Laycock, Donald. 2001. "Enochian: Angelic language or mortal folly?", *The Complete Enochian Dictionary*, pp. 19–64.

Loftus, E. F. and Ketcham, K. 1994. *The Myth of Repressed Memory*. St. Martin's Press.

Monrad-Krohn, G. H. 1947. "Dysprosody or altered 'Melody of Language' ". *Brain: A Journal of Neurology*. Vol. 70, No. 4, pp. 405–15.

Mori, Kentaro. 2010. "Spiritualism in Brazil: Alive and kicking. 'Counterclockwise' " Committee for Skeptical Inquiry web column. Available at: http://www.csicop.org/specialarticles/show/spiritualism_in_brazil_alive_and_kicking Accessed October 12, 2010.

Newburg, Andrew. 2006. *Psychiatry Research: Neuroimaging*. Vol. 148, No. 1, 22, pp. 67–71.

Nickell, J. 2004. "Abraham Lincoln: An instance of alleged 'Spirit Writing'. Investigative files". *Skeptical Inquirer*. Vol. 14, No. 3.

Nida, Eugene. 1966. "Glossolalia: A case of pseudo-linguistic structure available on nidainstitute.org. The 16 criteria for human language are listed". In Greenberg, Joseph (ed.) *Universals of Language*. MIT Press.

Poe, Edgar Allen. 1841. *The Murders in the Rue Morgue. The Dupin Tales*. Modern Library.

Price, H. 1940. *The Most Haunted House in England*. Longmans.

Randi, James. 1997. *An Encyclopedia of Claims, Frauds, and Hoaxes of the Occult and Supernatural*. St Martin's Griffin.

Reeves, R. and Norton, J. W. 2001. "Foreign accent-like syndrome during psychotic exacerbations: Neuropsychiatry". *Neuropsychology Behavioral Neurology*. Apr–Jun; Vol. 14, No. 2, pp. 135–38.

Rowland, Ian. 2008. *The Full Facts Book of Cold Reading: A Comprehensive Guide to the Most Persuasive Psychological Manipulation Technique in the World*. Ian Rowland Limited.

Sagan, Carl. 1997. *The Demon-Haunted World: Science As a Candle in the Dark*. Ballantine Books.

Samarin, William. 1972. *Tongues of Men and Angels: The Religious Language of Pentecostalism*. MacMillan Publishing Company.

Seattle Times. 2010. "Brain injury gives local mom a 'foreign' accent". *The Seattle Times*. Available at: http://seattletimes.nwsource.com/html/localnews/2008315220_foreign27.html Accessed September 16, 2010.

Shepard, Leslie. (ed.) 1984. *Encyclopedia of Occultism & Parapsychology*, second ed. Detroit, Michigan: Gale Research Co., s.v. "automatic writing" and "slate writing."

Stevenson, Ian. 1966. *Twenty Cases Suggestive of Reincarnation*. University of Virginia Press.

Stevenson, Ian. 1974. *Xenoglossy: A Review and Report of a Case*. University Press of Virginia.

Stevenson, Ian. 1984. *Unlearned Language: New Studies in Xenoglossy*. University of Virginia Press.

Stollznow, Karen. 2004. "The writing's on the wall". *The Skeptic*. Vol. 24, No. 2, pp. 34–37.

Stollznow, Karen. 2007. "Singing in tongues". *Australasian Science*. Vol. 28, No. 7, p. 46.

Stollznow, Karen. 2011. *Braco the Gazer. The Naked Skeptic*. Committee for Skeptical Inquiry web column. Available at: http://www.csicop.org/specialarticles/show/braco_the_gazer/ Accessed June 20, 2011.

Times of India. "UP village boy suddenly acquires American accent". July 14, 2007.

Thomason, Sarah. 1989. "Entities in the linguistic minefield". *Skeptical Inquirer*, Vol. 13, No. 4, Summer, pp. 391–96.

Thomason, Sarah. 1996. "Xenoglossy" In Stein, Gordon (ed.) *The Encyclopedia of the Paranormal*. Prometheus Books.

Van Praagh, James. 1999. *Talking to Heaven: A Medium's Message of Life after Death*. Signet.

Washington Post. 2010. "Fairfax woman developed Russian accent after head injury". Available at: http://www.washingtonpost.com/wp-dyn/content/article/2010/05/28/AR2010052801724.html?referrer=emailarticle Accessed September 16, 2010.

Wood, Frederic. 2003. (1939). *Egyptian Miracle*. Kessinger.

WWMT. 2010. Available at: http://www.wwmt.com/articles/woman-1384765-michigan-newschannel.html.

Zerner, A. and Farber, M. 2008. *The Ghost Writer Automatic Writing Kit: Messages from Beyond and Magic from Within*. Enchanted World.

Part III
Hidden Language

Introduction

Steganography is the practice of hiding a secret message within another message. The Greek historian Herodotus chronicles the earliest cases of steganography dating back to 440 BCE. In his book *Histories*, he tells the story of King Darius of Susa who shaved the head of a prisoner and wrote a secret message on his scalp. When the man's hair grew back he was sent to Miletus to present the hidden message to the king's son-in-law, Aristogoras. In the second account, a Greek soldier named Demeratus needed to warn Sparta that King Xerxes planned to invade Greece. In those days, writing involved printing text onto wax-covered tablets. Demeratus removed the wax from the tablet and wrote a secret message on the wood inside. He then sealed the tablet with wax and sent the message without it being detected. Ancient Romans used to write between the lines of letters using invisible ink made from fruit juice, milk, and urine. These messages were revealed when heat was applied to the writing.

Today, the use of invisible ink, microdots, null ciphers, and image substitution are all different methods for hiding messages. But sometimes, hidden messages are found where they may not exist. Televisions, computers, and recording equipment are believed to receive messages from aliens, angels, demons, and the dead. When played in reverse, recorded speech is said to reveal our subconscious desires and fears. Lyrics allegedly conceal satanic messages that can only be heard when a song is played backwards. Secret prophesies are thought to be hidden within the pages of the Bible.

This chapter explores hidden messages and meaning found in symbols, songs, speech, and the written word. We take a look at electronic voice phenomena, the Bible Code, the theory of reverse speech, secret symbols of the Freemasons, and claims that hidden messages prove that Paul is dead, but Elvis is still alive.

11
Voices of the Dead

,

The use of electronic devices for communicating with spirits is called instrumental transcommunication. Radios, televisions, fax machines, and computers are used to collect hidden messages that are purportedly of a paranormal nature. Audio recordings are the most common types of communication, known specifically as electronic voice phenomena (EVPs). These are said to be voice recordings of the dead, but recorded *after* the person has died. EVPs are believed by some to be evidence for the existence of life after death. Alternatively, they are held to be the voices of spirits, demons, angels, or aliens.

The light bulb goes off

Prolific inventor Thomas Edison is popularly credited as the father of EVPs and real-time spirit communication. There is an urban legend that while Edison was inventing the phonograph, the motion picture camera, and the electric light bulb, he was also in the process of creating an apparatus that would enable communication with spirits. This belief can be traced to an 1890 interview in which Edison spoke about the idea of communicating with the "life units" or atoms of the deceased. In an article published in *Scientific American* (1920), Edison speculated about the possibility of building a device that could communicate with the dead. He was quoted as saying:

> It is possible to construct an apparatus which will be so delicate that if there are personalities in another existence or sphere who wish to get in touch with us in this existence or sphere, this apparatus will at least give them a better opportunity to express themselves than the tilting

tables and raps and ouija boards and mediums and the other crude methods now purported to be the only means of communication.

(Clark, 1977)

Some believe Edison's talk of spirit machines was a marketing prank. He was agnostic, although he lived during the height of the Spiritualism movement, when belief in an afterlife and the ability to communicate with the dead was common, and disembodied voices manifested magically during séances. This legend is further fueled by gossip that Edison visited psychics and held séances. However, with over 1,000 patents, Edison never registered any machine for contacting spirits and there is no evidence to suggest that he built or was building such a device. The Edison National Historic Site dispels this myth:

> Did Edison make a machine that could talk to the dead? This seems to be another tall tale that Edison pulled on a reporter. In 1920 Edison told the reporter, B. F. Forbes, that he was working on a machine that could make contact with the spirits of the dead. Newspapers all over the world picked up this story. After a few years, Edison admitted that he had made the whole thing up. Today at Edison National Historic Site, we take care of over five million pages of documents. None of them mention such an experiment.

The ghost in the machine

The Spiritualism movement also spawned the practice of spirit photography. These were attempts to capture the images of ghosts on film. In 1941, photographer Attila von Szalay turned his attention from spirit photography to recording voices of the dead. He began experimenting with 78rpm records, but he didn't have success until 1956 when he started using a reel-to-reel tape recorder. Together with Raymond Bayless, the two designed a machine to collect EVPs. This was an insulated microphone connected to an external recording device and speaker. Using this machine, they collected many spirit messages including "This is G!" and "Hot dog, Art!" (Rogo and Bayless, 1980).

One day, Friedrich Jürgenson (1903–87) was recording bird songs when his tape also seemed to capture human voices, although there was no one else around. Inspired by this, he spent many years recording nothing. When these recordings were played back, they seemed to reveal human voices. Jürgenson wrote about these experiences in the 1964 publication *Rosterna fran Rymden* ("Voices from space").

The book caught the interest of Latvian parapsychologist Konstantin Raudive (1909–74). The pair began working together, and soon Jürgenson captured a voice that sounded like his mother, who had died a few years before. The voice even called him by the pet name she used for him. Jürgenson believed that he was recording voices of the dead, and so he wrote a second book in 1967, *Sprechfunk mit Verstorbenen* ("Radio-link with the dead").

Raudive voices

Raudive's belief in his own research was sealed when he recorded the message, "Va dormir, Margarete" ("Go to sleep, Margaret"). He believed this to be the voice of his recently deceased friend, Margarete Petrautzki. He wrote, "These words made a deep impression on me, as Margarete Petrautzki had died recently, and her illness and death had greatly affected me" (Raudive, 1971). This finding started a trend, and he soon began receiving messages from deceased family, friends, and famous people. These messages even captured different languages, including German, Latvian, and French. The Picasso of EVPs, Raudive collected over 100,000 recordings and eventually published his findings in *Breakthrough* (1971). His work was so prolific that today EVPs are also known as Raudive voices.

Raudive died in 1974, but of course, he soon showed up again in EVPs, along with Beethoven, aliens, and a lamplighter from eighteenth-century Philadelphia. These messages were all captured by Sarah Estep who founded the American Association of Electronic Voice Phenomena in 1982, popularizing modern beliefs and theories about EVPs. In the early 2000s, collecting EVPs was popularized by the movie *White Noise*, and TV shows such as *Ghost Hunters* and *Ghost Adventures*. Now anyone can hunt for EVPs.

Armed with various recording devices, EVP-seekers visit cemeteries, deserted buildings, historic sites, and other stereotypically haunted environments. The typical protocol is to leave a device to record for a period of time, or to invoke the responses of spirits by posing questions. They typically quiz the spirit with, "Who are you?", "Why are you here?", and ask for other information about the life and death of the spirit. If the spirits are believed to be aggressive, such as poltergeists, the ghost hunter may instead "provoke" the spirits, goading them with insults and threats. According to EVP theory, the spirit voices are hidden. They aren't heard during recording but are only heard after the recording is played back.

When the spirits do talk back, what do they say? Raudive (1971) believed that spirits speak "very rapidly, in a mixture of languages, sometimes as many as five or six in one sentence", while "grammatical rules are frequently abandoned and neologisms abound". In modern ghost hunting, spirits tend to be hard of speaking, so EVPs are characterized by single words, or short phrases that are barely audible. The dead have lost their personalities and the messages are never profound, specific, or useful. They usually consist of noises that that sound like stereotyped haunting messages, such as "Help me!", "Get out!", or "I'm sorry".

There is a system of classification for EVPs, but it is not standardized, due to the subjectivity of interpretation. Examples are classified from class A (best) to class D (worst), according to quality, audibility, and understandability. In an attempt to make these messages more audible, they are enhanced and amplified using audio software programs. This is ostensibly to clean up any ambient noise, but this can inadvertently, or purposefully, manipulate the recordings to make the results more persuasive. It's not that the messages are garbled or inaudible to begin with, it's that they aren't messages.

The causes of these recordings are natural, not supernatural. Most good quality EVPs are likely recordings of living people, background noise, or radio interference known as cross-modulation, when a device picks up incongruous snippets of human voices. Alternatively, messages can be heard by way of a psychological phenomenon called pareidolia, the misinterpretation of random, white noise. This is the audio version of seeing patterns in clouds. Overall, the best way to capture "voices of the dead" is to record them when the speakers are still alive.

The Frank's Box

A popular approach to spirit communication is to use a Frank's Box or similar device. Unlike televisions and recording equipment that are built with more practical purposes in mind, the Frank's Box is designed specifically to capture EVPs. However, it is not an audio recorder, this is a radio receiver. It is believed that the Frank's Box facilitates real-time communication between the living and the dead, not to mention extraterrestrials, angels, spirits, and assorted entities from other dimensions.

The Frank's Box is one of several incarnations. These devices are known by many names, including the Spiricom, the Telephone to the Dead, or the Shack Hack, according to the design and the manufacturer. Whether known as the Frank's Box, Ghost Box, Joe's Box, Spirit Box, or Mini Box, they all open a paranormal Pandora's box. To some people, Frank's Box is a revolutionary device that facilitates communication between the living and the dead, not to mention angels, aliens, and demons. To others, it's just a broken radio. But this radio is built to be broken. It is untunable, so you can't listen to an Elvis song, but if the claims are to be believed, you might just contact Elvis instead.

There were several forerunners to the Frank's Box, including vacuum tube radios, phonographs, and wire recorders that supposedly captured messages from the dead. In 1979, William O'Neil and George Meek created the Spiricom, a tone and frequency generator that promised two-way communication with spirits. O'Neil claims he built the device according to specifications received psychically from George Mueller, a scientist who had died in 1967. Using the Spiricom, O'Neil recorded long conversations with Mueller, but strangely, their voices never overlap as found in normal conversation. It turns out that the Spiricom was a hoax. The spirit "voices" were created using a mechanical larynx. O'Neil was also an accomplished ventriloquist.

In 1995, the do-it-yourself article "Ghost voices: Exploring the mysteries of electronic voice phenomena" appeared in *Popular Electronics* magazine (Konstantinos, 1995). This inspired amateur radio enthusiast Frank Sumption to build his Frank's Box. However, the credit can't all go to the article. Sumption claims a team of spirits also assisted him in the design and creation of his device. In accordance with the myth that Thomas Edison pioneered spirit communication, some even believe that Edison's spirit dictated the design of the Frank's Box to Sumption.

How it works (or doesn't work)

How does it work? The Frank's Box is a homemade radio receiver that continuously scans radio frequencies at a predetermined rate. This effect is like twisting the knob on a radio backwards and forwards quickly. However, the scan lock function is disabled, so the listener can't tune into a station. This "sweep method" creates a radio that plays erratic white noise. Random fragments of speech and music punctuate the rushing sound of unused frequencies when the scanner momentarily picks up a station. But who needs channels when you can channel spirits instead?

How does it not work? Sumption claims that the white noise creates what he calls "raw audio", which paranormal beings use to transmit messages intended for the listener. By his theory, the device tunes into some sort of cosmic radio station where the DJs are spirits.

"Radio-Sweep" is a technology that involves rapidly changing the tuning of a radio receiver to produce a sound track composed of bits of sound from whatever radio programming is on the air and from whatever radio station is detected by the radio at the time. In theory, the communicating entity somehow arranges for the radio programming of local stations to have the needed sounds and that the sweep will detect that sound at the right time to produce the desired message.

(Butler, 2010)

Sumption describes how he believes his device works as a kind of electronic medium.

This is simply another method of supplying "raw" audio that spirits and other entities can use to form voices. Raw audio is a sound source that contains bits of human speech, music and noise, and a convineint [sic] source of raw audio is a radio with it's tuning swept across the entire band, AM, FM, or shortwave. The sweep can be random, linear, or even done by hand.

(purplealiengirl.tripod.com)

Since radio stations provide any speech that's heard, the broader claim is that the spirits are controlling the airways on the off chance that a human is using a Frank's Box through which they can communicate. However, the Frank's Box doesn't have the capability of receiving earthly signals other than the AM or FM broadcast bands, let alone unearthly ones.

The Purple Princess

Sumption says he is in frequent communication with a number of "higher-level spirits" he calls "The Guys". These regular contacts include "Otto" and "about ten women with German names". The Guys deem him to be royalty and have dubbed him their "Purple Princess". This has inspired him to wear purple clothes, and he refers to himself as Purple, the Purple Space Friend, the Purple Princess, and the Purple Alien Girl.

"They" claim I'm their long lost Purple Princess, kidnapped from my home planet long ago when Earth had space flight by the ancient Egyptians. I couldn't be rescued at that time, so I was transported forward in time, to now, at the end of the current Earth cycle when I could go home. It gets wierd [sic] from there. Other entities that talk though the box claim they see a woman where I should be.

Some believe these devices can also predict the future. Sumption claims his boxes have revealed doomsday prophecies and predicted world events and natural disasters. The boxes can even be used to contact the victims of these events. Sumption's cronies also claim that the Frank's Box can be used for solving crimes, finding missing persons, medical research, and in the diagnosis and treatment of disease. One user reports: "I asked about Autism and I heard: 'Man made' and when I asked about vaccines being a cause I heard 'Yes'."

That which we call a Frank's Box by any other name . . . wouldn't work either

After Sumption, a paranormal investigator by the name of Christopher Moon is the biggest advocate of the Frank's Box. He was once a "primary tester" of the box, spurring Sumption to remark that Moon was the only person who understood how the device "should" be used. That is, until Moon turned the box into a business. He permanently borrowed a few Frank's Boxes from Sumption, installed the device in a fancy display case, and rebranded it as the "Telephone to the Dead" (Moon has since changed this name to the "Spirit Phone", and fashioned himself as a necromancer who "summons the dead"). For a considerable fee, Moon promises to contact the deceased loved ones of his clients. For an additional fee, he interprets these "messages" from beyond. Unlike the patched-together phrases and words that Sumption receives, Moon receives complete messages, but only Moon can hear them. His machine produces an incomprehensible snippet of sound, but he translates these into lengthy and detailed messages.

> Skeptical, Christopher met with Mr. Sumption at his workshop for a demonstration. Christopher was astounded to find that the device that Frank Sumption had built was actually designed through the EVP of deceased scientists. It quickly became obvious to Christopher what Frank Sumption had done; he had completed the infamous Thomas Edison Telephone to the Dead.
>
> (Moon, 2010)

Moon exaggerates the wild claims. Further to Sumption's belief that he has regular spirit contacts such as Otto, Moon developed the idea that each box has a sort of switchboard operator assigned on the other side, known as a "spirit technician". Contrary to Sumption's belief that the message is intended for and meaningful to the user only, Moon claims that only 30 people can correctly hear and decipher the "messages" with the assistance of these technicians. Fortunately, Moon, along with his spirit technician Tyler, is one of these mediums. Foolhardy amateurs who are not chosen run the risk of encountering evil entities and opening portals to demons.

Moon claims that Thomas Edison is one of these spirit technicians, and claims that he communicates with the deceased inventor via the machine. Sumption has made, withdrawn, and denied these claims over the years. His latest statement on the matter was: "I have in fact heard a voice that said 'Edison here' there was no real information conveyed that I could understand." Sumption suggests that these spirits could have been "mimicking" Edison's voice. However, Sumption disputes that Moon is in contact with Edison because he recorded the persuasive EVPs, "Grandpa Edison never spoke to Chris" as evidence (purplealiengirl.tripod.com).

Moon's strategy is to carry out personal or public readings and then to leverage this client list by contacting these people again and enticing them with, "The telephone is calling for you." But you'll have to pay for a session to receive the message. In personal correspondence, electrical engineer Paul Turner adds:

> Many of Moon's customers or victims have spoken out against him saying that they were not happy with the session, then weeks after the session he contacts them again saying he has talked to their loved one and that he has the information they were looking for. But it will cost an additional fee.

Jeannette Osborne, a former client of Moon's, was seeking "something tangible" to prove there is life after death. Osborne spent thousands of dollars having sessions with Moon. During these readings she was told her family was plagued by demons, and she underwent two exorcisms via the device, which she calls "Boxercisms". She received unsubstantiated warnings about her son, a soldier stationed in Iraq, and she even exposed Moon's deception by planting bogus information which he fed back to her as fact. She also recounts the heartbreaking story of nursing her dying brother, and how she created a code word for him to send from beyond the grave via the Telephone to the Dead. She never received the message.

Opening a Pandora's box

Sumption doesn't mass produce his Frank's Boxes or sell them. This has led enthusiasts to make or break their own radios, or to purchase one from the growing list of companies that manufacture these devices commercially. That is, if Sumption won't loan one of his boxes to you, as he did to me. Electrical engineer Paul Turner examined the gadget and provided the following analysis.

The Frank's Box Model 63 that you possess is an alleged Instrumental TransCommunication (ITC) device, the term would imply a two-way communication between the spirit world and that of the living. However, after examining the device and the builder's own schematics, I fail to see where or how this two-way communication occurs as the device itself is nothing more than an AM/FM receiver with modifications. The results that the builder claims would be a matter of personal belief in the metaphysical.

The First Circuit in the chain is a salvaged RCA AM/FM tuner card. It would appear to have come from an older tabletop style radio. The first thing that struck me as unusual about the card is that the builder placed two quartz crystals on the tuning coil using antenna lead and silicon to secure them between the coil and the housing. It is not possible for these crystals to interact with the tuner, except for the slight possibility the crystals, acting as spacers for the excess antenna lead, could slightly change the characteristics of the reception of the tuner, perhaps reducing its selectivity. Or this is an attempt by the builder to make the device seen more magical.

There are two hand wired circuit boards, which again seen to be populated with a combination of new and salvaged parts. These parts are wired to a proto-board, normally used for prototype circuits. One containing the modifications necessary to linear scan the tuner, this is accomplished using the XR 2206 function generator integrated circuit. This IC generates the sawtooth wave which enables the modified tuner to scan frequencies from top to bottom then back again. This is the same process as spinning a tuner knob on an old-style radio up and down the dial. The adjustment for the rate of scan is controlled by an attenuator on the front face.

This board also contains the preamps and microphone amplifier for an external echo box which is optional. The speaker for the echo box is driven by the RAW speaker output on the front panel, the volume being controlled by the RAW drive attenuator on the front panel. The return microphone from the echo box when the switch is engaged would only feed the line output jack, which then could feed a recording device.

The workmanship of the device is sloppy, it would appear to be an effort of trial and error as opposed to a well-thought out design. While some of the circuits are clever it is in no way elegant or innovative; perhaps a better classification would be haphazard. I speculate that the builder has a rudimentary knowledge of electronics, perhaps at a ham radio level or late 1970's trade school. So if entities indeed gave him the knowledge to build the device as he states in his schematics apparently they did not keep up with the technical journals.

In conclusion, the Frank's Box Model 63 does an adjustable linear sweep of the AM or FM band depending on which is selected. The result is a random noise generator. It does not have the capability of receiving any signals except that of the AM or FM broadcast band. It does not have transmit capability. Its sole function is to linear sweep the broadcast band producing bits and pieces of audio from those broadcast stations. Since the claim is that spirits speak through the random noise, I could well see that after a few moments of listening to this random audio, the sensory trait of pareidolia would come into play creating false positives. This is the only logical explanation to the builder's claims.

To Sumption and his followers, the Frank's Box is a scientific approach to hunting for ghosts. "It functions on the quantum level," he explained to me. "What do you mean by 'quantum'?" I asked. He shrugged his shoulders and admitted, "I don't know." The Frank's Box is no more technology than a Parker Brothers Ouija board, but with its underlying ethical problems, it's no game. The Frank's Box and similar devices are tarot cards for the technological age.

You say potato, I say gobbledygook

The "messages" received from the Frank's Box are composed randomly from the repertoire of radio stations. Proponents prefer listening to the AM band, and as a greater source of talk radio and news than FM radio, AM broadcasting produces a higher ratio of words to music. Amidst the radio static, the content includes music, advertisements, news, and talk. However, the scanner barely rests on a station before flitting to the next, so the output is arbitrary and consists of word fragments, single words, and short phrases, combined with language-like sounds from music and white noise. Listeners pick out these intelligible sounds selectively to form "messages".

As the results are subject to whatever is playing at the time, the "messages" are unpredictable and cannot be replicated. The Frank's Box may occasionally generate a clear, recognizable word in isolation, but most often, the output is nonsensical. Therefore, the data can only be interpreted subjectively. The output is construed and manipulated to suit the context and the agenda of the listener. Some of Sumption's favorite examples include: "Frank Sumption is keeping this", "C'mon Purple. Keep this box", "We love you Princess, this is Otto", "Purple, Good Morning", and "Purple Bitch. We use the radio". The messages are often disputed. At a paranormal conference I once attended a "certified EVP specialist" reported that he had recorded a spirit uttering, "I like ice cream." "No", corrected his colleague, "the spirit said 'I'm a nice kid!'"

Fans of the Frank's Box spend hours listening to the world's most unlistenable radio. For them, it is addictive, like a psychic slot machine. They are convinced by the pay-offs: the coincidental words and the more intelligible sounds. But these are merely better quality gibberish. If the listener doesn't hear anything but gobbledygook, Sumption argues they are simply listening the "wrong" way. Indeed, many believe there is a special way to "hear" the messages and that this ability requires practice, sensitivity, training, and time.

> When I first started making the linear sweep boxes, at first all I could hear was gibberish, then all the sudden I could hear "the guys" talking to me. It seems not everyone can hear it, especially just starting out. It takes time to tune in the ear, and maybe develop some intuition.
>
> (purplealiengirl.tripod.com)

Sumption explains that the ability to understand EVPs is "like learning a new language". But this is not authentic language. The Frank's Box generates bits of speech, and the results resemble speech, but collectively, these sounds don't constitute speech. The messages don't have the features that characterize natural language. They are pieced together selectively from a mixture of sounds, there is no grammar or consistency, and no agreed-upon meaning. The output is meaningless. That is, until someone gives it meaning.

Rorschach radio

The messages are meaningless from a semantic perspective, but the listener infuses them with meaning based in personal experience. However, sometimes this made up meaning can be shared artificially. Listeners are usually suggestible and want to hear something meaningful. There is a large emotional component to the practice and listeners are often driven by a personal expectation and desire to hear something, and any "message" is due to confirmation bias that the Frank's Box works. These are selective listeners who pay attention to the hits and ignore the misses and manipulate the data to fit their theories. Sometimes they even recognize the "voices". The voices don't have to sound like the deceased and the messages don't have to be profound for the believers to believe. In this mindset they have a tendency to be led, and to hear what others think they hear. This is known as priming, where the listener is prompted by others to see or hear something meaningful in something meaningless. Having others hear what you hear also seems to legitimize the results.

The messages received via Frank's Box are a type of pareidolia. Pareidolia is a well-understood psychological phenomenon, by which we identify meaningful patterns in random stimuli. This is known by various names, including apophenia, simulacra, Type I errors, and patternicity. People are pattern detectors, and in our attempts to detect signal from noise we often make perceptual errors. A common example of pareidolia is thinking we're hearing a phone ring when we're in the shower. The white noise generated by having a shower picks up a broad spectrum of sounds, including the ones that make up ringing tones, and we detect patterns corresponding roughly to our own ringtone (Alcock, 2004).

Frank's Box messages are the audio version of seeing Jesus on a tortilla, or the Virgin Mary on a cheese sandwich. We search for the familiar in the unfamiliar. Like the infamous Rorschach inkblot tests where a patient is told to identify images in meaningless visual patterns, Frank's Box listeners are hearing language in meaningless audio patterns. The Frank's Box is a kind of Rorschach radio.

Sumption himself provides the natural explanation for his invention, if we ignore the first part.

> [This is] simply another method of supplying "raw" audio that spirits and other entities can use to form voices. Raw audio is a sound source that contains bits of human speech, music and noise.
>
> (purplealiengirl.tripod.com)

Simply, the Frank's Box produces meaningless "human speech, music and noise" from which listeners create meaningful messages. The Frank's Box isn't a device that allows the living to communicate with the dead. It's just a broken radio.

12
Backmasking

Backmasking, otherwise known as backward masking, is the theory and alleged practice of planting messages into music. In cases of backmasking, the hidden messages can only be heard when the music is played in reverse. Some people believe that the messages are not perceived consciously when the music is played normally. Instead, they are absorbed subliminally. But they aren't urging you to "Drink Coca Cola", these messages order people to smoke marijuana, praise Satan, and commit suicide.

Thomas Edison and backmasking

As a rule, we don't listen to music played backwards, so how did this phenomenon start? Just like EVPs, Thomas Edison is often credited (or blamed) for backmasking. Edison invented the tinfoil phonograph in 1877. In experiments with his new device, he attempted reverse eduction, that is, he played sounds backwards. Edison played speech and songs in reverse, including a whistled version of "Yankee Doodle". He observed that music played backwards, "is still melodious in many cases, and some of the strains are sweet and novel, but altogether different from the song reproduced in the right way" (Blecha, 2004).

Edison and his colleagues were especially fond of a trick in which they would record the phrase "mad dog" and play it backwards to make it sound like "goddamn" (Feaster, 2006). But there is no evidence that this phenomenon was understood in terms of the occult. Instead, it was a novelty. Backwards effects demonstrated how the phonograph could create new sounds from existing compositions. These were sometimes described as a "musical kaleidoscope". A century later, backmasking would take on a different connotation.

133

The advent of reel-to-reel tape players in the 1930s made it easier to experiment with not only playing music but also recording music. In the 1940s, French composer Pierre Schaeffer became the first DJ by experimenting with sampling and backwards sounds. He pioneered backmasking in recording, known as *musique concrète*, which was a style favored by 1950s avant-garde musicians (Holmes, 2006).

We'll fuck you like Superman

The practice became mainstream when the Beatles incorporated backwards vocals and instruments into their 1966 album *Revolver*. These techniques were used specifically on the three tracks "'m Only Sleeping", "Tomorrow Never Knows", and the single "Rain". John Lennon claims he stumbled across the technique by accident when he was high on marijuana (Aldridge, 1991), while producer George Martin maintains he was experimenting with reverse tape effects specifically for the album (Giuliano and Vrnda, 1999). Whoever discovered the phenomenon first, it was used for artistic purposes only. There were no hidden messages until the fans, and fanatics, went looking for them.

When fans began hearing backwards music they were inspired to play the music backwards. Soon, they were finding cryptic messages in popular songs. One of their most famous messages can allegedly be found on "A Day in the Life", the last track on *Sgt. Peppers Lonely Hearts Club Band*. At the end of the song is a backward loop. When played in reverse, you can supposedly hear the chant, "We'll fuck you like Superman".

In the documentary *The Beatles Anthology*, George Martin demystifies the above claim. "A Day in the Life" culminates with an "orchestral orgasm" played by the London Symphony Orchestra. Trying to work out how to end the song after a long piano fade-out, Martin says,

> We had to have a bit of fun at the end of it, didn't we? So we just recorded a load of nonsense for two seconds. Every boy in number two studio was singing gibberish, and I tucked it in on the inner groove. And then people thought there was something significant in it. So we had to have our little joke.

There was a hidden message at the end of the song, but it wasn't for humans: "We even put in a frequency of 18 kilohertz just for dogs to listen to, and I guess some people read something into that too." Paul McCartney further denies any intentional message in the song, "we had certainly not intended to do that but probably when you turn anything backwards it sounds like something … if you look hard enough you can make something out of anything" (Miles, 1997).

Paul is dead

Some backmasking messages fed into urban legends and conspiracy theories, especially the myth that Paul McCartney had died in a car crash in 1966 and was replaced with a lookalike. The "Paul is dead" stories surfaced around 1969 when the Beatles were disbanding. The chief piece of evidence for Paul's death was the indistinct "turn me on, dead man" found backwards in the *White Album*'s "Revolution 9", an experimental cacophony of discordant music, choir singing, radio broadcasts, sirens, applause, and gunfights.

The band's experimentation came back to haunt them. Fans began searching for more clues and found them, even though they weren't there. "Paul is a dead man. Miss him, miss him, miss him," was discovered backwards in the song "I'm So Tired". During a long jam session at the end of "Strawberry Fields Forever" John Lennon supposedly admits, "I buried Paul." Lennon revealed to *Rolling Stone* magazine that he actually says "cranberry sauce" (Gambaccini, 1974). The Beatles had a penchant for surrealism in their lyrics. Lennon once heard that an English teacher at his former school was making students analyze Beatles songs. This inspired him to write the cryptic lyrics to "I am the Walrus" (Shotton and Schaffner, 1984).

Backmasking claims span the decades; from the Beatles in the 1960s through the 1970s, when Eric Clapton was believed to sing "I'm so wicked" backwards in "Cocaine", to the 1980s, when Queen encouraged fans to take drugs by singing, "It's fun to smoke marijuana" on "Another One Bites the Dust". But there was a price for hearing the hidden "messages". You had to destroy the record to play it backwards. Still, the myths have survived the death of records. Claims have continued into the 1990s, 2000s, and beyond, with suggestions that there is backmasking in songs by Eminem, Britney Spears, The Spice Girls, and many other modern songs. Using digital software any recording can now easily be reversed and "messages" found in everything.

Ironically, the claims actually created the phenomenon. As a result of the rumors, many bands began experimenting with backmasking for artistic or satirical effect. After being accused of embedding a message on *Eldorado*, Electric Light Orchestra deliberately engineered a message in "Fire on High", "The music is reversible, but time – turn back! Turn back! Turn back! Turn back!" In a parody of backmasking, Pink Floyd left the following message in *The Wall*'s "Empty Spaces": "Congratulations, You have just discovered the secret message. Please send your answer to old pink, care of the funny farm, Chalfont."

These engineered reversals are clear messages. Non-engineered "messages" are incomprehensible because they aren't real messages. The songs popularly accused of being backmasked aren't backmasked at all, while engineered reversals are genuine examples of steganography. Deliberate messages can be engineered in a variety of methods. A message can be recorded at a low volume or recorded at a different speed than the rest of the recording. The most common method is to record a message and play it backwards during the song.

Satanic panic

Backmasking is feared to have powerful effects on listeners, inducing loose morals and bad behavior. The messages are believed to be created by a rock band or producer, if not Satan himself. The practice is typically associated with the music industry, and specifically, rock, rap, heavy metal, or other genres perceived as deviant or subversive at one time or another. We probably wouldn't expect to find backmasking in a sample of folk music or country. As the joke goes, "What do you get when you play country music backwards? You get back your wife, your dog, your truck and your job."

One of the main claims is that backmasking is used to embed satanic messages in music. Many popular bands have been accused of this, including the Rolling Stones, Santana, Deep Purple, and Frank Zappa. The most infamous allegations include: The Eagles sang, "Yes, Satan organized his own religion", in "Hotel California"; Styx crooned, "Satan move though our voices" on "Snowblind"; and the following message can be found in Led Zeppelin's "Stairway to Heaven", "I live for Satan...the Lord turns me off...there's no escaping it...here's to my sweet Satan....there's power in Satan...he will give you 666."

There are a number of possible explanations for these occult connections. In 1966, Lennon made his infamous comment that the Beatles were "more popular than Jesus". This incited the "Jesus controversy" backlash against Lennon and the Beatles. The band, and by extension, rock "n" roll, was branded as sacrilegious, and thousands of albums were sacrificed in mass record burnings. As we have seen, Led Zeppelin was also accused of backmasking on the song "Stairway to Heaven"; similar accusations were made about their songs "Black Dog" and "Rock N' Roll". *Led Zeppelin IV*, the album on which these songs appeared, was rumored to be full of hidden occult messages, including the artwork which featured four "sigils" believed to be satanic symbols. It was popularly believed that the band members were black magicians who had entered into a Faustian pact with the devil to secure their success. In reality, guitarist Jimmy Page had a fascination with Aleister Crowley and was an avid collector of the mystic's memorabilia and occult paraphernalia. The link between Led Zeppelin and backmasking was probably bolstered by a quote from Crowley. In his 1913 book *Magick Liber ABA*, he recommends that black magicians in training "listen to phonograph records, reversed," to learn how to think and speak backwards.

Speaking backwards was a part of the fabled black mass, a ceremony said to be held during the witches' sabbath. During this rite, the participants mocked the Catholic Mass by invoking the principle of opposites. Black candles were used instead of white, crucifixes were inverted, and participants walked backwards over them. Litanies substituted the name of "Satan" for "God", prayers were recited backwards, and negatives and affirmatives were switched so that the Lord's Prayer was read as, "Lead us into temptation and deliver us not from evil" (Cavendish, 1967).

Stories of black masses featured prominently in allegations of satanic ritual abuse that surfaced during the 1980s. Unsurprisingly, the fear of satanic backwards messages in music gained momentum during this time. Fundamentalist Christian crusaders such as Gary Greenwald, Don Hutchings, and Michael Mills toured the United States, claiming that many popular songs contained backmasked messages. They feared that backmasking is an invasion of privacy, because the messages are understood subliminally when played normally. They preached that these messages exert a powerful influence on the listener, encouraging drug use, criminal behavior, homosexuality, sexual promiscuity, and satanism. Violent rallies, record-smashing sprees, and record burnings often followed these lectures. Greenwald and others claimed that religious materials are free of backmasking. However, a number of messages have been found and even engineered in Christian music, as revealed in Frank Oglesbee's *The Devil, You Say? Back-masking in Contemporary Christian Music*.

These preachers lobbied for legislation to label or ban backmasking. A bill was introduced in the US House of Representatives to label suspicious albums with a sticker that read: "Warning: This record contains backward masking that makes a verbal statement which is audible when this record is played backward and which may be perceptible at a subliminal level when this record is played forward" (Vokey and Read, 1985).

The bill passed in Arkansas and a similar bill was passed in California, but the success was fleeting and it was soon overturned.

The Judas Priest trial

The backmasking witch-hunt culminated with the Judas Priest trial. In 1985, 20-year-old James Vance and 18-year-old Raymond Belknap attempted suicide in Sparks, Nevada. The Judas Priest album *Stained Class* was implicated in the suicide of Belknap, who died after shooting himself in the face. Vance survived his suicide attempt. The boys were listening to the song "Better by You, Better by Me", which allegedly contained the backwards message "do it". Although there is no explanation of what the listener should "do" exactly, this message allegedly commanded the boys to attempt suicide, although they were intoxicated and high on marijuana at the time. The presiding judge ruled that the messages were there but were unintentional. Ultimately, the case was dismissed. Similarly, during the 1988 trial of Richard Ramirez, the serial killer claimed that AC/DC's "Night Prowler" inspired him to commit his crimes. He was unsuccessful in convincing the jury of this.

Some heavy metal bands really did experiment with engineered satanic messages, including Iron Maiden and Slayer. Cradle of Filth's "Dinner at Deviant's Palace" featured a reversed reading of the Lord's Prayer. Ironically, these bands don't mince words. Their lyrics about sex, suicide, drugs, and death are blatant. As AC/DC's Angus Young said of the Ramirez trial, "You didn't need to play the album backwards, because we never hid the messages. We'd call an album *Highway To Hell*; there it was right in front of them" (Simmons, 2004).

Testing, testing, testing

During the height of the panic, Vokey and Read (1985) conducted experiments to determine whether backmasked messages actually exist, and if they do, whether they can influence the listener or not. They recorded passages from Lewis Carroll's "Jabberwocky", the 23rd psalm, and other messages, including phrases in French and German. These were then re-recorded backwards and played to subjects to find out if they could be understood. The subjects could discern the sex of the speaker at 98.9 per cent accuracy and detect the language of the messages at 46.7 per cent accuracy. To test comprehension, the subjects were presented with individual words and asked if they had appeared in the passages. They achieved 55.8 per cent accuracy with this task; results no greater than chance. But the subjects were more successful at identifying syllables than words, so they were more likely reconstructing, rather than detecting words.

In another series of tests, the subjects were asked to judge the meaning of the messages, based on whether the messages were nursery rhymes, Christian, satanic, or pornographic in content. Again, the results were no greater than chance, and the meaning of the backwards messages didn't appear to have been understood at any level, conscious or otherwise. Nor was there evidence that the listeners were influenced, consciously or unconsciously, by the content of backward messages.

In a final test, the researchers identified some plausible-sounding messages in the backwards speech, including the phrases "Saw a girl with a weasel in her mouth" and "I saw Satan". They also invented control messages that didn't fit the phonological patterns of the samples. The subjects were instructed to listen for these phrases. They didn't hear the control messages, but they did hear the phonologically plausible phrases at a rate of 84.6 per cent, but only *after* they were pointed out. The results of the study demonstrate that people really do hear messages where they don't exist, but not any random phrase they are induced to hear, only plausible-sounding interpretations. Vokey and Read conclude that backmasking messages aren't caused by producers or Satan, they are found by the listeners themselves, "the apparent presence of backward messages in music is a function more of active construction on the part of the perceiver than of the existence of the messages themselves".

They have it backwards

Songwriters haven't had any success in writing lyrics that make sense both forwards *and* backwards. Even palindromes, words that look the same forwards and backwards, such as *kayak*, sound different when played in reverse. The syllables and stress will be different, especially when said in phrases. Hearing words in backwards lyrics is similar to mishearing lyrics. In Jimi Hendrix's "Purple Haze" the lyrics, "Scuse me, while I kiss the sky" are mistaken for, "Scuse me, while I kiss this guy". These misheard lyrics are popularly called mondegreens. Similarly, when people believe they hear messages in backwards music, they are hearing word-like sounds because they are comprised of human speech sounds. Speakers are able to hear something intelligible without the message being there.

This is another example of pareidolia. Like EVPs, the brain searches for recognizable patterns in the chaos. When we hear music played backwards we mistakenly identify words amongst the noise. Hearing messages is aided by suggestion, when someone else points them out to us. As Vokey and Read explain, Greenwald didn't just ask his audiences to listen to the reversed passages and hear the messages. Before the music was played people were presented with an interpretation of what they were about to hear. Under these conditions, it is not surprising that most listeners "hear" the messages they've been primed to hear.

13
Reverse Speech

Everyone knows Neil Armstrong's famous first words on the moon. But did you know that they say something else when played backwards? Armstrong's words, "That's one small step for man" reverses to say, "Man will space walk." This is a reflection of his logical thoughts at the time. Man will continue to walk into space.

(davidoates.com)

David Oates discovered the phenomenon of reverse speech (RS). This is the theory that regular speech contains hidden messages that can only be heard when it is played backwards. It is believed that unconscious thoughts, memories, and experiences are embedded in our spoken language, and we can reveal these by recording speech and playing it in reverse (Oates, 1991). This is backmasking without a soundtrack.

The theory of reverse speech

Oates claims that RS occurs every 10–15 seconds of speech, producing two messages simultaneously. The "overt mode" is spoken forwards and is heard consciously, while the "covert mode" is not under our conscious control, and is only heard when speech is played backwards. These two modes of speech are dependent upon each other and cannot be fully understood in isolation. When combined, they communicate the total psyche of the person, both conscious as well as subconscious.

We don't always say what we really think, whether we conceal our thoughts deliberately or we communicate ineffectively. According to Oates, RS breaks down the communication barriers that language creates. Oates believes that RS is invariably honest and he promotes it as the "ultimate lie detector". The human mind is no longer private. If a lie is spoken forwards, the truth will be spoken backwards.

RS is touted as a linguistic truth serum that reveals intention and motivation. It can be used as an interrogative tool for police and courts, to reveal the guilt or innocence of a suspect. It will coax an offender to confess, point to the evidence, and expose any accomplices. By analyzing RS, the media can examine political speeches for falsehoods, and employers can evaluate job candidates. Doctors can accurately diagnose their patients, while RS can also be used as a tool in child psychology, behavioral therapy, and self-improvement. If the claims made about RS could be proven, it would be a groundbreaking discovery with many practical applications.

Oates isn't a linguist or a psychologist. He discovered RS by accident in 1983, when he dropped a cassette tape into a toilet. He fished it out of the bowl and cleaned it, but found that the damaged tape only played in reverse. Strangely, Oates could still hear language, but these messages seemed to have a different meaning to the normal speech. He was likely inspired by the backmasking craze of the previous two decades, but Oates insists that backmasking is intentional whereas RS is unintentional.

An Australian by birth, Oates spent most of the 1990s living in California, promoting his theory via books, lectures, workshops, and counseling. Oates once pushed "reversing machines", which were basically tape players that could play in reverse. However, with the advent of digital recorders, most software programs can play recordings backwards. Today, there are many "RS practitioners" who are qualified by Oates' courses. Advocates claim that the theory works with all natural languages, and there are practitioners who perform RS analysis in Dutch, Spanish, and French.

Out of the mouths of babes

Oates believes that covert speech develops before overt speech, and that children speak backwards before they speak forwards. He claims that children as young as four months old produce single words in reverse, such as "Daddy", "hungry", and "help". He cites examples of a four-month-old child whose vocalizations played backwards say, "Mommy, Mommy". However, these noises don't constitute language, especially when played in reverse. The babbling stage begins at approximately 5–8 months, when the baby's vocalizations begin to sound like phonemes, but these do not yet represent meaning. At the end of the first year, babbles begin to sound like words. Even then, they may not have any specific meaning attached to them.

Oates' claims contradict everything linguists know about first language acquisition. Oates also claims that by 13–14 months, babies form complex sentences in reverse. However, until 18 months, babies are still in the one-word stage. At two years, infants start producing sentences without grammar; after 30 months, they enter the multi-word stage and begin making sentences. A recording of a baby crying supposedly says "Daddy help", but crying isn't language. RS analyses of children's speech are subjective interpretations of the kind of thing a child might say.

Oates also contradicts our understanding of neuroscience. He says that the left hemisphere of the brain produces forward speech while the right hemisphere produces RS. He doesn't provide any evidence of this latter claim, and Kimura (1968) reports that both forward and RS sounds are identified most accurately by the left side. It isn't as simple as the left brain controls language, and the right brain controls thinking. Young people who sustain damage to the left side of the brain can develop speech control by the right hemisphere to some extent and language deficits can occur after right hemisphere damage. In 30–40 per cent of left-handed people, and 5 per cent of right-handers, the right side of the brain is used for language.

RS is gibberish. Similar to Frank Sumption's claim that deciphering EVP is like learning another language, Oates' argues there is no "gibberish", only RS that isn't understood yet. But it is not objectively meaningful; it is all in the interpretation. It is only language in the sense of what it was before it was modified. It is no longer natural language.

Interpretations of RS tend to reflect the expectations of the analyst and the content of the forward speech. For example, a woman talked about her experiences in an RS workshop. Her backwards speech was said to reveal the message, "the source to give help". Amazingly, many reversals flatter Oates. His nine-year-old daughter says in reverse, "I am the power. I am Oates." He cautions us to be careful in what we say to our kids, citing one child who repeats curse words in RS, "Hey fucking hell." Like backmasking and EVPs, Oates' reversals are often sensational and vulgar. A man who wanted a business relationship with Oates says in his reversed speech, "I'm so full of shit." A woman in her 50s wonders how she managed to keep the interest of her toy boy, and her subconscious replies, "He's wanting old pussy."

Celebrities reversed

Other analyses are said to reveal lies when the RS contradicts the statement. During her life, actress Anna Nicole Smith said of her controversial marriage to an elderly oil tycoon, "I turned him down. I said that I wanted to try and [make something out] of my life." But her RS reveals the unspoken truth, "I have a scam."

RS analyses often reflect well-known facts or scandalous accusations, especially about public figures. Bill Clinton once said, "I try to articulate my position as clearly as possible." Oates' analysis reveals that he "really" said, "She's a fun girl to kiss." Oates has done the talk-show circuit many times revealing his analyses of celebrities; with appearances on *Coast to Coast*, *Larry King Live*, and CNN news. He has a penchant for analyzing assassins and serial killers, including Charles Manson, David Koresh, and Ted Bundy. According to Oates' analyses, O. J. Simpson and Scott Peterson admit they murdered their wives, Tiger Woods' public apology for his infidelities was insincere, and Queen Elizabeth II is glad that Princess Diana died.

Oates also analyses music and has concluded that Eric Clapton sings "I'm so wicked" in "Cocaine", in "Help" the Beatles admit, "Now he uses marijuana," and Led Zeppelin's "Stairway to Heaven" reveals, "It's my sweet Satan. The one whose little path would make me sad whose power is fake. There was a little toolshed where he made us suffer, sad Satan." Not one to miss a trend, Oates' analyzed *Stained Class*, the album made infamous by the Judas Priest trial. Unsurprisingly, Oates found the hidden "do it, do it" message too, and much more. Oates' (1991) says, "I found over 72 speech reversals on this album, only two of which were quoted at the trial. The attorney for the plaintiff completely overlooked the most striking reversals, 'God is evil. An innocent man help us. Get out of it, get out of it. Say, am I sexy. Give us the truth. You silly fuck. I took my life.' "

Hceeps esrever

The most feasible word-like sounds we could hear in backwards speech would be palindromes; words like "madam" and "racecar" that sound almost the same when spoken in reverse. Other phonetic coincidences may be found, such as corresponding forms that are the approximate reversal, like "say" and "yes". However, to lend credence to his theory, Oates' denies that palindromes and other coincidences represent true RS. Of course, he and his cronies are the only ones who know the difference, although their distinctions between genuine and coincidental reversals are inconsistent.

People complain about the use of slang and "bad grammar", but if we are to believe Oates our RS is far worse. When we speak backwards, entire sentences are reduced to awkward, ungrammatical, and nonsensical phrases. Oates and his followers have collected such examples as, "Ate sickness," "You see the luck solid," "I don't love the shark with error," and "See the wolf fallen in the lake."

Most "messages" are ambiguous, so Oates began finding metaphors in reversed speech. Oates and his analysts then translate these metaphors, especially for use in hypnotherapy. In his *Reverse Speech Metaphor Dictionary* (2000) he provides definitions for metaphors he believes are commonly found in reversed speech. These are often animals, such as wolves, and religious references. For example, a reversal recording of an official speaking weeks after the 9/11 terrorist attacks is interpreted as, "Brave eagle, we're sad", and "eagle" is explained as a metaphor for the United States. Oates also uses RS as another kind of divination. Instead of tarot cards or tea leaves, a segment of speech is used to read the personality, past, present, and future of a subject. Clearly a believer in all things paranormal, Oates' calls RS the "seventh sense".

Oates allows his beliefs to bias his analyses. He uses RS to support popular conspiracy theories, including UFO fears about Area 51 and the belief that the moon landing was a hoax. Oates claims that officials in Washington DC showed interest in his research, until his team uncovered the Desert Storm code word "Simone" embedded backwards in one of former President George Bush's speeches. Oates' assistant Scott Jones sent a "secret memo" (that is publicly available online) to then secretary of defense Dick Cheney. Oates believes he was silenced because he knew too much.

Instead of having practical applications, there are many dangers to RS. Its use in a court of law would be unjust, its use in employment would be discriminatory, and its use in medicine would be dangerous. Newbrook (2005) reports the case of a woman who analyzed a sample of her daughter's speech, inspired by her husband's attendance of an RS workshop. Her analysis supposedly revealed that her husband was molesting her daughter. She reported him to a child protection authority, and when this failed, she sought to gain sole custody to prevent contact between father and daughter.

Speak for yourself

Oates also claims that RS enables communication with nonverbal people. RS bears similarities to facilitated communication, also known as supported writing. This is the practice of assisting communication with patients suffering from autism, brain damage, or diseases such as cerebral palsy. This involves a facilitator who stabilizes the patient's hand so they are able to type a message on a keyboard or device that features letters, words, or other symbols. Astonishingly, these patients often reveal an extraordinary degree of literacy. Some convey sentences, while others pen poems and short stories, or even complete college courses. Facilitated communication seemed to reveal the hidden world of uncommunicative people and to suggest the true cognitive and linguistic skills of the underestimated patient.

However, there were some suspicious elements to the practice. Strangely, facilitated communication would only work with a facilitator, but not with the patient's parents. It would work even though the patient had never learned how to read or write, and sometimes the patient wasn't even looking at the keyboard when the messages were typed. Like RS and repressed memory therapy, facilitated communication has resulted in false allegations of sexual abuse. Multiple studies haven't been able to validate the claims of facilitated communicators. For example, one study presented subjects with visual or auditory stimulus, but the subject couldn't identify the stimulus if the facilitator had not also witnessed it (Beck and Pirovano, 1996).

It was the facilitators, not the patients, who were typing the messages. The message board became an Ouija board for the uncommunicative. While often well intentioned, the operators impose their own beliefs, thoughts, and expectations upon the subject. Similarly, RS practitioners believe they are analyzing a subject's speech, but they are only speaking on behalf of their subjects.

Straight talk about backwards talk

Newbrook and Curtain (1997, 1998) examined Oates' claims by replicating and refining one of his own experiments. Oates claims that any listener can hear RS, but he primes them with the messages they should hear. Using Oates' favorite examples, the researchers set out to see if the messages can be heard without prompting. The results showed that unprompted listeners couldn't hear the messages in RS. The backmasking study by Vokey and Read (1985) supports this, showing that subjects who hear recordings of words played in reverse are unable to identify the words.

Newbrook and Curtain also found that it is possible to condition listeners to hear different messages in the same example, as long as the sounds are similar. The authors observe that, "the power of suggestion is an important factor in the recognition of RS sequences". They conclude that the claims regarding RS are implausible and unsupported by the empirical evidence. In a later synthesis of the existing literature on RS, Byrne and Normand (2000) also conclude that there is no data to support the claims.

Early in his career, behaviorist B. F. Skinner (1936) invented a device called the Verbal Summator. This was a phonograph that played meaningless patterns of vowel sounds repeatedly. This machine evaluated a patient's responses to random stimuli, supposedly to reveal their hidden emotions. Skinner described this machine as a kind of auditory inkblot. Like the Rorschach test, the sounds had subjective meaning and interpretation. Similarly, RS is best explained as pareidolia. Like EVP and backmasking, hearing language in backwards speech is making meaning of abstract sounds. When the meaning is shared, it is aided by suggestion. It is easier to hear words and phrases when an RS analyst deciphers the message and points it out to you. All in all, it's the theories behind RS that are backwards.

14
The Bible Code

Were modern events such as the Holocaust, the moon landing, and the assassination of President John F. Kennedy prophesized in the time of Adam and Eve, Moses, and Noah? Proponents of the Bible Code (also known as the Torah Code) believe that the "Word of God" also reveals the hidden word of God. These are messages said to foretell modern events that were encoded thousands of years ago in the Old Testament. The Bible Code is alleged to be the "fingerprint of God".

Jewish mystics believed that God dictated the Torah to Moses, so it has been a favored sources for bibliomancy and other forms of prophecy. Advocates like to say that even scientist Isaac Newton scoured the Bible for prophecies, but that was during the seventeenth century and he also practiced alchemy. Others search through scriptures like they're trying to break a cipher. Taking a large block of text, they hunt for words, especially names, places, phrases, and dates.

Equidistant letter sequencing

One such person was Torah scholar and mathematician Rabbi Michael Weissmandel (1903–56). He searched the 78,064 words in the Book of Genesis in Hebrew and discovered the word TORAH hidden within the text. A few decades later, the messages allegedly coded by God could be decoded with computers. Researchers Doron Witztum, Eliyahu Rips, and Yoav Rosenberg did just that. In 1994 they published an article in *Statistical Science*, claiming they had found hidden messages embedded in the Torah using a method called equidistant letter sequencing. This is a type of skip code. A block of text is chosen and spaces and punctuation are omitted. Then the text is searched for sequences of letters spaced at equal intervals throughout text. For example, isolating every second letter in *troops* reveals *tops*. Using this code on the Hebrew Book of Genesis, the authors discovered the names of several famous rabbis, in close proximity to their birth and death dates. They claimed the probability of obtaining these results by mere chance alone is one in four million.

Michael Drosnin and *The Bible Code*

In 1992, journalist Michael Drosnin was introduced to the method by mathematician Elihyahu Rips. In his own experiments with searching the Old Testament he found the words "Yitzhak", "Rabin", "assassinate", and "Amir". Believing these words foretold the future assassination of then Israeli Prime Minister Yitzhak Rabin, he sent a warning to Rabin that went unheeded. Sure enough, Rabin was murdered in 1995; by a man named Yigal Amir.

In 1997 Drosnin released his book *The Bible Code*. Drosnin tweaked the original theory, claiming that related words found in close proximity constitute prophecies and that the Bible contains hundreds of hidden messages and predictions. Among these, Drosnin claims that the Bible contains references to Adolf Hitler, the Apollo 11 spaceflight, Bill Clinton, and the global economic collapse of the 2000s. Drosnin explains, "The Bible is constructed like a giant crossword puzzle. It is encoded from beginning to end with words that connect to tell a hidden story" (Drosnin, 1997).

Reading between the lines

On closer inspection *The Bible Code* findings aren't so amazing. Drosnin had 304,805 Hebrew letters of the Bible as an inventory. His match for "Yitzhak Rabin" was found using the skip code with an interval of 4,772, meaning the letters of apparent significance were almost 5,000 words apart (Thomas, 1997).

As for Drosnin's foretelling of the Israeli prime minister's assassination, Rabin was at serious risk in his role, and many political and psychic predictions of his murder had already been made. Moreover, Drosnin didn't provide any specific information about the date of Rabin's death, which was 4 November, or the place, a rally in Tel Aviv. Drosnin's actual warning to Rabin was ambiguous, "I believe you are in real danger, but that danger can be averted" (Drosnin, 1997). Other predictions of Drosnin's went unfulfilled. *The Bible Code* was released in 1997 and predicted the end of world in 2000. The year 2000 came and went, so he moved the goalposts and the 2002 sequel the *Bible Code II* prophesized the end of the world in 2006. Drosnin is just another failed Doomsday prophet.

Rips has distanced himself from Drosnin's theory, and denied the implication that they worked together. He said,

> I do not support the book as it is or the conclusions it derives. All attempts to extract messages from Torah codes, or to make predictions based on them, are futile and are of no value. This is not only my own opinion, but the opinion of every scientist who has been involved in serious Codes research.
>
> (Van Biema, 1997)

As for the predictions of past events, it is easy to predict the future after the fact. Foretellings of world events and the births and deaths of rabbis are backdated predictions. To get a scientifically meaningful statistic you need to state in advance exactly what you're looking for, otherwise you're just fishing for results to fit the hypothesis. This is just a kind of data mining, and these would-be code-breakers are confusing word combinations with predictions.

The searching is done using readily available computer programs that perform endless combinations seeking something meaningful. This is similar to hacking software that cracks passwords. Like a giant word search puzzle, lines of text are placed into randomly chosen matrices creating an inconceivable number of possible random lines of text. This matrix of letters can be read in any direction; forward, backward, horizontally, diagonally, and vertically. This is a type of word game known as acrostic. These are texts in which a hidden sequence of letters spells out a word or phrase. It is nothing new for people to search for acrostics in the Bible. But there are no rules for this game.

These trials on endless combinations of letters occasionally spell out a meaningful word. The chances of finding accidental words is high, especially for short words. In biblical Hebrew it is easier still, given that the alphabet is an abjad, meaning that the letters are primarily consonants. In what is known as *matres lectionis*, several consonants may also be used to indicate vowels, while diacritics known as *niqqud* are also used to mark vowels. If this wasn't complicated enough, Hebrew has multiple permissible spellings for names.

Sometimes "related" words are found nearby in clusters, if we take a generous view of what we perceive as nearby. More than one word can be semantically appropriate, for example *evil* can mean *bad* or *ill*. Grammar is optional, which allows for creative phrasing. From these innumerable combinations, words are created, then phrases are created, and then meaning is created. In many ways, equidistant letter sequencing is similar to hearing messages in backwards music or speech, and unearthing hidden messages is a kind of pareidolia.

The good word

In a *Newsweek* article Drosnin issued a challenge to skeptics, "When my critics find a message about the assassination of a prime minister encrypted in Moby Dick, I'll believe them" (Begley, 1997). And so they did. Using the novel *Moby Dick*, mathematician Brendan McKay not only predicted the assassination of Yitzhak Rabin, but the assassinations of Prime Minister Indira Gandhi, Soviet exile Leon Trotsky, the Reverend Martin Luther King, Abraham Lincoln, John F. Kennedy, and the death of Lady Diana, former princess of Wales (Bar-Hillel, Bar-Natan, and McKay, 1998). To demonstrate that patterns appear by chance in any book, McKay even found a tongue-in-cheek "prediction" of the murder of Drosnin, where he found the author's name near the phrase, "Him to have been killed."

Then McKay and colleagues turned to the findings of Witztum, Rips, and Rosenburg. Witztum et al. were accused of statistical tuning in a paper that was published (ironically) in *Statistical Science*. This is subtly reshaping data in a way that can influence the result (McKay et al., 1999). The rabbis named in the study could go by many different names in Hebrew. To give an example from English, "Bill Clinton" could go by many alternative names that still denote the same person: "Bill", "William", "Mr Clinton", or "president of the United States". In the Witztum et al. study one rabbi alone was known by 11 different names. Similarly, dates can appear in more than one form, for example, "January first", "the first of January", and "New Year's Day". The shorter words, the grammar, and the flexibility of Hebrew spelling can create multiple potential "hits", and there was no protocol behind the spellings selected for the study. McKay and colleagues attribute the success of Witztum et al.'s experiment to these ambiguities.

Even more damning, McKay et al. found that they couldn't replicate the results of the study when they used variants of the rabbis' names and dates. They provided no statistically significant clustering. However, they did find the same rabbis' names and dates in the Hebrew translation of Tolstoy's *War and Peace*, although this book had been the control text in the Witztum et al. study (McKay et al., 1999). Rather than being a low probability of chance, the authors concluded that any patterns are the result of pure random chance.

The original paper wasn't even taken seriously by the journal in which it was published. The editor stated, "The paper is thus offered...as a challenging puzzle" (Witztum et al., 1994). From scripture to romance novels, hidden messages can be found anywhere if we search long enough in a text that is big enough. In the end, the Bible Code isn't a divine puzzle to be solved. It is a human-made word puzzle with many possible "solutions".

15
Secret Symbols

Signs and symbols are different things. Signs are natural, while symbols are created. We're not talking "STOP" signs, we're talking signs that are natural indicators. For example, smoke can be a sign of fire, while a sore throat can be a sign of a cold. Conversely, symbols are referents made by us. The letter Q, the number 13, and the word "custard" are all symbols. In a sense, all languages are a kind of shared code. Sounds, letters, words, sentences, and all the components of language are symbolic. The symbol K is representative of the sound /k/, and the symbol 7 represents the concept of the number following six and preceding eight. But what happens when one symbol is misrepresented as another? This chapter looks at some famous hoaxes, myths, and urban legends about hidden messages in symbols.

Elvis is alive?

Musical legend Elvis Aaron (or Aron) Presley was born January 8, 1935, and died August 16, 1977. That is, if you believe he is dead. Conspiracy theories abound about Elvis, but the enduring legend is that the legend is still alive. Aside from Elvis sightings that are as common as Bigfoot sightings, the main evidence hinges on one small detail, the spelling of his middle name on his headstone. On his birth certificate, Elvis' middle name is spelled "Aron", while the spelling on his headstone is "Aaron". This "inaccuracy" supposedly suggests that the King is not buried there. Fans (and fanatics) interpret this as a sign that Elvis hasn't yet left the building.

Elvis was named after Saint Ailbe, a sixth-century Irish priest. "Ailbe" is anglicized as "Elvis", while the saint is often known as Elvis of Munster. The Presleys were a fervently religious family, and Elvis was heavily influenced by gospel music. The Presleys were congregation members of the Assemblies of God Pentecostal church, and Elvis' middle name was chosen after their family friend and fellow churchgoer Aaron Kennedy (Guralnick, 1994). Some sources claim Elvis' father misspelled this name on the birth certificate. However, it appears Vernon and Gladys spelled the name as "Aron" to parallel the spelling of Elvis' twin brother Jesse Garon Presley, who was stillborn. Aron appears on his record contracts, marriage license, and other legal documents until 1966, when Elvis decided to favor the biblical spelling, Aaron. When Elvis died, Vernon used the new preferred spelling on his son's tombstone.

However, there were some genuine misspellings in this story. Dr William Hunt, who delivered Elvis, recorded the births in his ledger. He misspelled Elvis as "Evis", and Garon as "Garion". On baby Jesse's death certificate he misspelled Presley as "Pressley". Ironically, the latter was the original spelling of the family name (Nash, 2010). There are simple excuses for these various misspellings and different spellings but, for the conspiracy theorists, Elvis will still be alive well after it would be impossible for him to be alive.

Freemason symbols

You're probably seen the iconic Masonic square and compass symbol on homes, offices, license plates, jewelry, and tombstones. Signs of the Freemasons are everywhere, like their all-seeing eye symbol, and yet they have an air of mystique to them. I once worked for a company that operated from a former Masonic Hall. My colleagues told stories of the meanings behind the symbols, and gossiped that when they first moved into the building they found evidence that satanic rituals had taken place there. Many believe that the Freemasons are a secret society with secret rituals, secret symbols, and a secret language. Do their symbols have hidden meanings?

The Freemasons are the world's largest and oldest international fraternal order. Not quite old enough to be descendants of the Knights Templar, as some claim, but the order began in 1717, and may have links to medieval stonemason guilds. The Freemasons have had many prominent brethren, including George Washington, Sir Arthur Conan Doyle, Mozart, and John Wayne. They teach lessons of social and moral virtues based on the symbolism of the tools and language of the ancient building trade, using the design and construction of a structure as a symbol for building character in men (Hodapp, 2010). And they don't see themselves as a secret society.

Masonic codes

According to legend, the Freemasons are a clandestine organization with mysterious powers, and they have been branded a cult, a religion, and a global conspiracy. The order has been linked to the illuminati, satanism, Nazism, communism, Zionism, and the Ku Klux Klan. It is also believed that Walt Disney was a high-ranking Freemason, and planted Masonic symbols throughout Disneyland. Like the fresh interest garnered by Drosnin's *The Bible Code*, Dan Brown's fictional *The Lost Symbol* has rekindled modern interest in the Freemasons and embellished the legends.

Many myths have arisen about the Freemasons. It is believed they adopt secret oaths at initiation to favor the order over society, so that the accused or witnesses in court only need give a secret sign to the judge who will be obliged to rule in his brother's favor. There is an urban legend that Masonic "Indians" saved white Americans who were at the point of being ritually killed because the prisoner had given a secret Mason symbol (Ridley, 2011). There are tales of Masons being spared when they reveal their brotherhood to a fellow Mason in power. As an example, Masons can speed in Wales yet not receive a fine!

During the American Civil War, General William Tecumseh Sherman and his troops embarked on their famous March to the Sea campaign across Georgia, burning and pillaging houses along the way. However, a few antebellum homes and towns were left unscathed. Urban legend attributes this to the Masonic symbols found on these homes, because Sherman himself was a Mason faithful to the codes of his brethren (Henken, 2003). However, there is no evidence that Sherman was a Mason.

Masonic symbols

Many Masonic symbols are highly recognizable but misunderstood. The unfinished pyramid on the reverse side of the Great Seal of the United States, as seen on the US one dollar bill, is believed to be a Masonic symbol but it isn't. There are Egyptian-themed Masonic lodges in existence, but pyramids don't have a role in Masonic symbolism (Hodapp, 2010). There are elements that share a connection to Masonic symbols, such as the all-seeing Eye of Providence design symbolizing "divine omniscience". But this is a commonly found symbol that appears across cultures and its meaning is open to interpretation.

The pentagram occasionally appears in the symbolism of Freemasonry. This symbol dates back to Mesopotamian writing from 3,000 BCE, and has been adopted by the Baha'i Faith, Christianity, and the Church of Jesus Christ of Latter Day Saints. Aleister Crowley and Neopagan groups such as the Wiccans also adopted the pentagram. As a result, it is often associated with the occult. However, the pentagram is a five-pointed star that is so common it appears on the US flag 50 times. The pentagram is most prominently the symbol of the Order of the Eastern Star, where it represents the Star of Bethlehem. It is believed that Masons use a pentagram that is right-side up or inverted, but these don't appear in traditional Masonic symbols (Hodapp, 2009).

The skull and crossbones feature in the older designs of the Knights Templar order of the York Rite of Freemasonry. Historically, the skull and crossbones symbol was used to denote cemeteries, especially as a warning to trespassers during the Black Death. The symbol was sewn onto on the tunics worn by the Knights Templar in their battles against the Muslim people. This probably explains the belief that the Freemasons evolved from the Knights Templar. Known as the Jolly Roger, it was associated with pirates, and today the symbol is associated with poisons. It features prominently in art and, as Masonic symbol, it serves as a *memento mori*, that is, a reminder of death and mortality.

As for the classic Masonic logo featuring the set of compasses and square, these represent the two primary tools. There are various interpretations of the symbol. The main theory is that the compass represents geometry and building. The compass is to "circumscribe and keep us within due bounds towards all mankind" (Duncan, 2004). A metaphorical interpretation of the square is that Masons should "square their actions", or aim to be accurate. There are many variations of this symbol, usually featuring a "G", representing "God" or "geometry", or numerous other emblems such as animals, flowers, tools, and open books.

The Freemasons also have symbols of recognition such as handshakes, passwords, and references that only initiated members would understand. This is to identify each other from non-members who might claim membership and its benefits. But there are many different orders and practices today, and the Freemasons suffer from a dwindling membership. Today, these codes are used more out of tradition.

There is nothing sinister about the Freemasons, which is essentially a collection of social clubs and charitable institutions. The disputed history, urban legends, and in-group markers have created fertile grounds for speculation and rumor. In this age of technology there is high visibility of Freemason symbols and their hats, jewelry, and bumper stickers;

and their "secret" rituals, symbols, and words are revealed in books available to the public. There is nothing truly clandestine about the order today. It seems that the final secret of the Freemasons is that they have no real secrets anymore.

The Proctor and Gamble symbol

Procter and Gamble (P&G) is one of the world's most successful consumer goods company in the world. Some people believe that these makers of such wholesome products as toothpaste, laundry detergent, pet food, and diapers are also a band of devil worshippers.

P&G was born in 1837 when brothers-in-law William Procter, a candle maker, and soap maker James Gamble became business partners. Within two decades the company was worth one million dollars. During the American Civil War (1861–65) the company supplied the Union Army with soap and candles. They soon began diversifying their product line, producing vegetable oil, laundry detergent, shampoo, toilet paper, and coffee. They even produced the first toothpaste that contained fluoride.

The company also popularized consumer advertising and daytime programming by sponsoring and later producing serial TV dramas. These became known as "washboard weepers", "dishpan dramas", "drainboard dramas", and "soapy sagas", but are better known today as soap operas (Cox, 2005). However, the company's once squeaky-clean image has been tarnished by rumors that they are linked to various cults and satanism.

In 1979, stories began to circulate that P&G were secretly controlled by the Reverend Sun Myung Moon's Unification Church, better known as the Moonies. For concerned consumers, the strange image of the man in the moon featured in the company's logo seemed to link the company to the Moonies, even though the logo was already a century old. The Unification Church had just purchased a property in Florida, and some feared they had also purchased P&G (Kimmel, 2004).

Trademark of the devil

Within a year the hearsay had morphed into the claim that the company was involved with witchcraft and the devil. The proof was found in the company's moon and stars logo that was thought to be a symbol of satanism. This seemingly innocuous logo of an old man's bearded face in a crescent moon facing 13 stars was allegedly full of hidden messages.

The evidence could be found in Revelation (12:1), "And there appeared a great wonder in heaven; a woman clothed with the sun, and the moon under her feet, and upon her head a crown of 12 stars." The logo was believed to be a mockery of the Bible passage, featuring a man's face in the moon instead of the woman in the sun, and 13 unlucky stars instead of 12.

More clues could be found in the logo. The old man became a "sorcerer" while the curls of his beard and the arrangement of the stars was said to spell out the number 666 when the image was held up to a mirror. This is the Number (Sign or Mark) of the Beast according to the Book of Revelation (13:18). When connected to one another, the stars would also form 666. The folds of the curls were seen as satanic ram's horns or goat's horns, an apparent symbol of the "false prophet".

P&G has a less-sinister explanation for the logo. In 1851, barge workers along the Ohio River began marking crates of Star brand candles (a P&G product) with a cross. These images were carved or burned onto crates to identify the products inside. In the mid-nineteenth century, literacy rates were not as widespread as today and brands were often identified by trademark symbols rather than company names. Soon the logo evolved into a five-pointed star in a circle, and then 13 stars to commemorate the original US colonies. In 1859 they added the man in the moon, which was a popular design of the day. This symbol had become a fad, much like the "Have a nice day" smiley face of contemporary times. The logo continued to evolve until 1932, when it stabilized into the elaborately bearded man in the moon surrounded by 13 stars.

A devil of a time

In the 1990s the satanism claims were reinforced by an urban legend. A rumor began that the president of P&G appeared on a TV talk show and admitted he had a pact with the devil to ensure the company's success. One version of this story tells that a representative appeared on the *Donahue Show* and admitted that the company donates a portion of its profits to the Church of Satan. When asked if this revelation would damage his business he sniffed, "There are not enough Christians in the United States to make a difference."

Over the years the story was also linked to the *Jenny Jones Show* and the *Sally Jesse Raphael Show*. The rumors were denied by the TV talk shows. Simply, company executives don't make interesting guests. Maurice Turnick, the executive producer of the *Sally Jesse Raphael Show*, responded to the rumor.

There is no truth to the rumor that the CEO of Procter & Gamble appeared on the Sally® Show and embraced satanism. Nothing about this rumor is true.

Ed Glavin of the *Jenny Jones Show* also denied the rumors.

It has come to our attention there is a rumor that the President of Procter & Gamble appeared on The Jenny Jones Show® discussing satanism. This is absolutely untrue. Neither the President of P&G, nor any other representative of P&G, has ever appeared on The Jenny Jones Show®. I encourage anyone who hears of such a rumor to let people know this never happened.

Phil Donahue himself wrote:

It seems impossible that the rumor of an appearance by the President of Procter & Gamble on DONAHUE is still circulating after more than a decade. There is absolutely nothing to this rumor. The president of P&G has never appeared on DONAHUE, nor has any other P&G executive. Anyone who claims to have seen such a broadcast is either mistaken or lying. It never happened!

Curiously, a nearly identical rumor circulated about the McDonald's corporation in 1977 (Kimmel, 2004). In 1990, the rumor transferred to fashion designer Liz Claiborne who became dogged by the story that she appeared on Oprah and admitted to donating 40 per cent of her company's profits to the Church of Satan.

P&G officials denied these claims fervently, and insisted that their profits go to stockholders, not Satan. At any rate, the company profits are a matter of public record, and any satanic support would be apparent in their financial records. There is no evidence that P&G have links to the Church of Satan or any other occult organization.

Hell to pay

The P&G logo controversy was a hoax. It is hard to pinpoint the exact source of the rumors, but it appears to have been spread by religious groups. The stories surfaced in the days before the internet, so this was a campaign spread via circulars delivered door-to-door, fliers placed in supermarkets, and by word-of-mouth. Ministers of fundamentalist churches sent newsletters to their parishioners throughout the Bible belt, urging them to sign petitions against the company, and to boycott their products and brands. P&G were faced with a public relations nightmare, and were flooded with tens of thousands of calls and letters every month. The company decided to fight hellfire with hellfire and enlisted Jerry Falwell and Billy Graham to quell the rumors, but they persisted.

P&G's competitors were also responsible for spreading the urban legend. The company's satanic connections were a devilish rumor spread by distributors from the multi-level marketing company Amway. In 1995, individual Amway distributors had forwarded the rumors via a company voicemail system, rekindling the scandal. This gossip was in turn repeated to thousands of customers to deter them from using P&G's household products, and persuade them to use Amway's equivalent products. Once the company found out this source of some of the rumor-mongering, P&G initiated a series of lawsuits against a few people who were identified as making false and defamatory statements linking the company to satanism. Finally, in 2007 P&G won a civil lawsuit against four former Amway distributors.

There is no evidence that P&G had links to satanism, or that there were hidden messages in the company's man-in-the-moon trademark. However, in 1985, after using the symbol for 100 years, P&G reluctantly decided to abandon the historical logo in an attempt to quell the rumors. Regardless, the rumors have survived the internet age and occasionally make a resurgence. As is typical with urban legends, the folklore always outlives the facts.

References

Alcock, James. 2004. "Electronic voice phenomena: Voices of the dead?" The Committee for Skeptical Inquiry. Available at: http://www.csicop.org/specialarticles/show/electronic_voice_phenomena_voices_of_the_dead/

Aldridge, Alan. 1991. *The Beatles Illustrated Lyrics*. Houghton Mifflin.

Allen, Tom. 1982. *Rock "n" Roll, the Bible and the Mind*. Horizon House.

Bar-Hillel, Maya, Bar-Natan, Dror, and McKay, Brendan. 1998. "The Torah codes: Puzzle and solution". *Chance*. Vol. 11, No. 2, pp. 13–19.

Beck, A. and Pirovano, C. 1996. "Facilitated communicators' performance on a task of receptive language". *Journal of Autism and Developmental Disorders*. Vol. 26, No. 5, pp. 497–512.

Begley, Sharon. 1997. "Seek and ye shall find". *Newsweek*. 9 June, pp. 66–67.

Blecha, Peter. 2004. *Taboo Tunes: A History of Banned Bands and Censored Songs*. Backbeat Books.

Brown, Dan. 2010. *The Lost Symbol*. Anchor.

Butler, Tom. 2010. "Radio sweep: A case study". *Association Transcommunication Journal*. Available at: http://atransc.org/journal/radiosweep_study.htm

Byrne, Tom and Normand, Matthew. 2000. "The demon-haunted sentence: A skeptical analysis of reverse speech". *Skeptical Inquirer*. Vol. 24, 2 April.

Cavendish, Richard. 1967. *The Black Arts. A Concise History of Wicthcraft, Demonology, Astrology, and other Mystical Practices Throughout The Ages*. Perigee Trade.

Clark, Ronald W. 1977. *Edison – The Man Who Made the Future*. G. P. Putnam's Sons.

Cox, Jim. 2005. *Historical Dictionary of American Radio Soap Operas*. Scarecrow Press, Inc.

Crowley, Aleister. 1913. *Magick Liber Aba* (Book 4). Weiser Books.

Drosnin, Michael. 1997. *The Bible Code*. Simon and Schuster.

Duncan, Malcolm. 2004. *Duncan's Masonic Ritual and Monitor*. Kessinger Publishing.

Edison National Historic Site. 2014. http://www.nps.gov/edis/index.htm

Feaster, P. 2006. *The Following Record: Making Sense of Phonographic Performance, 1877–1908*. Ph.D. thesis, Indiana University.

Gambaccini, Paul. 1974. "The Rolling Stone interview with Paul McCartney". *Rolling Stone*.

Giuliano, Geoffrey and Vrnda, Devi. 1999. *Glass Onion: The Beatles in Their Own Words*. Da Capo Press.

Guralnick, Peter. 1994. *Last Train to Memphis: The Rise of Elvis Presley*. Little, Brown.

Henken, Elissa. 2003. "Taming the enemy: Georgian narratives about the civil war". *Journal of Folklore Research*. Vol. 40, No. 3, pp. 289–307.

Hodapp, Christopher. 2009. *Solomon's Builders: Freemasons, Founding Fathers and the Secrets of Washington DC*. Ulysses Press.

Hodapp, Christopher. 2010. *Deciphering the Lost Symbol: Freemasons, Myths and the Mysteries of Washington, Part III*. Ulysses Press.

Holmes, Thom. 2006. *The Routledge Guide to Music Technology*. Taylor & Francis Group.

Kimmel, Allan J. 2004. *Rumors and Rumor Control: A Manager's Guide to Understanding and Combatting Rumors*. Psychology Press.

Kimura, D. 1968. "Neural processing of backwards-speech sounds". *Science*. Vol. 839, pp. 395–96.

Konstantinos. 1995. "Ghost voices: Exploring the mysteries of electronic voice phenomena". *Popular Electronics*. October issue, pp. 37–41.

Lilienfeld, Scott. 2007. "Psychological treatments that cause harm". *Perspectives on Psychological Science*. Vol. 2, No. 2, pp. 53–70.

Marlinki, Edward. 2000. *How to Read His Writings: The Unauthorized Guide to Decoding Edward Leedskalnin's Works*. Passels Information Network.

McKay, Brendan, Bar-Natan, Dror, Bar-Hillel, Maya, and Kalai, Gil. 1999. "Solving The Bible Code puzzle". *Statistical Science*. May Issue.

Miles, Barry. 1997. *Paul McCartney: Many Years from Now*. MacMillan.

Moon, Christopher. 2010. "What is the telephone to the dead?" *Haunted Times*. Vol. 4, No. 3, Winter.

Nash, Alanna. 2010. *Baby, Let's Play House: Elvis Presley and the Women Who Loved Him*. It Books.

Newbrook, Mark and Curtain, Jane. 1997. "Oates' theory of reverse speech". *The Skeptic*. NSW: Australian Skeptics. Vol. 17, No. 3.

Newbrook, Mark and Curtain, Jane. 1998. "Oates' theory of reverse speech: A critical examination". *International Journal of Language and the Law*. Vol. 5, No. 2.

Newbrook, Mark. 2005. "Reverse speech". *Skeptical Inquirer*. Vol. 15, No. 2, June.

Oates, David. 1991. *Reverse Speech: Hidden Messages in Human Communication*. Knowledge Systems.

Oates, David. 2000. *Reverse Speech Metaphor Dictionary*. EBook.

Oglesbee, Frank. 1987. *The Devil, You Say? Backmasking in Contemporary Christian Music*. Popular Culture Association Annual Meeting, Montreal, Canada.

Poundstone, William. 1983. *Big Secrets*. William Morrow and Company.

Raudive, Konstantin. 1971. *Breakthrough*. Colin Smythe.

Ridley, Jasper. 2011. *The Freemasons: A History of the World's Most Powerful Secret Society*. Skyhorse Publishing.

Rogo, D. Scott and Bayless, Raymond. 1980. *Phone Calls from the Dead*. Berkley Books.

Shermer, Michael. 2008. "Patternicity". *Scientific American*. December.

Shermer, Michael. 2009. "Telephone to the dead". *Scientific American*. January.

Shotton, Peter and Schaffner, Nicholas. 1984. *John Lennon: In My Life*. Thunder's Mouth Press.

Simmons, Sylvie. 2004. "AC/DC celebrate their Quarter Century". *MOJO*.

Skinner, B. F. 1936. "The verbal summator and a method for the study of latent speech". *Journal of Psychology*. Vol. 2, pp. 71–107.

Smith, Jacob. 2010. "An unnatural sound in village". *Short Film Studies*. Vol. 1, No. 1, pp. 135–37.

Stavro, A. 2005. *Koraïïu Pils. Edvarda Liedskalnina Koraïïu Pils Ir Uznemta Amerikas Savienoto Valstu Vesturisko Vietu Nacionalaja Registra*. LA izdevnieciba.

Thomas, David. 1997. "Hidden messages and the Bible code". *Skeptical Inquirer*. Vol. 21, No. 6.

Thorne, S. B. and Himelstein, P. 1984. "The role of suggestion in the perception of satanic messages in rock-and-roll recordings". *Journal of Psychology*, Vol. 116, No. 2, pp. 245–48.

Van Biema, David. 1997. "Deciphering God's plan". *Time*. 9 June.

Vokey, J. R. and Read, J. D. 1985. "Subliminal messages: Between the devil and the media". *American Psychologist*. Vol. 40, pp. 1231–39.

Witztum, Doron, Eliyahu, Rips, and Yoav, Rosenburg. 1994. "Equidistant letter sequences in the Book of Genesis". *Statistical Science*. Vol. 9, No. 3.

Part IV
Non-human Language

Introduction

From the sneaky serpent in Genesis to Mr Ed, animals in popular culture can often talk. However, some people believe that animals, including undiscovered animals, really can talk. Not only do aliens and Bigfoot exist, but they have language. If that wasn't strange enough, objects can talk, and we can talk back to them.

These chapters explore bizarre claims about non-human language. According to one man and his followers, English-speaking reptilian humanoids live among us. Pet psychics believe they can talk to the animals while psychic pets can talk back to us, with their minds. We encounter apes that use sign language, languages of the birds and the bees, and feral children without language. We meet clever horses, dogs, and pigs, and a talking mongoose named Gef.

16
Talking Animals

Is language unique to humans? What about those apes that use sign language, and those horses that can understand human speech? This chapter takes a look at animal communication and stories of animals that appear to have human-like language. We read about how cuttlefish communicate with color, and herrings may communicate by flatulence. Why did Genie and Victor, the "wild children", never fully develop language? We reveal the truth behind the legends of Clever Hans the horse, Koko the gorilla, Alex the talking parrot, and Nazi talking dogs.

Gef the talking mongoose

James Irving lived with his wife Margaret and 12-year-old daughter Voirrey in Cashen's Gap, near the hamlet of Dalby, on the Isle of Man. A former sales representative, Jim settled on this isolated piece of land to raise sheep. The family lived a quiet life, until one day in October 1931 when a strange, weasel-like animal appeared on the farm. The creature soon entered the house and kept the family awake at night by growling and snorting from its new home behind the wall paneling. Jim began calling the creature "Jack" and attempted to communicate with it. He discovered that Jack could mimic the sounds of other animals, including human speech.

> Its first sounds were those of an animal nature, and it used to keep us awake at night for a long time as sleep was not possible. It occurred to me that if it could make these weird noises, why not others, and I proceeded to give imitations of the various calls, domestic and other creatures make in the country, and I named these creatures after every individual call. In a few days' time one had only to name the particular animal or bird, and instantly, always without error, it gave

the correct call. My daughter then tried it with nursery rhymes, and no trouble was experienced in having them repeated. The voice is quite two octaves above any human voice, clear and distinct, but lately it can and does come down to the range of the human voice.

(Price and Lambert, 1936)

The animal proved to be a fast learner. Soon, he was fluent enough in English that he could introduce himself. His name wasn't Jack, it was "Geoff", although he spelled it phonemically as "G-E-F". He said he was "an extra, extra clever mongoose" born in New Delhi, India, on June 7, 1852. Gef's language skills improved exponentially, and soon he was swearing, singing songs, and telling jokes. "A mongoose can speak if he is taught", he explained to the Irvings (Price and Lambert, 1934). He was also a clever mongoose, by his own admission. "If you knew what I know, you'd know a hell of a lot", he bragged. Before too long, Gef was bilingual.

In succession, Gef sang three verses of "Ellan Vannin," the Manx National Anthem, "in a clear and high-pitched voice"; then two verses in Spanish, followed by one verse in Welsh; then a prayer in pure Hebrew (not Yiddish); finishing up with a long peroration in Flemish.

(Price and Lambert, 1934)

Gef quickly developed an excellent command of English, but his manners left a lot to be desired. He urinated through cracks in the walls. He played pranks on the family and once locked Voirrey inside her room. He was often disrespectful to the Irvings. Once Gef lost his temper when Jim took too long opening the morning paper, crying out "Read it out, you fat-headed gnome!". And he rudely called Mrs Irving, "Maggie the witch woman, the Zulu Woman, the Honolulu woman!" (Josiffe, 2011). Gef even bit her once, but he apologized afterwards, and instructed her to "put some ointment" on the wound.

Like Bigfoot and all other talking cryptid poltergeists, Gef liked to throw objects about. He tossed stones at the windows and hurled coins, kitchen utensils, and even furniture around the house. Jim believed that Gef could also shape-shift into other animals, and had the power of invisibility. Concerned for the safety of his family, Jim tried to kill the creature on several occasions, at first with poison, and then with a gun. Gef howled and groaned in terror, so Jim took pity on him and spared his life. The Irvings discovered that Gef had two fears: being killed, and being captured and "put in a bottle" like a genie (Josiffe, 2011).

After the attempted murders, Gef and the Irvings finally formed a truce and he was adopted into the family. Like putting out snacks for Santa, they left out food for him, including candy, cookies, and chocolates. Gef could even be useful on occasion. He was a skilled hunter who caught and killed rabbits for the family's dinner. He caught so many they could supplement their meager income by selling the rabbits for seven pence each. Gef even checked the clock for Jim when he asked for the time. But Gef still retained his bad habits for outsiders. He threw stones and spat at people who entered the house or merely passed by. But he always disappeared when a guest visited. Occasionally he warmed to a visitor, and amused them by peering in through a crack and calling "heads" or "tails" on a tossed coin (when none of the Irvings were in the room).

Like a naughty child, Gef was often heard but rarely seen. Gef had the most contact with Voirrey. He kept hidden from view out of his fear of being killed or caught. He was rarely heard by visitors, and he was never spotted by anyone but the Irvings. They described him as nine inches to a foot long, with yellow-brown colored fur, a long, bushy tail, tiny ears, a flat nose, and hand-like paws with three fingers and a thumb. Jim mused that Gef was a cross between a native rodent and an Indian mongoose. Such a strange cross-breed wasn't likely, although a mongoose on the Isle of Man was possible. Neighbor Eary Cushlinn had introduced the animal in 1912 to control the rabbit population (Josiffe, 2011). Gef described himself as, "a ghost in the form of a weasel", and a creature "from the fifth dimension". He once said, "I am a freak. I have hands and I have feet, and if you saw me you'd faint, you'd be petrified, mummified, turned into stone or a pillar of salt" (Lambert and Price, 1936).

The Dalby Spook

Townspeople called Gef the "Dalby Spook" and he was very unpopular. He was a gossip who spied on the neighbors and then reported back to the Irvings. Gef seemed to know many things he shouldn't have known. He also had the reputation of being a thief, and he played pranks on the townsfolk by hiding their personal possessions. To this day, when something disappears or is seemingly moved from where it was, people say, "That will be the Dalby Spook then" (Jossife, 2011). In general, the villagers began to blame Gef for their misfortunes. He also attracted unwanted attention to the town. The story received extensive press coverage, especially from tabloid newspapers that called Gef the "Man-Weasel". J. Radcliffe, a reporter for the *Isle of Man Examiner*, visited

Cashen's Gap where he heard a "piercing and uncanny voice". Believing it came from Voirrey he accused her of ventriloquism, although the Irvings denied this and said the noises came from elsewhere in the house.

Doubting Gef

The events also attracted paranormal investigators from around world, including Nandor Fodor from the International Institute for Psychical Research. He stayed for a week and didn't see or hear anything, but he still believed the Irving's story (Josiffe, 2011). The most infamous visitor was Harry Price, of Borley Rectory fame. Price wasn't the most skeptical researcher but he was still too skeptical for Gef, who said disapprovingly, "He's got his doubting cap on!". Gef wouldn't talk in the presence of "doubters". He was like the singing Michigan J. Frog, the Warner Brothers character who would only perform for his owner. Perhaps Gef (or someone else) was less afraid of death or being bottled than being exposed as a hoax.

Author Richard Lambert accompanied Price to the investigation and over the five weeks of their stay they never saw or heard Gef. However, Irving kept diaries of the events, so the investigators collected enough anecdotes to write *The Haunting of Cashen's Gap – A Modern Miracle*. The Irvings also mailed them evidence of Gef's existence, including a sample of his hair and casts of his paw prints. This was some 50 years before DNA testing became common, but the samples were sent for analysis to F. Martin Duncan of the Zoological Society of London. He concluded, "I can very definitely say that the specimen hairs never grew upon a mongoose, nor are they those of a rat, rabbit, hare, squirrel, or other rodent...I am inclined to think that these hairs have probably been taken from a longish-haired dog" (Lambert and Price, 1934). The Irving's had a pet sheepdog named Mona.

The clay casts showed a remarkable disparity in size between Gef's front and hind paws. The front paws measured almost ten centimeters, which was remarkable for an animal said to be only 30 centimeters in length. Strangely, the casts didn't show the markings expected from an animal's paw prints. It was suggested that one of the Irvings had drawn the imprints using a stick.

The Irvings captured several photographs of Gef. These are of poor quality, but of course, Gef didn't want to be photographed. One image seems to show a creature, but this is just the effect produced by blades of grass in the foreground (Josiffe, 2011). In several other photos a more visible yet blurry creature bears a resemblance to a weasel, ferret, or skunk. However, it could also be a stuffed animal, animal pelt, or a toy. With distorted photos and samples collected from dogs, the evidence for Gef is much like the poor quality evidence for modern sightings of Bigfoot. There was only anecdotal evidence and no good physical evidence to support Gef's existence. He was never reliably heard or seen by anyone.

Gef continued to remain elusive and so the public interest in him waned. By 1938 he had disappeared altogether. The Irvings returned to their quiet lives until 1945, when James Irving died and Voirrey and Margaret left the village. Leslie Graham became the new owner of the farmhouse and claims he occasionally heard strange noises around the property, but he never witnessed anything. That is, until one day in 1946 when he saw a three-foot-long, black-and-white weasel disturbing his chickens. He killed the animal with a club. The creature doesn't fit the usual descriptions, but many people believe that he had killed Gef (Josiffe, 2011). Gef was never seen again, but then he was never really seen at all. Like a mongoose Elvis, others believe that Gef might be alive somewhere still.

Mongoose is as good as yours

Cashen's Gap has since been demolished, and today, the strange events of the 1930s are mostly forgotten. Many doubt that Gef ever existed, but if the story was a hoax, who was behind it? Most people point the finger at Voirrey because she was closest to Gef. She was also known to kill rabbits on the moors with a club, which would explain the bunny booty supposedly caught by Gef. For believers in the paranormal, Voirrey was a pubescent teenager, which fits the profile of a poltergeist protagonist. However, following the newspaper article that accused her of ventriloquism, most townspeople believed she was pulling a prank. She was ostracized by the community and teased in school as "the spook" (Josiffe, 2011). Voirrey stayed out of the public eye for the rest of her life and died in 2005, but in her last interview she maintained her innocence.

> It was not a hoax and I wish it had never happened. If my mother and I had our way we never would have told anybody about it. But Father was sort of wrapped up in it. It was such a wonderful phenomenon that he just had to tell people about it.
>
> (McGraw, 1970)

As a swearing, singing, storytelling creature, Gef didn't have the vocabulary typical of a teenager, much less the vocabulary of a mongoose. However, he did have the vocabulary and experiences of a well-traveled, 60-something Manx-speaking man. McGraw (1970) reports that "the animal learned not only English, but to use the many foreign phrases that the widely traveled Jim Irving used – as did Voirrey, following her father's example". Suspiciously, a lot of the phenomena seemed to involve Jim. He often heard Gef when no one else was around, and curiously, his illness in his final years coincided with the disappearance of Gef (Josiffe, 2011). Gef seemed to know things that Jim knew, such as the time Jim went for a walk with Lambert, and "Gef" tagged along, overhearing the conversation that took place. Perhaps Jim *was* Gef?

In his *Confessions of a Ghost Hunter* (1936) Price mentioned an interesting event that he neglected to include in *The Haunting of Cashen's Gap*. On the second morning of his investigation he was awoken with, "Hullo! Hullo! Come along! Come along! and some chattering which I could not interpret." It turns out that the Irvings also had a pet parrot that mimicked human speech. Could this parrot have been the source of at least some of the voices attributed to Gef? In defending the Irvings, most people argue that there was no financial gain from Gef, so there was no motive for a hoax. Maybe the lonely life at Cashen's Gap was motive enough, especially for a storytelling traveler. Perhaps Gef the talking mongoose was a cryptid composite inspired by the pets, people, and imagination of the Irving family.

Clever Hans

Clever Hans was the original Mr Ed. In 1900, retired German schoolteacher Wilhelm von Osten revealed his horse prodigy to the public. Clever Hans, "Kluge Hans" in German, seemed to understand human language and to be able to perform mathematical calculations. People flocked to see Clever Hans calculate square roots, tell the time, and recognize people by name. He responded to questions requiring mathematical calculations by tapping his right hoof. These amazing feats were achieved without a whip and only with the gentle encouragement of bread and carrots. Clever Hans became so famous that he appeared on postcards and liquor labels, and his name was even mentioned in vaudeville.

Clever Hans attracted the interest of the academic community, and in 1904 a group of investigators known as the September Commission was assembled. Professor of philosophy C. Stumpf headed the team, and concluded that there was no evidence of direct signaling by Hans' handlers, either intentional or purposeful. Still suspicious, his colleague, psychologist Oskar Pfungst, investigated the claims independently and reached an entirely different conclusion. Instead of just examining Clever Hans, Pfungst observed the relationship between human and horse. He saw that when Clever Hans couldn't see the person who knew the answer to a question, he didn't respond correctly. And when the correct answer wasn't known to anyone present, Clever Hans didn't know the answer either.

If Clever Hans was tested with blinders on he would make strenuous attempts to see the questioner. He was clearly responding to visual clues, not auditory clues. Clever Hans wouldn't react if the questioner stood still, but if the person stooped over slightly, the horse would start to tap, whether or not he was asked a question. Clever Hans couldn't understand German. He was being tipped off by the subtle body language of his owners and other observers, who bent at the waist slightly with every hoof beat, and stood erect when Hans arrived at the correct number (Candland, 1995).

Pfungst reached the hypothesis that Clever Hans was trained, either accidentally or purposefully. "It is evident therefore, that the horse requires certain visual stimuli or signs in order to make correct responses" (Pfungst, 1911). Embarrassed, Professor Stumpf retracted his original claim. Pfungst had discovered the process of unconscious cuing, now known as the Clever Hans phenomenon, and created an interest in nonverbal communication and behaviorism.

Straight from the horse's mouth

In the days before the behaviorist movement there were many other "sapient animals". In England in the late sixteenth-century Marocco (also known as Morocco) became known as the "thinking horse" and the "talking horse". He was no Mr Ed, but he could walk on two legs, play dead, call the totals on a pair of over-sized dice, add and subtract, point out people in the audience, and drink a bucket of water or urinate on command. Marocco was owned and trained by William Bankes, who took his show on the road and traveled across Europe.

In Orléans, France, Bankes was arrested and sentenced to execution for consorting with the devil to produce a magical horse. He was given one last show to redeem himself. During the performance, Marocco knelt down before a cross held by a priest in the audience (Bondeson, 1999). Both horse and owner were spared the stake. Marocco became so famous that he was even mentioned as "the dancing horse" in Shakespeare's *Love's Labour's Lost* (Randi, 1997).

Other animal attractions included Zarif (owned by Karl Krall, who bought Clever Hans after van Osten died), the German horse that could extract the cube roots of numbers. Beautiful Jim Key cited Bible passages where horses are mentioned. Princess Trixie could count change back from a cash register, and Mascot the "talking horse" could shake hands and pull a lever. Not only have there been many eloquent equines, but also many smart swine. In the 1780s, the Learned Pig of London could spell words and answer math problems by picking up cards in its mouth (Jay, 1998). This gave rise to the Pig of Knowledge, Toby the Sapient Pig, and many other "Toby's", which became the standard name for a clever pig.

All of these animals stamped their hooves to spell or count. And all were responding to cues from their trainers. These "intelligent" animals are products of intelligent training, but there is no doubt that these animals are smart. Clever Hans couldn't understand language and mathematic concepts, but he learned how to respond to subtle muscle movement. He was able to transfer this skill to read other people too, and ignore all distractions. Clever Hans was still clever, and Pfungst was pretty clever too.

"Wild" children and language

If we're not raised with language, will we develop it anyway? It was once believed that if babies were raised without hearing language, they would naturally speak some sort of original God-given language. In *Histories*, Herodotus reports the story of the Egyptian Pharaoh Psammetichus who tested this theory more than 2,500 years ago. Two newborn babies were placed in the care of a shepherd who was instructed not to talk to them. With only the company of the mute caretaker and a herd of goats, the babies eventually uttered something that sounded like "bekos". This was interpreted to be a Phrygian word meaning "bread". Phrygian, once spoken in what is now modern Turkey, was thus believed to be the original tongue (Yule, 2010). However, the infants were probably mimicking the bleating of the goats. King James IV of Scotland conducted a similar experiment around 1500. He reported that the children began speaking Hebrew spontaneously. This simply confirmed his religious belief that Hebrew had been spoken in the Garden of Eden.

Since no study would get past an ethics committee today, all we have to examine are anomalous examples. There are several cases of children raised outside of culture and civilization. These unwitting subjects are often called "savage", "wild", "wolf", or "feral" children. Victor, the wild boy of Aveyron (c.1785–1828), spent his entire childhood alone in the woods near Saint-Sernin-sur-Rance in France. He eventually emerged from the forest in his early teens and was integrated into society, but he never developed language. More recently, Genie spent the first 13 years of her life locked inside a dark bedroom. She suffered severe abuse at the hands of her father, who beat her with a stick if she vocalized, and barked and growled at her like a dog to keep her quiet. When she finally escaped with her mother in 1970, she was only capable of speaking a few words and phrases, including "stop it", and "no more". Genie never learned functional language.

Without exposure to language in their early years, children seem to grow up into adults without functional language. These cases have given rise to the idea that humans are born with a language acquisition device, an innate biological device for language. It is also believed that childhood is a critical period for acquiring language, and if individuals don't acquire language before their teenage years, they will never do so properly. According to this theory, the "switch" for language was not activated in these wild children. However, we also need to keep in mind that they were psychologically scarred by their experiences and are not typical examples. The nature versus nurture debate about language is ongoing.

Nonhuman primates and human language

But is language unique to humans? Since the late nineteenth-century researchers have tried to teach human language symbols to nonhuman primates. As our nearest relatives, these species were a natural choice. In 1892, Richard Lynch Garner attempted to teach Moses the chimpanzee the words "mamma", "feu" (which is French for "fire"), and "wie" (German for "how"). Despite bribes of delicious corned beef, Moses never learned how to speak these words (Candland, 1995). Other nonhuman primates have been taught a word or two, but their thick ape accents are difficult to understand. They don't have the vocal apparatus that we have and need to be able to produce the range of sounds used in human language.

However, modern researchers have had great success teaching modified sign language and symbol recognition to chimpanzees, bonobos, gorillas, and orangutans. Many of these apes are so famous they are known on a first name basis. Sarah, Sherman, Michael, Kanzi, and Koko are like the Madonnas of nonhuman users of human language. Many of these apes have shown an incredible ability to learn and use signs and symbols. Trainer Francine Patterson claims that Koko the gorilla is able to understand 1,000 symbols in American sign language and understand some 2,000 words in spoken English. According to Sue Savage-Rumbaugh, Kanzi the bonobo can understand some 3,000 English words, and hundreds of picture symbols known as lexigrams. Some apes have even learned how to teach these to other apes, such as Washoe the chimpanzee who taught her adopted son Loulis. Roger Fouts, the co-author of *Next of Kin* (1998) further shows that these primates display unique personalities, complex emotions, and intelligence.

Unlike primates in the wild, these animals are enculturated into our world. They undergo intensive training for most of their lives to achieve these abilities, but not all respond to the learning process. They don't develop, acquire, or expand the use of symbols in the same way that humans do. Some researchers have been accused of overstating the abilities of animals, and in the process of trying to see if nonhuman primates can be more human, many have been treated inhumanely. However, the concept of language is not black and white, but grey, spotted, striped, feathered, and furry. Before we're accused of "Homo sapiens chauvinism", maybe we need to readjust our ideas of language and communication.

Ludwig Wittgenstein (1953) said, "If a lion could talk, we could not understand him". Researchers have tested these animals against our standards, when they already have their own methods of communication. Perhaps we need to understand them in terms of their own communication. These systems are sufficiently expressive for their needs. Like us, their language evolved for survival, and also for culture and play. Like us, these communication systems involve gestures, facial expressions, and vocalizations.

Nonhuman primate language

All of our hominoid relatives have communication systems. Chimpanzees have a large repertoire of gestures with over 60 distinct signals. They have also learned attention-attracting sounds to get responses from parents or human caretakers. Gorillas have some 25 different vocalizations, including grunts and barks that indicate location in the dense forests. Their screams and roars signal warnings. Bonobos have unique vocalizations that are learned and differ across groups, like a kind of dialect. They also engage in conversation-like exchanges. During confrontations, males alternate screams at each other. To advertise their status to the group, like a honeymoon, mating gibbon couples produce loud calls known as duetting, involving vocally complex booms, barks, and bitonal screams. As a mating strategy, male orangutans make long calls, a series of grumbles, roars, and sighs that can last for minutes and be heard up to a kilometer away. Orangutans are probably most famous for blowing raspberries. We tend to interpret these as a rude noise or a tickle, but this is a spluttering sound made by orangutans of all ages when they build nests.

Many species of monkeys have a range of vocalizations, but this isn't monkey business. Many of these are alarm calls to alert the group to predators. However, vervet monkeys use acoustically different alarm calls for specific predators. Leopard calls cause them to run into trees, while they hide in bushes and look skywards in response to eagle calls, and look down on the ground for python calls. Like young children who call every animal a "dog", baby vervets mistakenly give eagle calls for other kinds of birds, and snake alarms when they see snake-like objects. They're punished when they give the wrong call, while parents give positive reinforcement for correct calls by repeating the alarm (Seyfarth et al., 1980).

Eagles and leopards are also predators of Diana monkeys, who have developed distinct alarm calls that even other species can understand. Yellow-casqued hornbills can recognize these calls, and take action when they hear the call for their mutual enemy the eagle (Rainey et al., 2004). The putty-nosed monkey call "pyow" is an alarm response to leopards, while "hack" means that there is an eagle nearby. This is a small vocal repertoire, but these monkeys show it's what you do with it that counts. Researchers suggest that these calls can be combined into sequences to mean something else entirely. It seems as if the putty-noses have developed a mini monkey grammar (Arnold and Zuberbühler, 2008).

Language evolved over millions of years, and gestures and vocalizations preceded language for we Homo sapiens. When we look at the similarities we share with our primate relatives, it's easy to agree with Fouts, who observes, "Language did not descend from the gods. It emerged from our animal ancestors." It is going to be interesting to see where evolution takes us all.

Animal language

Communication systems aren't limited to primates. To find food, bees need to communicate with other members of their colony, that is, the honeybee society. They use movement, scent, and even food exchanges to communicate. Scout bees hunt for pollen and nectar and if their hunt is successful they return to the hive and perform a "waggle dance". The bees shake their abdomens and produce a buzzing sound with their wings. This isn't for show; the speed of this movement indicates the distance of the foraging site. To show where the food is, the dancing bee also aligns her body in the direction of the food. After this display, the bees may share their foraging food, to demonstrate the quality of the supply. Bees also use odor cues to communicate with members of their colony. The queen bee emits pheromones that attract the male drones to mate with her, but also keep female workers disinterested in mating. And when a worker bee stings, it produces a scent that alerts fellow workers to the threat.

Ants also communicate using pheromones in ways similar to bees. Anyone who has murdered ants as a child knows that crushed ants emit an alarm pheromone. This warning smell is capable of sending nearby ants into a frenzied attack. Scent is also used as a map to lead ants home, to a new location, or to a new food source. A forager leaves a scent trail leading back to the food, a path that will be reinforced as it attracts more ants until the source is exhausted.

Cuttlefish are the chameleons of the sea. These cephalopods communicate using their ability to change color and communicate using this. They control the pigment in their skin and change their pattern and texture to camouflage themselves so they don't become sea sushi. Like a neon light show, cuttlefish flash messages in color. During mating rituals, males develop zebra-like patterns but they are two-faced about it. One side shows a dominant display towards other males, while the other side shows a calm display towards potential mates. Females show their interest by turning a gray-color, and develop luminescent cells that circle their beaks like green lipstick. Cuttlefish use their brains to develop these colors; they are literally thinking the color onto their bodies. We can only do this when we blush. But all they perceive are contrasts in color. Ironically, cuttlefish are colorblind.

Humans talk by making sounds with our bodies, and animals also do what they can with what they have. Herrings have a unique system of communication. To form protective groups at night they create high-frequency sounds by releasing air from their anuses. It appears that herrings use flatulence as a contact call. Researchers say this sounds like "high-pitched raspberries". They've dubbed these "fast repetitive ticks", making for the mischievous acronym FRT (Wilson et al., 2004).

Toothed whales use a process called echolocation to locate and identify objects and creatures in the murky ocean. This is a kind of hearing used for seeing, also used by birds and bats, although sound travels faster through water than air. These whales emit calls into the water and listen for the echoes that return from objects around them. Humpback whales communicate using whale song and sperm whales communicate with clicks. These various vocalizations are used for the purposes of mating and identification. Dolphins have a signature whistle to identify themselves, much like a dolphin name. Like whales, they also use echolocation, and make a number of vocalizations, including whistles, whines, and clicks that are produced by muscles within the blow hole. They are also capable of imitating the signature whistles of other dolphins. Some dolphins have learned an artificial language based on gestures and been taught simple rules of grammar (Herman, 2010).

The most sincere form of flattery

Other animals are adept at imitating human speech sounds. Psychologist Irene Pepperberg studied Alex, an African grey parrot, for 30 years until his death in 2007. Alex developed a vocabulary of some 150 words. This number isn't as high as that reached by other parrots, but Alex could also identify objects, colors, and shapes, recognize quantities up to six, and understand opposing concepts including bigger versus smaller. Pepperberg claims that Alex didn't just mimic, he could actually think. However, parrots are famous mimics, and it seems that Alex's skills were a result of mimicry, rote learning, and unconscious cues from Pepperberg, just like Clever Hans. Alex was being trained to imitate human speech. He was undoubtedly an intelligent bird, and Pepperberg's research has clearly demonstrated that birds aren't birdbrains.

Hoover the "talking seal" was a harbor seal who imitated human speech. Harbor seals usually make snorting, sneezing, growling, and hissing sounds, but most of these vocalizations are made underwater. Hoover grew up spending a lot of time around people, before he was moved to an aquarium in Boston. He would entertain visitors with vocalizations that resembled "Get outta here!" and "Well, hello dear!" in what sounded like a thick New England accent. Other animals produce sounds that mimic human speech, including talking cats Tiggy and Oh Long Johnson, whose vocalizations sounded like he was singing, "All the Live Long Day". Batyr the "talking" Asian elephant had a vocabulary of 20 words in Russian and Kazakh. He could manipulate his tongue and jaw with his trunk to say his own name, request food and drink, and count up to three. Kosik, a fellow talking elephant, was taught to say "yes" and "no" in Korean.

During World War II, Adolf Hitler established the *Tier-Sprechschule* (animal talking school). This dog training school conducted research into animal communication, including human–canine mental telepathy. The Nazis hoped to breed an army of educated dogs that could read, write, and talk, and one day serve alongside Nazi troops. They claimed to have amazing success in teaching language to the dogs. A German pointer named Don could say in a human voice, "Hungry! Give me cakes!". Another dog was asked in German, "Who is Adolf Hitler?" to which he responded, "Mein Führer!" (Bondeson, 2011). Like parrots and elephants, these dogs were taught to mimic language, but not speak language.

Through training, some animals are also capable of responding to human language. Dogs can be taught to respond to human vocal commands. Some have displayed an ability to respond to hundreds of words, including the border collies Betsy, Rico, and Chaser. However, this is not language comprehension. Animals learn by repeat behavior, the reinforcement of correct responses, and a reward system. This is training, rather than education. Animals "talk" to each other and to us in their own ways, and comparing the numerous forms of nonhuman communication to human communication is like comparing the proverbial apples to oranges.

17
Pet Psychics and Psychic Pets

Lord Carnarvon funded the legendary expedition to locate the tomb of Egyptian Pharaoh Tutankhamen. The apparent victim of a curse, Carnarvon died in Cairo. It is said that his pet dog Susie howled and died at the exact moment of his death, even though she was thousands of miles away in England.

Some people believe that animals have extrasensory perception. Punxsutawney Phil, otherwise known as Groundhog Phil, is like an animal almanac who is believed to predict the weather. Phil lives on a hill named Gobbler's Knob, and every February 2 he is encouraged to emerge from his burrow. Superstition dictates that if he "sees his shadow" and returns to his burrow there will be six more weeks of winter. If he doesn't see his shadow, spring will arrive early. Phil is the Peter Pan of groundhogs. He has allegedly lived to the biblical age of 120 years, despite the average lifespan of a groundhog being only eight years. Legend has it that every year Phil is fed "groundhog punch" that lengthens his life by another seven years.

For thousands of years, people have believed that animals can predict earthquakes, volcanic eruptions, and other natural disasters that scientists can't yet foretell. Aelian's *De Natura Animalium* ("On the nature of animals") is the earliest written account of this phenomenon. The Roman author reported that mice, snakes, and weasels deserted the Greek town of Helice in 373 BCE, just five days before an earthquake dropped the land into the Corinthian Gulf.

There is much anecdotal evidence of animals behaving strangely before a disaster. Dogs bark for no reason, nervous cats hide, and other animals display erratic behavior that should be heeded as warning signals. But people tend to only remember the unusual behavior after a catastrophe has taken place, not the strange behavior that occurs at

other times. The US Geological Survey conducted animal behavior studies in the 1970s, documenting changes in the behavior of birds, mice,
and domestic animals before earthquakes. The results suggested these
were reactions to weather changes rather than predictions of quakes.
Some recent research suggests that sea snakes may anticipate typhoons
(Liu et al., 2010) and toads may anticipate earthquakes (Grant and
Halliday, 2010), but not in any supernatural way.

Some pets are believed to sense when disaster is about to strike for
their owners, by way of a telepathic connection. People argue that their
cats know when they're about to be taken to the vet, and their dogs
know when they are about to be walked. However, these pets are probably responding to subtle cues, like the owner who glances at the closet
containing the cat carrier, or a dog that is used to the regular routine of
an afternoon walk.

Lady Wonder the "psychic" horse

Lady Wonder (1924–57) took the "clever horse" claims one step further. Lady was believed to possess psychic powers. This mind-reading
mare could understand English, answer questions, and make predictions
by nudging alphabet blocks with her muzzle. Lady was also trained to
operate a piano-sized, typewriter-like device with levers that activated
alphabet cards and numbers. Lady would sway her head over the keys,
and then nudge them one at a time with her nose to spell out her
answers.

Mrs Claudia Fonda of Richmond, Virginia, was Lady Wonder's owner.
Charging one dollar for three questions, she made the horse oracle available to the public. Over 150,000 people paid a visit to the farm. There
are many stories about Lady Wonder's amazing accuracy. It is said she
predicted the election of Franklin D. Roosevelt, the United States' entry
into World War II, and the correct outcome of the World Series for 14
years (Kollatz, 2007). She was particularly talented at locating lost items.
Then Lady Wonder became a pet psychic detective, spelling out clues as
to the whereabouts of missing children, including a four-year-old boy in
Massachusetts, and two children from Illinois (Candland, 1995).

Biologist-turned-parapsychologist Joseph Banks Rhine (1895–1980)
and his wife Dr Louisa Rhine investigated Lady Wonder in 1927.
Concerned that trickery was involved, they tested Lady's abilities and
declared there was no cheating, but concluded that Lady Wonder was
telepathic. During a second investigation the Rhines did a more thorough job of testing, by preventing voluntary and involuntary cues
between horse and owner. This time they concluded that Lady Wonder

wasn't psychic... anymore. They theorized that she *had* been psychic but she'd since lost her psychic abilities.

Lady Wonder didn't have any psychic abilities in the first place. This was another example of the Clever Hans phenomenon. The magician Milbourne Christopher (1962) also investigated the case and discovered that when Fonda didn't know the answer, Lady Wonder didn't know the answer either. As a test, he provided Fonda with the false name "John Banks". (This was a reference to Bankes, the owner of Marocco the horse.) Sure enough, when Christopher asked Lady, "What is my name?" she nudged the levers to spell out B-A-N-K-S.

In another test a number was written down, which Lady Wonder then predicted. Christopher suspected that Fonda was using an old mentalist trick called "pencil reading". This involves observing the subtle movements of the pencil to guess what was written. He pretended to write a bold "9", but only touched the paper on the down stroke to draw a "1". Predictably, Lady predicted incorrectly that the number written down was "9". Finally, Christopher observed that Fonda gave a "slight movement" of her training rod whenever Lady's head arrived at the correct letter. That was enough to cue the swaying mare to stop and nudge that lever.

As for Lady's predictions, the stories are more flattering than the reality. She wrongly predicted the victory of presidential candidate Thomas Dewey over Harry S. Truman, as did the political pundits of the time. Similarly, Lady's psychic detective predictions reflected current media speculation and police activity. When Lady Wonder predicted that the Illinois police would find the body of a murdered boy in the DuPage River, the authorities were dragging the river at that time. Therefore, Lady's predictions were Fonda's predictions, influenced by the media.

Fonda says she originally bought Lady Wonder to plow her farm. Instead, she ended up treating her as a pet. She babied Lady Wonder, feeding her milk from a bottle and playing with her like a child, spending hours building block houses and spelling out words in front of her. Fonda had previously owned and trained Shetland ponies to perform simple tricks According to the *Richmond Times-Dispatch* (1927), Fonda handpicked Lady Wonder, saying to her husband, "I want that colt. I believe I can educate her. I believe that mare has sense." This was another case of an intelligent trainer training an animal to be intelligent.

Jaytee the "psychic" dog

My father once told me the story of a friend of a friend who owned a psychic cat. Every day, the cat would sit in the window knowing precisely when the owner was about to return from work. One day, the cat didn't sit in the window. It was soon discovered that the owner had died in an accident. The cat sensed that he wasn't coming home. It is an urban legend that animals can detect when their owners are coming home, and most of us have heard variations on this theme. One of the most famous of these stories is Jaytee the "psychic" dog. He is also the most researched case.

Parapsychologist Rupert Sheldrake (1994) suggested that pets might have psychic abilities to perceive when their owners are returning home. An Austrian TV company tested this theory with Pamela Smart from Ramsbottom, England, and her five-year-old terrier Jaytee. Smart lived with her parents, who noticed that Jaytee seemed to sense when she started her journey home, and would sit on the porch until her return. The experiment showed that at the moment Smart decided to go home, Jaytee went to the porch and stayed there until she arrived. The media and the public decided that Jaytee was a clairvoyant canine, who knew telepathically when his owner had decided to return, or had left for the trip home.

Psychologist Richard Wiseman (1998) and his team wondered if there were natural instead of supernatural explanations behind Jaytee's behavior. It was possible that he was aware of her routine and responding to cues from his owners about her return, or perhaps he was guessing when she was coming home. The researchers conducted a series of controlled experiments to test the claim. They found that Jaytee wasn't only going to window when his owner was coming home, he went to the window a lot. There were many doggy distractions, and Jaytee traveled to the window for a variety of reasons. He watched people and other dogs walking past. He watched cars pulling up outside, including an exciting fish delivery van. Or he would go to the window for no obvious reason.

In all of the experiments Jaytee failed to detect when Smart had decided to return or when she actually left for home. He wasn't reading her mind and intentions. Jaytee made frequent trips to the window, suggesting that selective memory and multiple guesses were giving the owners the impression he had psychic powers. Sheldrake (1999) conducted his own tests but imposing his own beliefs on the study and ignoring observations that contradicted these beliefs, he determined that Jaytee was telepathic. Sheldrake argued that Jaytee was frequently at the window when Smart returned home; therefore, something psychic was obviously afoot. However, Wiseman responded that this was such a regular occurrence he'd be more surprised if Jaytee wasn't at the window when his owner returned home.

N'kisi the "psychic" parrot

Like Alex in Chapter 16, N'kisi (in-key-see) is another African grey parrot who can say more than "Polly want a cracker". Inspired by Alex, owner Aimee Morgana began training N'kisi to use language from five months old. N'kisi was an excellent student and developed a vocabulary of more than 1,000 words. Morgana believes he even invents words to explain new concepts. Unfamiliar with the aromatherapy oils Morgana wore one day, N'kisi combined the words "pretty smell medicine" to name them. She also believes that N'kisi has a sense of humor and can laugh. According to Morgana, her parrot's skills surpass those of Alex, because N'kisi is also psychic.

Morgana reports that N'kisi can read her thoughts, and those of her husband. Enter Rupert Sheldrake (2004) of the Jaytee case, who believes that N'kisi is telepathic. There is plenty of anecdotal evidence to attest to N'kisi's psychic powers. One day, N'kisi was in his cage and out of view while Morgana watched television. A car commercial began, whereupon N'kisi remarked, "There's my car!" as though he was seeing what she was seeing. During a movie, Jackie Chan was perched precariously atop a skyscraper, so N'kisi warned him, "Don't fall down!". When Morgana and her husband merely think about going out, N'kisi says, "You gotta go out, see ya later." Another time, Morgana picked up her phone as she looked for her friend Rob's number to call him. N'kisi read her thoughts and said, "Hi Rob!". Then N'kisi began seeing Morgana's dreams. She was dreaming of an audio tape deck and awoke to N'kisi's instructions, "You gotta push the button." On another occasion Morgana dreamed she was holding a medicine bottle, when N'kisis woke her up by with, "See, that's a bottle!".

Sheldrake conducted a series of experiments to test N'kisi and Morgana's psychic connection. To avoid sensory cues, owner and pet were placed in different rooms and on different floors. Both subjects were videotaped during 147 two-minute sessions. In each trial, Morgana opened a randomly selected envelope containing a photograph, and studied each image for 20 seconds. N'kisi was to read her mind and state out loud appropriate keywords to describe the picture Morgana was viewing. A set of 19 keywords were used that were common to N'kisi's vocabulary, including "keys", "teeth", and "water". According to the study, N'kisi uttered one or more of the keywords in 71 of the trials. Of these, 23 were counted as direct hits, when the word corresponded directly to the picture. Sheldrake concluded that the results "imply that N'kisi was influenced by Morgana's mental activity while she was looking at particular pictures". For example, when Morgana was looking at a picture of two people on the beach wearing swimsuits, N'kisi said, "Look at my pretty naked body."

Upon closer inspection, this wasn't so amazing. Throughout the trials, N'kisi said "naked body" a total of 11 times. N'kisi said "doctor" a total of 16 times, but didn't say the word the two times that a doctor actually appeared. Two images and two words appeared with high frequency. A photo of a flower appeared 17 times, and N'kisi said "flower" 23 times, with ten hits. An image of water appeared ten times, and N'kisi said "water" 12 times, having two hits. Almost half of N'kisi's hits were with these two words alone. He often repeated specific words, suggesting that these were high frequency words in his normal repertoire. Sheldrake argues, "N'kisi repeated key words more when they were hits than when they were misses." But it seems this parrot was merely parroting words.

Moreover, in 60 of the 147 trials N'kisi gave no response or said non-keywords. These trials were discarded as "nonscorable". Therefore, 40 per cent of the trials were discarded, when they should be counted as misses. Sheldrake maintains that excluding silence and irrelevant words is standard practice when testing young children and animals. However, it's disingenuous to construe non-keywords and silence as "nonscorable", but then interpret the timely utterance of keywords as "psychic". Sheldrake's study appeared in the *Journal of Scientific Exploration* (2003), although even the editor remarked that its statistical significance is less than compelling. Meanwhile, a BBC article entitled, "Parrot oratory stuns scientists" was retracted, because scientists weren't stunned, and N'kisi doesn't appear to be psychic.

Morgana's claims of N'kisi's psychic abilities are anecdotal, and there are lots of possible natural explanations. When N'kisi said to his owners, "You gotta go out", he was probably responding to their regular routine. When N'kisi commented on a car commercial he couldn't see, perhaps he had *heard* the car instead. When N'kisi guessed that Morgana was about to call Rob, perhaps he was a friend she called frequently. When N'kisi "saw" the bottle in Morgana's dream, she neglected to admit that "bottle" is an everyday word in his inventory, like "car", "phone", and the other words that allegedly prove his telepathy.

Finally, a lot of N'kisi's powers are in the interpretation. His "speech" isn't always clear, and this is because it isn't speech. Morgana is N'kisi's teacher, but also his translator. N'kisi's conversations are most intelligible when they're translated by her *before* they've been heard by someone else. Therefore, the listeners have been primed to hear something specific. In this case, some of N'kisi's vocalizations are misconstrued as words. Sheldrake's study only presented subjective interpretations of what the parrot said and meant. In the end, N'kisi's skills were already remarkable. He didn't have to be psychic to be smart.

Oscar the "psychic" cat

Oscar is one of the resident cats at the Steere House Nursing and Rehabilitation Center in Providence, Rhode Island. Since 2005 he has lived in the dementia unit on the third floor of the hospital. However, he isn't the kind of cat you want to attract with, "Here kitty, kitty!". Oscar is a bad omen. According to staff, he has the uncanny ability to sense when a patient is about to die. This black-and-white tabby has been branded the "furry grim reaper" and the "four-legged angel of death" for his fatal purr-dictions.

It all started when, as a kitten, Oscar leaped onto the bed of a patient and fell asleep. The patient died later that day. Since that time, he has presided over the deaths of 50 people. Like the nurses and doctors, Oscar does the rounds of the patients, but not to administer medication or clean bedpans. He's looking for a warm (soon-to-be cold) body to curl up to. He wanders in and out of each room but never lingers, until he identifies a dying patient. He then makes his prediction by jumping onto the patient's bed and curling up in a ball to sleep beside them during their final hours.

According to witnesses, Oscar keeps vigil over the dying person until they have passed. Many patients and family members find his presence to be comforting, and he has been given an award for being a "compassionate cat". Occasionally, the family will request that the morbid moggy be removed from the room. When this happens, Oscar meows miserably, clawing at the door to be let back in, and pacing the halls in protest. If he's left in the room he stays until the funeral director leaves with the body, and often follows the solemn procession to the hearse.

However, it wouldn't be so heart-warming to be told your loved one is about to die because a cat sat on his lap. When Oscar selects a bed the act is interpreted as a sign that the patient has less than four hours to live. In response to the cat's actions, the next-of-kin are notified, and a priest is called to deliver the last rites. This would be a terrible prediction to get wrong, or right. Geriatrician David Dosa (2010) boasts that Oscar is never wrong. He has never taken the time to test his hypothesis, but he has taken the time to write a book about Oscar's alleged abilities. He claims that Oscar has been accurate in 50 cases, but he doesn't provide any data or any names, and he doesn't mention any failures to predict deaths.

Dosa attests to this accuracy by saying that Oscar is generally not a friendly animal and tends to be aloof. This Oscar "the grouch" is in contrast to his portrayal as "compassionate" and "comforting". Suddenly, he isn't the kind of cat to sit on your lap, unless you're dying. Dosa's colleague Mary confirms that, "Oscar only spends time with patients who are about to die." However, the hospital staff are busy people, and perhaps they are only noticing the hits and not the misses. The book contradicts itself by revealing that during the two-thirds of the day that he's asleep, Oscar also sleeps on the doctor's tables and on the beds of patients who *aren't* about to die. In his original *New England Journal of Medicine* essay, Dosa admits that Oscar sometimes curls up to a patient who doesn't die, and leaves while the patient is still alive. Dosa asks the reader to forgive Oscar for these "occasional mistakes".

If Oscar is indeed attracted to dying people, there are lots of theories about his motives. Laurie Cabot, the "official witch" of Salem, believes Oscar is a "familiar" with a psychic connection to dying patients, and the ability to help them cross over (Moore, 2007). Dosa hypothesizes that there is a biochemical explanation for the behavior: Oscar can "smell" death.

> As cells die, carbohydrates are degraded into many oxygenated compounds, including various types of ketones – chemical mixtures known for their fragrant aroma.... Could it be that Oscar simply smells an elevated level of a chemical compound released prior to death? It is certainly clear that animals have a refined sense of smell that goes well beyond that of the ordinary human.

Researchers are hoping to harness the heightened sense of smell of animals for diagnosis. Dogs and mice may be able to detect cancer, while honey bees and the African giant-pouched rat may be able to sniff out tuberculosis (Pflumm, 2011). These studies are still experimental.

Perhaps there are other grounds for Oscar's attraction, such as cues from staff, patients, or family. He could be imitating the behavior of staff. Maybe he is placed or coaxed into patients' rooms. If Oscar is drawn to the rooms of dying patients, perhaps the extra blankets, the additional activity at times, or the more quiet surroundings in these rooms lure him. But we can't take it all too seriously. Dosa's essay and book are only collections of anecdotes and inspirational stories. He even admits that he "made some changes that depart from actual events" for narrative purposes, and that the characters in the book are composites of different patients. In the end, Dosa admits that he can't explain Oscar's behavior.

> I don't really pretend to know the nature of Oscar's special gift – I am not an animal behaviorist nor have I rigorously studied the why and how of his behavior. Whether he is motivated by a refined sense of smell, a special empathy, or something entirely different – your guess is as good as mine.

The reality seems to be that Oscar is a cat who occasionally sleeps on the beds of people who die in a hospice where all of the residents are dying. Perhaps there isn't anything to explain.

Paul the "psychic" octopus

Psychic powers aren't only for furry or feathered pets. Paul was an octopus oracle that successfully predicted seven out of seven winners of the 2010 FIFA World Cup. Paul was an English common octopus living in a commercial aquarium in Oberhausen, Germany. His feeding behavior was used to predict the outcome of the German national football team's matches. Paul was presented with two boxes containing his lunch, a portion of mussels. Each box was labeled with a national flag representing the two warring teams. Whichever box Paul gravitated to first would be his "prediction" of the winner, because of course, he went on to eat the contents of the other box too.

There have been several rival psychic animals, including Mani the parakeet, Leon the porcupine, Anton the tamarin, and Sonny Wool the psychic sheep. However, none enjoyed Paul's perfect record when it came to selecting winners. (And everyone tends to forget that he made two inaccurate predictions for the UEFA Euro 2008.) With only two choices, Paul's successes are explained by chance. However, there are theories that his decision-making was guided by other factors. Octopuses are colorblind, but they are capable of discerning brightness, as well as an object's shape and size, so Paul may have been attracted to a particular flag for these reasons. After all, octopuses are the most intelligent of all invertebrates. They are known to poach lobster traps and unscrew jars with their tentacles, just like Paul did as he'd open the box to get to the mussels.

Not everyone loved this psychic cephalopod. By unintentionally guessing the winner, some believed that Paul determined the outcome of each game. Paul received several death threats, including recipes for his cooking, and when he selected Germany to win against Argentina, some Argentineans wanted to put Paul into their paella. Before he could be tuned into calamari, Paul retired and died at two years old, the average lifespan of the common octopus.

Pet psychics

For doting owners whose pets enjoy spa days (but don't enjoy their organic raw diets) there are other popular pet services, including animal homeopathy, acupuncture, aromatherapy, chiropractic, and pet psychics. Also known as animal communicators, animal intuitives, pet psychologists, pet psychiatrists, or interspecies telepathic communicators, they claim to be able to talk to the animals…literally. Like a psychic Dr Doolittle, they believe they can understand animals, and make themselves understood to animals. They claim to be able to solve emotional and behavioral problems, diagnose and treat sickness, find lost pets, and even contact dead pets.

Pet sounds

Pet psychics are not only fluent in cat and dog, but they can converse with all creatures great and small. Most often, they read household pets and livestock. Pet psychics act as a voice for the pet, but they also claim to hear the pet's "voice" via clairaudience or mental telepathy. Some believe they can translate the animal's thoughts and emotions into words, but others claim the animal actually "speaks". Dogs don't communicate in barks, or cats with meows; according to some pet psychics, animals speak in a human voice. The vocalization usually befits the animal. Big dogs have deep, gruff voices, while cute little kittens speak in a child-like voice (Applebome, 2006). Amazingly, they always speak in the same language as the psychic.

But they don't speak out loud so the rest of us can hear them too. Instead, pet psychics use metaphysical methods to communicate with their pet patients. They use their hearts to connect with the pet's soul, they tune into a pet's energy, or a spirit guide mediates the communication. Animals are often credited with having a "sixth sense" or "heightened awareness", just as psychics claim to have. They profess to use senses that are underdeveloped in the rest of us, including clairvoyance, a kind of psychic sight. The psychic claims to have visions of the pet, or the animal shows mental images to them, like a kind of movie reel. They may also use clairsentience, a murky sense of knowing, commonly called intuition, sensitivity, or gut feeling. Some pet psychics report to be empaths, that is, they literally feel what the animals feel.

Never work with animals or psychics

Celebrity pet psychic Sonya Fitzpatrick says that she simultaneously experiences the animal's thoughts, emotions, and sufferings.

> If they are hurting or hungry, I feel those sensations in my own body. A pleasantly full sensation tells me the animal is being regularly fed, while gnawing hunger pangs tell me just the opposite. If the animal has an ear or bladder infection, or is stiff with arthritis, I feel the exact symptoms in the correlating parts of my own body.
>
> (Fitzpatrick, 1997)

Fitzpatrick reports some incredible phenomena. She believes she can communicate with nonverbal people, including autistic children and coma patients. She became a pet psychic after a visitation from Saint Francis of Assisi. Even though he died in 1226, the patron saint of animals visited her in 1994, and told her that she'd soon be doing "God's work with animals". But she is selective about what constitutes an animal. She only communicates with nice animals that have a "single consciousness". Spiders and flies are to be swatted at every opportunity because they have a "mass consciousness" and therefore can't be read psychically. However, she also believes in reincarnation, so by that theory Fido may be reborn as a spider.

Fitzpatrick was once outsmarted by a turtle. She was called in to have a consultation with Jean Lafitte, a sick turtle. "Speaking in a small, tinny voice he told me he had outgrown his aquarium tank." He requested a larger tank, cleaner water, a green plant, "and a small fish for a companion". His owner purchased these items, including a goldfish. Within days, Jean Lafitte's new fishy friend had disappeared. Fitzpatrick was called in again to investigate the curious situation, and discovered that sneaky Jean Lafitte had wanted food, not friend. "I've eaten him," the turtle confessed to her. "I knew I would never get the fish if I'd told you I was going to eat him." Fitzpatrick was mortified by her unwitting part in the fish's murder, and angry at Jean Lafitte's deception. "To this day, I haven't forgiven myself for my role in the hapless goldfish's death. He really deceived me, that turtle" (Fitzpatrick, 1997).

For some pet psychics to be able to establish communication the animal needs to be present during the reading. To prevent little accidents in the office or studio, others conduct remote readings, and only require a photo of the animal or just the pet's name and breed. For others, the pet doesn't even need to be alive. These pet psychics are also pet mediums who use channeling or séances to contact pets that have "crossed over". During these readings, the pets allegedly send comforting messages to their owners. These include "I love you", assurances they are not angry they were put to sleep, or that they still take walks and play fetch in that giant dog park in the sky.

According to some psychics, owners can also learn to communicate with their pets using mental telepathy. This is an especially useful way to correct bad behavior. Forget obedience school, if Buster won't be house-broken, just imagine him going to the toilet outside on the lawn instead of the bed. Perhaps Daisy the dog won't stop chasing Max the cat. Rather than calling her in vain, simply visualize the pooch returning to you and sitting calmly at your feet, and she will (Nadzan, 2005).

Animal whisperers

Animal whisperers also believe they can talk to the animals. They don't usually claim to have psychic abilities, but they use various methods to communicate with an animal for the purposes of training and behavior modification. The most common types are horse whisperers who practice the tradition of "natural horsemanship", such as Daniel Sullivan, Monty Roberts, and Pat Pirelli. Whisperers for dogs are also common, especially since the appearance of "the dog whisperer" Cesar Millan, the reality TV host.

Dog whisperers claim to achieve astonishing results, especially with the rehabilitation of dangerous and aggressive pets. Many of their techniques involve confrontational methods based on dominance theory. But this ability isn't as mysterious as it first seems. Animal whisperers are self-taught handlers. There is no intuitive connection or supernatural understanding between whisperer and animal, even thought the name suggests something mystical. However, professional behaviorists criticize these methods because they are based on outdated and irrelevant research into the behavior of wolves. Modern behaviorists prefer positive training methods to punishment-based techniques, which can come back to bite dog owners.

The ballad of Jed

Since our pets aren't as talkative with us as they appear to be with psychics, most owners take the psychics at their word. So I once decided to test the claims of a pet psychic, to see if she might really be talking with the animals. But there was a slight problem. I didn't have a pet. So, I borrowed Tennessee Jed, a large tabby cat owned by my neighbors Matt and Bekah. I enlisted the services of feline fortune teller Ann Savino, who communicates with animals via clairvoyance. She asks questions of the pets and they "answer" with images.

I asked Savino to tell me about Jed's past, implying that I didn't know his background. She guessed correctly that he was from a shelter. This was her only correct response, although it was an assumption because I didn't appear to know. She told me that Jed was one year old, when he was actually three. She concocted an unhappy background story, that he was a stray cat who lived on the streets, foraging for food, when at 12 weeks he went straight from shelter to owner. She said he had had three uncaring owners before me, and was previously called "Buttons". However, Jed has always had the same owners, and only one name. "Buttons" didn't even correspond to any of his many nicknames, including Beastly One, Tiger, and Tubbs.

I asked if I should acquire another cat as a friend for Jed, but Savino said he was too shy, "sweet and gentle", and "couldn't handle another cat around". This was probably because he was acting uncharacteristically quiet in his unfamiliar surroundings. However, he already had a companion cat by the name of Bizzy, and Jed is the dominant cat in the home. He is known for being aggressively playful, and once lodged a claw in his owner's eyelid. Savino also warned me that Jed had stomach problems, which was disproven by a recent visit to the vet. As for me she incorrectly "saw" that I had once miscarried a baby.

Savino asserted that Jed was born in Marin County, California, where the reading took place. In fact, he was born over 2,000 miles away in Jackson, Mississippi. I finally asked her if Jed felt at home in the apartment (that wasn't his home). "He's happy here. He feels secure and safe. He definitely feels at home." She paused, "This is the most secure he's ever felt. He knows that this is his home. Jed's secure, happy, and safe in this home. He knows he's loved. He knows that you're his mummy" (Stollznow, 2009).

However, as Bekah loaned Jed to me she said to him in parting, "Goodbye son. I'll be back soon." It was very clear that *she* is the cat's mother. As confirmed by Jed's owners, Savino was completely inaccurate in her reading of Jed's age, place of birth, background, behaviour, and state of health, not to mention my own health. Most damning of all, her pet psychic abilities didn't tell her that Jed wasn't my cat. It seems she was making basic observations and guesses about Jed, and she wasn't communicating with him via clairvoyance.

Pet peeve

Pet psychics can be extremely dangerous to the animal's health, when owners opt to consult a psychic instead of a veterinarian. Many pet psychics don't do medical readings because the claims can be disproved, and the psychic exposed. Pet psychics can be unethical when they are asked to make life or death decisions for a pet. Like many other psychics, Sonya Fitzpatrick is a Dr Kevorkian for animals who advises owners on end of life issues. One time she "communicated" with a circus tiger suffering from cancer. He "told" her that he would rather enjoy the last few months of his life than undergo chemotherapy (Jansen, 2011). The treatment may have extended or saved his life, but the tiger died four months later. Fitzpatrick is biased. She believes that veterinarian medicine and commercial pet foods are the predominant causes of animal disease (and she has her own line of pet food). The outlandish claims of pet psychics can also be offensive. One psychic told a client that her cat's bad behavior should be excused because of its previous life. Apparently, the cat had been a prisoner in the Dachau concentration camp during the Nazi holocaust (MacLean, 2012).

Whether they are aware of it or not, it appears as though pet psychics are using cold reading techniques to perform their readings. These are a combination of generalizations and animal stereotypes. For example, claiming that Tiger "said" he prefers tuna to tinned food. They use a basic knowledge of animal behavior; that Buddy hates to be left alone at home during the day, which is why he tears up the curtains. They use guesswork based on observations, as when Savino assumed that Jed has a shy personality. They also glean information from the client, as when she guessed Jed was a rescue animal, based on my question. These readings are then validated, not by the pets, obviously, but by the owners, who already believe. Pet psychic readings are like psychic readings for people, but only easier for the psychic, because the furry, feathered, and scaly clients can't disagree. Surely our best friends deserve better than a fake voice.

18
Monster Language

Human characteristics are attributed to many legendary creatures, and as part of this anthropomorphization they often have language abilities. Fairies, elves, gnomes, goblins, and genies of folklore speak human languages, usually in addition to their own tongues. Many fiction writers have created artificial languages and writing systems for these creatures, including J. R. R. Tolkien's Elvish languages and Eoin Colfer's Gnommish fairy script. As for the undead, vampires retain the language skills they had when they were still alive. Zombies are no longer great conversationalists but they can still mutter "brains!". In popular paranormal theory, ghosts and spirits can communicate with the living, although they often require a medium or a device designed to contact the dead.

Cryptids are animals whose existence has not been proven scientifically, like the Loch Ness monster. Some cryptids are believed to have language skills too, especially hybrid-human creatures, such as spring-heeled Jack, the Mothman, mermaids, monkey men, lizard men, and goat men. An early version of the mythical goat-sucking *chupacabra* (Spanish for "goat sucker") could allegedly understand Spanish, although not speak it. A monster called the *popobawa* (Swahili for "bat wing") of Zanzibar is believed to both speak and communicate via mental telepathy. Its modus operandi is to rape men, then warn them that they must spread the news of their violation to others, lest they be subject to more savage attacks. There are numerous anecdotal reports that the Indonesian cryptid the *orang-pendek* (Indonesian for "short person") communicates using vocalizations similar to nonhuman primates (Freeman, 2004). What about the most infamous cryptid of all . . . Bigfoot?

194   *Non-human Language*

Bigfoot language

The evidence for Bigfoot is plentiful but not compelling. There is a wealth of eyewitness and folkloric evidence, while cryptozoologists and Bigfoot hunters have collected numerous examples of physical evidence, including Bigfoot tracks, samples of hair and blood, and photographs and videos of a putative Bigfoot. However, proving the existence of Bigfoot is not about quantity of evidence but quality, and the quality of evidence is poor. The images are blurry and unconvincing and the footprints prove to be pranks. Through DNA testing the physical samples are revealed to come from bears, dogs, or other animals, and specimens of Bigfoot bodies or bones are never found. Despite the ongoing controversy surrounding the 1967 Patterson-Gimlin film, the evidence for Bigfoot is invariably revealed to be cases of mistaken identity or hoaxes.

A fascinating category of evidence involves claims of a Bigfoot language. Eyewitnesses report hearing howls, whoops, growls, screams, mumbles, whistles, and other strange vocalizations in the wild, and attribute these to Bigfoot. Variant forms of Bigfoot are found across cultures, and the Sasquatch, Himalayan yeti, and Australian yowie are similarly believed to produce vocalizations. Other reputed forms of Bigfoot communication include the mimicry of wildlife and forest sounds, wood-knocking, rock-knocking, and rock-throwing. Bigfoot are also thought to form patterns with sticks and rocks as a kind of writing system. In wilder claims about wild men, Bigfoot are believed to have the ability to communicate telepathically, and use their large feet to send infra-sound communication over long distances. Bigfoot are also thought to speak and understand human languages, and to have their own Bigfoot language.

The Sierra Sounds recordings

There is little evidence to support these claims, other than the anecdotal kind. The Sierra Sounds recordings, also known as the Berry/Morehead tapes, are one of these rare pieces of data. In fact, they are touted as the gold standard of evidence for a Bigfoot language. During a number of expeditions to the Sierra Nevada mountains between the years 1972–75, Alan Berry, Ronald Morehead, and their crew captured audio recordings of alleged Bigfoot encounters. They recorded a total of 90 minutes of Bigfoot vocalizations and wood-knockings using a microphone dangled from a tree branch attached to a reel-to-reel recorder. Over the years they also found 18-inch footprints of Bigfoot, and experienced many sightings... just not during the recordings! Bigfoot was supposedly heard, but never seen at these times.

Of the Sierra Sound recordings, a two-minute-long clip known as "samurai chatter" is celebrated as the "Patterson-Gimlin of audio evidence for Bigfoot". The recording purportedly captures a creature in conversation with Morehead. The "Bigfoot" utters short speech-like sounds, to which Morehead replies by mimicking the sounds. The unidentified creature sounds a little like a Muppet. The vocalizations have a human-intonation, so the dialogue sounds like a conversation of questions and answers. Listeners speculate that the "language" sounds like Japanese, hence the name. There is also a theory that the language evolved from an indigenous American dialect.

A paper written by a graduate student is often cited to validate the Sierra Sounds recordings (Hertel, 1978). The study analyzes unspecified clips to estimate the vocal tract length of the speakers and determine whether they could be of human origin. The findings are inconclusive, although three speakers are identified in the recordings and the author surmises that one of these is "nonhuman". It is later clarified that this "nonhuman" speaker is "of larger physical size than an average human adult male," which certainly doesn't preclude humans! Samples of "Bigfoot whistles" are also analyzed, and it is found that they "could either have been produced with some kind of a musical instrument or by the creature using only part of its vocal tract". This is a poorly written and sensationalized student paper, but it is most likely that the voices are of human origin.

The other Sierra Sounds recordings feature a range of unidentified sounds. These were all heard independently of sightings, yet they are attributed to Bigfoot. They could likely be explained as other wildlife noises, including, coyotes, bears, elk, owls, raccoons, wolves, and big cats. In one clip "Bigfoot" is believed to mimic a bird, although the simplest explanation is that it's just a bird. In another recording an "English-speaking Bigfoot" allegedly threatens the expedition with, "You're not welcome!". This is likely an example of pareidolia where speech is mistakenly heard among the ambient wildlife sounds.

Morehead and Berry (until his death in 2012) staunchly deny that the recordings are a hoax. However, for a number of reasons, it is highly probable that they are a hoax, or that the crew was hoaxed. The expeditions were undertaken specifically to hunt for Bigfoot. Bigfoot was heard but never seen when the recordings were made. Clearly, animals made some of the sounds, while the wood knocks are easy to hoax. The "language" itself is unconvincing. The vocalizations are an amateur impression of how a proto-language evolved by nonhuman primates would sound. "Bigfoot" is likely human, and the Sierra Sounds a combination of hoax and misidentification, like all of the other evidence for Bigfoot.

The Sierra Sounds are copyrighted and available for sale. With a lack of scientific research to support their theories, Berry and Morehead rely on customer and "expert" testimonials to support the authenticity of the recordings. One of these authorities is Nancy Logan, a self-proclaimed linguist whose qualifications include bilingualism, and that she is so proficient at mimicking accents that "I have a Russian friend... she thinks I'm a Russian... the bottom line is I have a very sensitive sense of hearing." On the basis of this she concludes, "I don't think these tapes are fake" (Logan, 2012). In one clip an airplane goes overhead and the "Bigfoot" utters some sounds excitedly. Logan speculates that these are "Sasquatch swear words".

Logan also muses, "I don't think Homo sapiens can make all of these noises." American English has about 36 phonemes (the basic sound units we usually represent as individual letters, e.g., /k/ or /s/). This in itself is a large inventory, but then other languages have even more phonemes. Some indigenous African languages are complex due to their large number of *click* consonants (*tsk!* is one of the very few clicks we use in English). These "click languages" have upwards of 100 different phonemes. Humans have developed techniques to produce complex and unique vocalizations, such as the overtone singers and throat singers of Asia and Europe. Of course it is possible that humans can make the noises captured in the Sierra Sounds recordings.

(Big) Foot in mouth

"Bigfoot language expert" R. Scott Nelson has taken the Bigfoot language claims one step further. As though it is the Linear B of Bigfoot language to be deciphered, Nelson has created a transcription of the Sierra Sound recordings. He is a retired US Navy cryptologic technician interpreter who speaks Russian, Spanish, and Persian. He also believes he can speak "Bigfoot".

Nelson claims he has identified not only vocalizations such as whistles (W), grunts and snarls, but also individual phonemes, the sounds that combine to create words. Nelson has created a pronunciation key for these phonemes, and he uses the Latin alphabet, diacritics, and various other symbols, such as delta and theta, to represent these sounds. He calls this the Sasquatch phonetic alphabet or the unclassified hominid phonetic alphabet. All of these sounds have been described in the international phonetic alphabet, so it is unclear why he doesn't use this standardized representation of the sounds of spoken language.

According to Nelson, Bigfoot language has some interesting sounds, including an alveolar trill, the rolling "r" sound that occurs in Spanish and older forms of Scottish English. It also has the voiceless velar fricative that appeared in Old English but is now mostly known for being the final sound in Scottish English *loch*. He has also included symbols for glottal stops and click consonants, making "Bigfoot" a very complex language phonologically! Nelson also claims he can identify the gender and age of the Bigfoot, and determine whether an utterance constitutes a statement, command, question, or answer. He even believes he can detect when a Bigfoot is using rhetorical techniques such as persuasion, instruction, or aggression.

Here is an example of Nelson's transcriptions.

0:08.62	(W) (W) (W)
0:15.11	RAM HO BÄ RÜ KHÄ HÜ
0:16.70	WAM VO HÜ KHÖ KHU'
0:17.52	NÖ U PLÄ MEN TI KHU
0:18.82	NÄR LÄ
0:20.21	NA GÖ KÜ STEP GÄ KÜ BLEM
0:21.25	Ü KÜ DZJÄ
0:21.76	FRrÄP E KHÜK LE

(Nelson, 2011)

According to Nelson, Bigfoot language is spoken twice as fast as any known language. He says, "the creatures mentally process information at a much higher rate than humans do, or at least they are able to communicate their ideas much faster" (Nelson, 2011). This rapid "speech" only appears in some of the recordings and is reminiscent of speaking in tongues. The structure is simplistic and features the rapid repetition of basic consonant-vowel combinations such as "gu", "du", and "ku". It's easier to speak faster if you're talking gibberish.

Nelson has broken down the sounds into "syllables". If we listen to a foreign language it sounds like a continuous stream of sound, without clear breaks between words. Therefore, if we don't know a language we can't accurately pick out the words. The Sierra Sounds recordings feature unintelligible sounds, so there is no way to determine word boundaries because there are no words. Nelson has merely made guesses, and then taken it upon himself to standardize these subjective sounds. Fortunately, he didn't attempt to translate the language. However, he believes that Bigfoot words have English cognates, suggesting that they are historically related.

Nelson gushes, "We have verified that these creatures use language, by the human definition of it." No, we haven't. Before creating a transcription of this "Bigfoot language", Nelson first needed to demonstrate that this is language. He has tried to authenticate the recordings, rather than analyze them in an unbiased way. Unknown sounds don't immediately qualify as "language", any more than an Unidentified Flying Object must be extraterrestrial. If this is indeed an undocumented language, an anthropological linguist would be needed. This linguist would do field-work to document the language, by working with the data and with user communities. However, as we can see, there is no user community, and insufficient data.

It appears as if cryptozoological fans confuse "crypto-linguistics" as research into cryptids and language. Being bilingual and working as a translator doesn't qualify someone to identify or describe undocumented languages. The Bigfoot community prematurely labels Nelson's work a "breakthrough". The Sierra Sounds are used not only to support the claim of a Bigfoot language, but to legitimize claims of Bigfoot's existence. As Nelson argues, "The existence of the Sasquatch Being is hereby assumed, since any creature must exist before his language." However, there are still prior questions. Does Bigfoot exist, and if so, could Bigfoot speak?

Off on the wrong foot

As we discussed above, nonhuman primates can be trained to learn symbols, such as the signs learned by bonobos, gorillas, and orangutans. Many primates have also developed their own communication systems, like the gestures of chimpanzees, and the alarm calls of Diana monkeys. However, language differs from vocalizations in that human sounds are made with the vocal apparatus (lips, tongue, teeth, roof of the mouth, vocal folds) to form speech. Nonhuman primates do not have the anatomical flexibility that Homo sapiens have with our vocal apparatus, and therefore they don't have the capabilities for a large repertoire of sounds.

For argument's sake, if Bigfoot did exist, the species would likely have developed its own system of communication. Similar to the claims of the *orang-pendek*, Bigfoot would likely communicate using vocalizations.

Without the physiology to produce a wide variety of speech sounds, it is unlikely that Bigfoot would have developed language, let alone be able to speak existing human languages. But this is putting the cart before the Bigfoot. There is no solid physical evidence to support the existence of Bigfoot. Before we establish the existence of Bigfoot language, we need to establish the existence of Bigfoot.

19
Alien Language

In popular culture we've created aliens in our own image. They may be little green men, Men in Black, or the Greys, but they have bodies similar to ours. And like us, they usually have the ability to communicate with each other, and with us. From Percy Greg's *Across the Zodiac* (1880) to Vulcan, Ferengi, and the other tongues of the *Star Trek* universe, science fiction has produced many constructed languages, known to nerds as *conlangs*.

Some of these invented alien languages are simplistic, such as the limited Martian vocabulary of "Ack! Rack!" in the movie *Mars Attacks*. Other sci-fi languages are impressively elaborate, like Klingon (tlhIngan Hol), as spoken by the Klingon race in the *Star Trek* films and TV series. Klingon initially consisted of a handful of words created by "Scotty", actor James Doohan. Linguist Marc Okrand expanded Klingon into a fully-fledged language with its own syntax, vocabulary, phonology, and even alphabet (tlhIngan pIqaD). There is a Klingon dictionary, and Shakespeare's *Hamlet* and *Much Ado About Nothing* have been translated into Klingon. The language actually has a small community of speakers. There is a Klingon language institute that publishes *HolQeD*, a journal of language and culture, and *jatmey*, ("scattered tongues") a magazine of poetry and fiction, and even holds an annual conference.

Xenolinguistics

If we earthlings encounter an extraterrestrial species, obviously, we will want to communicate with them. But it is unlikely they are going to make it easy on us by saying, "Take me to your leader!" in the Queen's

English. Xenolinguistics (also exolinguistics and astrolinguistics) is the speculative study of hypothetical alien languages. In his search for intelligent life beyond Earth one researcher explored intelligent life already on Earth. Dr. John C. Lilly (1915–2001) conducted pioneering work with dolphins in the hope that interspecies communication could be the key to undertaking extraterrestrial languages we might encounter in the future. He founded the Order of the Dolphin, a semi-secret society of which Frank Drake and Carl Sagan were members. Lilly's approaches soon drifted away from the mainstream. Living in a house flooded with seawater, his assistant Margaret Howe taught Peter the dolphin how to pronounce an approximation of the words 'hello', 'one', 'work' and 'play.' In his lab on St. Thomas in the US Virgin Islands, Lilly subjected his dolphins to invasive experiments on their brains and injected them with LSD to see if it had any effect on their vocalizations, which it didn't. He came to believe that dolphins are aliens who share our planet, and he tried to talk to them using mental telepathy. Rather than a think tank of academics, most often it is science fiction that tackles the human–alien communication barrier.

Some believe there might be an intergalactic language common to all, known as a lingua franca. Galactic Basic is spoken galaxy-wide in the *Star Wars* films, although it sounds remarkably like English. Others suggest we could invent some sort of pan-cosmic Esperanto. However, if we encounter aliens, and they have a comparable communication system, it is likely that we would develop a new language with them. These are called contact languages because they form when two groups meet but don't have a lingua franca. You probably know them as pidgins and creoles. Such a language would be a mix of their existing languages and ours. So, the new language might have a human vocabulary and an alien grammar.

If there's no common tongue, a popular theory is the idea of a machine translation device, such as the babel fish in *The Hitchhiker's Guide to the Galaxy*. When placed in the ear, this small yellow fish allows the person to instantly understand anything said in any form of language. The TARDIS time machine from *Doctor Who* allows its passengers to speak and understand foreign languages and writing systems. The protocol droid C-3PO is a universal translator in *Star Wars*, and fluent in some six million different languages. *Star Trek*'s universal translator offers instant translation between languages, although conveniently, the device doesn't work when Klingon is being spoken for the purposes of privacy. In the "Darmok" episode of *Star Trek*, the device translates the language of the Tamarin race. However, the language is based on metaphor from Tamarin folklore and it is completely obscure when translated directly into English. This story illustrates the difference between knowing a language and understanding a message in it.

Unless miscommunication is essential to the plot, these translation devices are precise, unlike the translation programs in existence, where you seem to learn how to say "hello" but end up propositioning a complete stranger. These sci-fi inventions are workarounds to avoid dealing with the enormous problems posed by interstellar translation. Human-to-human translation is difficult enough. There aren't quite the six million languages found on *Star Wars*, but there are over 6,000 human languages today. These unique languages represent different ways of talking about and thinking about the world. However, as humans, we all still have some common ground.

An alien view

Living in another galaxy tends to influence your worldview. An alien species will have taken a different evolutionary path to humankind. There will be radical differences in biology and ecology that will have had an effect on culture and cognition. Human-to-alien translation wouldn't be the same as human-to-human translation, and would be difficult in the absence of common experiences and knowledge. Would we even recognize alien language as language? There are theories that aliens might use a nonverbal communication system involving gestures, or a system based on chemicals, like insects or plants. Their communication could involve color, like chameleons, or methods based on taste, touch, smell, or electrical impulses. There won't be a "Rosetta Stone for Alien" anytime soon.

In the search for a universal language to communicate across cultures and (literally) space, some believe that a constant such as mathematics may offer a solution. A formal language could feasibly circumvent cultural bounds, as illustrated by the math-based language in Carl Sagan's *Contact*. Dutch logician Hans Freudenthal assumed that aliens, and humans, could learn a self-teaching, logic-based language, so he created Lincos (*lingua cosmica*) for use in radio transmissions. Formal languages could possibly work, provided aliens have human-like thought. But it is overly optimistic to think that a simplified language based in math and logic could convey abstract concepts and culture-specific terms, such as *grande decaf soy caramel macchiato with an extra shot of espresso*.

Musical tones are used to communicate in *Close Encounters of the Third Kind*. A universal language might involve pictures or song, although these so-called universals could pose problems. Music won't work if the aliens don't have hearing, and pictures won't work if they don't have sight. Some people with the neurological condition synesthesia see letters and numbers as colors, and stimuli might be interpreted differently by another species too. For example, sounds could be perceived as colors, or images seen as three-dimensional (Mossop, 1996).

Another popular belief is that extraterrestrial communication would be more advanced than terrestrial communication. They would certainly have language, but it would be more evolved and complex than ours. Perhaps they could be capable of mental telepathy, the language of thought. They would transmit their ideas via thought, rather than mere speech. The idea of telepathy or mind transference is explored in science fiction, such as *Star Trek*'s Vulcan mind meld. When using this telepathic link the minds of two individuals temporarily share the same thoughts, like a remote support or desktop sharing between minds. For telepathy to work beyond science fiction, both the sender and receiver would probably have to share a language, because thought projection wouldn't necessarily include automatic translation. And thoughts or mental pictures wouldn't be a replacement for language. While it is possible to think in pictures, much learning and abstract thought is mediated by language.

An alien tongue

Alien communication in science fiction isn't science fact. Fans of Klingon know it's fantasy (well, most of them do!) but there are some people who believe extraterrestrial languages exist, and they can speak them. Beyond the conspiracy theories, science has made a genuine attempt to search for life beyond earth. Since 1985, The Search for Extraterrestrial Intelligence (SETI) has searched for alien communication, without success. But this hasn't stopped some people from claiming they have had close encounters of the linguistic kind. They call themselves contactees, abductees, experiencers, starseeds, star children, or "the chosen one" to help initiate "first contact". Strangely, there are many chosen ones and many contacts have been first.

As we saw in Chapter 7, nineteenth-century Swiss psychic Hélène Smith (Catherine-Elise Müller) claimed to be able to talk to Martians. During trance sessions she would write automatically using the Martian language and alphabet, and describe scenes of life on Mars. Psychologist Théodore Flournoy (1900) and Ferdinand de Saussure, the founder of modern linguistics, examined these samples of Martian, and concluded that it was a badly designed artificial language. The grammar, sounds, and vocabulary of Martian resembled French, Smith's native language. In Flournoy's book *From India to Planet Mars* he joked, "Martian is only disguised French."

Even today, there are still unknown languages and undeciphered writing systems, including the Linear A script used in Crete about 4,000 years ago, the unknown writing on the Phaistos Disk also found in Crete, and Rongo Rongo used to write the Rapa Nui language on Easter Island. If we can't decipher the writing of our ancestors, we'll probably have difficulty understanding the language of species from other worlds. Alien languages will likely sound very alien indeed, and probably exhibit unfamiliar structures and unfamiliar sounds. To make Klingon "sound" alien, Okrand chose features that occur infrequently in natural languages (Okrent, 2009).

Alleged alien languages are as artificial as those invented by sci-fi writers; they just haven't admitted it yet. But these discovered alien languages aren't as convincing as conlangs. They seem to represent the contactee's simplistic idea of what an alien language might be like. The writing systems resemble exotic ones, like hieroglyphs, or they are blatant rip-offs of existing human languages. Contactee Betty Luca's (formally Andreasson) alien language is more of earthly origin. Upon analysis, the "mystical language" taught to her by "the Elders" is a mix of Latin, Greek, and other classical languages. Less convincing still, the words are in citation form, that is, the unmarked words that you'd find in the dictionary (Newbrook, 2004). Therefore, there is no grammar and the "language" is just a list of words, probably plucked straight out of *Greek for Beginners*.

Sheldan Nidle claims that he has experienced multiple visitations and abductions. During these sessions he was educated on board the alien spacecraft. In these classes, he was taught six "star languages", Sirian, Pleiadean, Andromedan, Herculean, Centaurian, and Lyran. Nidle also claims to have alien implants in his body that have given him advanced knowledge about mathematics and physics. To prepare us for first contact, Nidle teaches that "hello" is *selamat ja* in Sirian, and *selama'at jara* in Herculean (Nidle, 2009). Curiously, these phrases bear a close similarity to *selamat*, a common greeting word found in Indonesian and Malaysian that is derived from the Arabic *salam*, meaning "peace". Languages only hundreds of miles apart can be vastly different and unrelated. Sirius is a star almost nine light years away from us, and Hercules is a constellation many light years away, but if we are to believe Nidle, his alien languages are not only related to each other but also to languages here on earth.

Following repeated abductions by aliens, Australian Tracey Taylor believes she became spontaneously fluent in a star language. Taylor's "language" is a characteristic example of glossolalia. She murmurs meaningless sounds that bear a resemblance to Japanese; unsurprisingly, Taylor spent time living in Japan (Newbrook, 2004). She was a patient of hypnotherapist Mary Rodwell who has conducted over 1,000 hypnotic regressions with alleged alien abductees. Like Taylor, Rodwell (2010) reports that many abductees suddenly speak in unknown tongues and write strange symbols after encounters with aliens. Abduction stories are often the product of fantasy, delusion, or hallucinations caused by sleep disorders such as sleep paralysis and night terrors. They can also be created by regression therapists like Rodwell who both invent and validate false memories of anal probes and weird languages.

Are we alone?

David Icke believes that not only are we not alone, but the aliens are already among us. These aren't your average "Greys", these are blood-drinking, shape-shifting reptilian humanoids from the Alpha Draconis star system (Icke, 2000). Reptilians are common in science fiction, but also common in conspiracy theories. They usually hide in underground bases, although Icke believes that many prominent figures are reptilian. Not only can they speak English but apparently they can earn an MBA at Harvard and govern a country. According to Icke, former US President George Bush is a reptilian, and so is the entire British royal family. The first sighting of reptilians involved Herbert Schirmer of Nebraska who claimed to have been taken aboard a UFO by reptilian aliens in December, 1967. Interestingly, *Star Trek* introduces a reptilian alien called the Gorn in the episode "Arena" that aired January 19 and July 6 of that year.

Aliens are elusive to science, yet a select few are harassed by them constantly. Stan Romanek claims he has been abducted by aliens many times, has fathered hybrid-alien babies, and had a peeping Tom alien peer in thorough his window. Then an alien began leaving messages on his answering machine and tape recorder. One of these was an unintelligible "low, rumbling growl, as if an evil creature was going to come ripping out of the tape recorder", but Romanek believed it contained a hidden message. He played it at "seven times the original recording speed" and it revealed a female saying clearly, "Starseed, it's time" (Romanek and Danelek, 2009). I took the original recording and sped it up, but due to data loss, the high-speed version doesn't match Romanek's message. Therefore, the message was clearly recorded first, and then slowed down. Most importantly, in all recordings the "alien" sounds exactly like "Audrey", the synthesized British English female voice available through AT&T Natural Voices text-to-speech software.

Benjamin Crème of Share International heads a cult that merges existing religions and ufology. He believes that extraterrestrials from Venus and Mars visit us frequently, but space sisters and brothers or space people are preferable terms, because "aliens" and "little green men" are discriminatory. He teaches that the Messiah, Christ, Buddha, and Krishna are all names for the same being: Maitreya, who will reappear on earth soon. At that time, Maitreya will "overshadow" the planet, that is, he will establish telepathic communication with everyone on earth at the same time, in the native language of each person (Stollznow, 2010). This sounds like the original biblical speaking in tongues that occurred at the feast of Pentecost (Chapter 8). While we wait for Maitreya's appearance, crop circles aren't a human hoax but are "love letters" written by space people to earthlings.

It seems as though these people have read one too many science fiction novels. It can be fun, and frustrating, to speculate about the existence of alien languages but we are talking about a hypothetical language from a hypothetical species. Like the claims about Bigfoot language, let's find the aliens first.

20
Talking Objects

Talking to plants is believed to help them to grow. We name our boats, planes, and hurricanes, and sometimes even our genitalia. We yell at the car when it doesn't work and swear at the chair when we stub our toe, but some believe that objects can talk back to us. Some religions believe that everything has a spirit or life force, including inanimate objects. This chapter is about talking to objects, and talking objects. We explore possessed possessions, and why we're more likely to have a haunted watch than a haunted toaster. We also look at haunted items believed to have language abilities, including talking paintings, talking dolls, and a haunted dress that has a story to tell.

Talking to plants

Like animals, plants are animate, although they certainly don't have "language" as we understand it. But we know that plants respond to light, while scientists also know that plants use chemicals to communicate with each other. Recent research into plant bioacoustics also suggests that plants produce and respond to sound and vibration, constituting a form of communication (Gagliano et al., 2012). However, some people believe that plants also have emotions and that talking to them can promote healthy growth.

Luther Burbank (1849–1926) was a highly successful horticulturalist who created hundreds of new varieties of fruit, vegetables, grains, and ornamental plants. He also believed plants are capable of understanding speech, and can respond to speech. In his efforts to develop the spineless cactus he comforted his plants with, "You have nothing to fear. You don't need your defensive thorns" (Sackman, 2005). There is some evidence that plants might respond to the carbon dioxide emitted from our breath as we talk "on" them. However, this technique would require hours of daily chit-chat to be effective.

Charles, Prince of Wales, not only talks to his plants but he listens to them too. He was quoted as saying half-jokingly, "I just come and talk to the plants, really. Very important to talk to them; they respond, I find" (*Daily Telegraph*, December 22, 1986). This affinity with plants is nothing new to the English monarchy. It was widely believed that King George III (1738–1820) tried to shake hands with an oak tree, thinking it was the King of Prussia (Ayling, 1972). George III suffered from mental illness in his later years and of course, talking to objects or hearing objects talk can be symptoms of various mental health conditions, including schizophrenia.

Planting a seed

Another popular belief is that playing music to plants encourages them to grow. In an episode of the TV show *Mythbusters* the team conducted controlled tests to see if greenhouse plants respond to recordings of speech and music. They exposed separate groups of plants to endless loops of "positive" speech, "negative" speech, classical music, and death metal music. A control greenhouse had no soundtrack at all. In the end, the plants subjected to sound grew slightly better than the control sample, and the theory was found to be plausible. The plants liked death metal music best, although a few in this group died when their watering system failed. Overall, it seems that plants prefer sunlight and water to good conversation. In practice, it is possible that people who talk to their plants are more likely to care for them diligently in other ways too, ensuring they thrive.

She's the cat's mother

As a social convention we personify objects by naming them, especially beloved personal possessions. B. B. King named his Gibson guitars Lucille, while Steve Vai has Ibanez guitars named Evo and Flo. Stephen Colbert jokingly names his gun "Sweetness". It is common to name our childhood toys and our cars, computers, or boats, but we probably wouldn't hame a toaster or a fridge. We also name machines after people, such as "Lisa", the predecessor to the Apple Macintosh, which was named for Steve Jobs' daughter. We name technology, like the Mars exploration rovers "Spirit" and "Opportunity". We even paint these names on their "bodies". Personification is a rhetorical device popular in literature, where inanimate objects are given feelings, sensations, and physical traits. We often attribute human emotions and characteristics to the objects we name, so that a car is described as "stubborn" or "temperamental". We also name hurricanes, because Sandy, Andrew, and Katrina are more memorable than latitude–longitude identification methods.

Naming objects tends to give them gender too. Unlike French and German, nouns are not marked for gender in English. However, we often refer to possessions by using gender-marked pronouns, but we aren't assigning gender in any grammatical way. Ships are "she", the environment is "Mother Nature", and nations are "mother countries" or "fatherlands". Sometimes we assign gender to animals when the sex is unknown, so dogs are often referred to as "he" and cats as "she". By extension of our bodies, some people name their genitalia for the purposes of play, humor, or euphemism. These names usually reflect gender. A man's penis will probably be bestowed with a masculine-sounding name like "Mr Happy" rather than "Bertha". As a euphemism, breasts are popularly called "the twins" or "the girls", while testicles are "the boys".

When we name objects we don't do so because we perceive them as animate, we are only showing our affection for them. We can also reveal our frustration by talking to objects. We talk to our cars and computers when they don't work, but not with the expectation that they will work again because of it. We probably swear at the chair if we bump into it and injure ourselves, and we might even kick it back as "punishment". As a rule, we don't expect these objects to talk back to us.

May the (life) force be with you

Some belief systems and cultures teach that everything has a spirit or life force. The native American Algonquian people believe that everything has a spirit called a Manitou, including machines and plants. In ancient Egypt, this life force or life energy was known as *"ka"*. In modern India it is called *"prana"*, while in China it is *"qi"* (chi). *Qi* is central to the Chinese practice of feng shui (meaning "wind water"). This is the belief that everything has an inherent force that is either negative (*yin*) or positive (*yang*). These forces must be kept in balance to create positive qi in the home, workplace, and society. Feng shui teaches that certain colors, numbers, and styles of architecture attract good fortune. In accordance with feng shui principles, the careful display of possessions, such as wind chimes, mirrors, and statues of fish and dragons, is believed to bring health, wealth, and happiness. Alternatively, some objects and places are thought to attract misfortune. As living beings, we have "*yang* energy", and should avoid spending too much time near places that contain negative "*yin* energy", including slaughterhouses, prisons, hospitals, and cemeteries.

Possessed possessions

Prisons, hospitals, and cemeteries are places that are often stereotyped as being haunted. So are castles, spooky-looking houses, and other sites, such as battlegrounds where tragic events took place. Sometimes it's not the building but the contents that are believed to be haunted. A popular claim among the paranormal community is that objects in houses can be a source of paranormal activity, and we're not talking about the Haunted Mansion at Disneyland. Certain things are stereotypically haunted too. Your toaster probably won't be haunted, although likely candidates include jewelry, furniture, clothes, musical instruments, religious artifacts, second-hand items, family heirlooms, and children's toys.

So-called haunted objects are usually items that have sentimental value to the owner. According to ghost-hunter theory, Grandpa haunts his walking cane because haunted objects are imprinted with the residual energy of former owners. My good friend Reed Esau displays a "haunted clock" in his home that was given to (forced upon) him by a colleague. She thinks that the clock stopped at the exact moment of her mother's death, so she fears it is possessed by her mother's spirit. Some people also believe that evil spirits can possess objects. These possessed possessions are allegedly created when an object is used in an occult ritual. Haunted items are accused of causing poltergeist and paranormal activity and even relationship problems and bad luck in the home.

Why are some objects more haunted than others? Old items are especially thought to be haunted, and this is probably because they are connected to the history of their owners. Antique, estate items, and second-hand objects are often believed to be haunted too, probably because they have an unknown and questionable past. A haunted history can be easily fabricated, as in the case of psychometry. In this practice, a psychic performs a cold reading of a person, using a personal object as a tool. If the owner doesn't know the history of the item, the psychic can simply invent a story.

The Baker Mansion in Altoona, Pennsylvania, has a "haunted wedding dress" in its collection. Visitors and staff believe that the dress "moves" in its display case as though it is being worn by a woman. The popular theory is that former resident Anna Baker haunts the dress, but it wasn't even hers. Later occupant Elizabeth Dysart was the owner of the dress. So, why is the dress attributed to Baker? Allegedly, her father forbade her from marrying a man of lower social standing. Baker stayed true to her lost love and never married, and so the would-be bride is said to haunt the dress to this day. Folklore aside, there is a natural explanation for the movement of the dress. The display case once rested on rickety floorboards, so when people approached the dress shook, giving the appearance of being animated (Nickell, 1995). The staff seems to have stumbled across this explanation, as the dress is no longer on display.

Talking dolls

Some objects are targeted as being haunted simply because they have an eerie appearance. Dolls are especially "haunted", possibly because of their ethereal, vacant-looking expressions or permanent smiles. Sometimes, haunted objects are even believed to "talk". Dolls, clowns, and other human-like toys that become animated are a common theme in horror movies, such as "Chucky" in the *Child's Play* movies. Robert the Doll was the inspiration for this character. In 1906 in Key West, Florida, a Bahamian servant of the Otto family gave 4-year-old Robert Eugene a handcrafted doll dressed in a sailor suit and clutching a stuffed lion. He named the life-like doll 'Robert' after himself, and the pair became inseparable. Strange activity soon began in the house. Robert's parents overheard him talking to the doll, and an evil-sounding voice responded. The doll was also said to giggle and change its expression from innocent to wicked. Glassware smashed and furniture upturned in the boy's presence, but whenever he was accused of mischief, he pointed at the doll and cried, 'Robert did it!' (In Key West this remains a common expression for shifting blame.) It was then feared that the servant was a voodoo practitioner, and that the doll was cursed. Robert grew up and became a famous painter and author in Key West. When he died in 1974, Myrtle Reuter moved into the home, and discovered the doll sitting in a chair in the attic. She soon claimed that it moved about her room and even attempted to attack her, so she donated him to the Fort East Martello Museum. Today, Robert is housed in a locked case, although the staff swears it doesn't stop him from getting up to his old tricks. Visitors ask Robert for his permission before they take a photo, but if they neglect to do so and snap a picture anyway, they are said to meet with misfortune. Letters addressed to Robert arrive at the museum frequently, apologizing and begging for his forgiveness to end the bad luck.

Annabelle the doll can't speak but some believe she can write instead. In 1970, Donna received 'Annabelle', a Raggedy Ann doll, as a birthday gift from her mother. After a few days, Donna and her roommate Angie started noticing bizarre things about the new toy; the doll appeared to change its position and move to different rooms. Messages appeared around the house that read, 'Help us' and 'Help Lou', which was a plea to Donna's friend Lou. The handwriting looked like it belonged to a small child and was scribbled in pencil on parchment paper, although the girls didn't keep either in the house. Annabelle's behavior soon turned sinister. Donna discovered blood on the doll's hands, and one night it allegedly attempted to strangle Lou. Paranormal researchers Ed and Lorraine Warren investigated the case and concluded that a demon attached itself to Annabelle, giving the illusion that the doll was alive. They believed that the demon wanted to possess Donna's soul, so they subjected the doll to an exorcism. The Warrens then quarantined Annabelle, who now resides in the Warren Occult Museum in Monroe, Connecticut, in a glass case with a sign saying, 'Warning. Positively Do Not Open'. Annabelle has a cameo in the movie *The Conjuring*, but Hollywood replaced the original rag doll with a gory, grinning doll whose face is marred by scars.

Of course, many toys can actually "speak". To make dolls more realistic, early examples of talking dolls would cry "Mama!" through bellows or a weighted mechanism. Thomas Edison experimented with tin and wax phonographs that sang a verse from "Twinkle, twinkle, little star", but each phonograph had to be recorded individually. Later dolls contained tiny plastic phonograph records that enabled them to speak a repertoire of phrases and sing nursery rhymes. Doll-makers in the mid-to-late twentieth century favored a pull-string mechanism, as used in the Chatty Cathy dolls. Modern toys are implanted with microchips that store numerous phrases, while many newer toys are interactive and contain voice recognition software so that dolls can recognize "Mommy's" voice.

Paintings and mirrors are popular "haunted" objects. The Myrtles Plantation in St Francisville, Louisiana, is said to be one of the most haunted places in America. The mansion boasts a haunted mirror in which it is believed that murder victims are trapped because their handprints appear on the mirror's surface. However, it has been shown that these markings are caused by deterioration and that the "victims" died of natural causes (Stollznow, 2013). Most commonly, haunted paintings are portraits where the sitter's eyes appear to follow you, although this is an optical illusion. Anecdotally, the subjects in some creepy-looking portraits are said to speak, cry, or even age.

This brings to mind *The Picture of Dorian Gray*. In this novel by Oscar Wilde, the young and handsome aristocrat Dorian Gray becomes the subject of a lifelike portrait. He ponders that he'd like to enter into a Faustian-like pact to sell his soul so that the portrait would age, instead of him. This wish is fulfilled, and he goes on to live a life of debauchery. Each immoral act he commits is reflected in the painting as age or disfigurement, while Dorian himself remains youthful and attractive. Perhaps cases of haunted paintings are influenced by this famous tale. They might also be influenced by religious paintings and statues that "weep" tears of blood or oil, and statues that "drink" milk. Alternatively, some people believe that paintings are haunted because they feel fear or sadness when they view the artwork. In these cases, it seems that the artist has simply been successful at evoking these emotions.

Without a musician to guide them, haunted instruments are said to play tunes. Haunted pianos are a particularly popular claim, but these could simply be self-playing pianos. A "haunted" piano in Fort Francisco, La Veta, Colorado, was caused by loose parts and people walking across loose floorboards, much like the "haunted" dress in the Baker Mansion. To attract tourists, many establishments capitalize on their haunted reputations, or simply invent them. A similar phenomenon has taken place online. Until 2012, eBay listed thousands of "haunted" items for sale, including toys, ornaments, and jewelry. Other websites still sell these items. What better way to get rid of those hideous earrings from Aunt Ethel and make some extra cash? Some items are advertised as being cursed, and appeal to the curio collector. Despite the promises, a spirit won't be attached to the items, but elaborate stories are – an astounding number of dolls were formerly owned by little girls who died tragically, while an amazing amount of objects were used in satanic rituals. Not everyone wants an evil Ouija board, so rings, pendants, and amulets are instead charmed or blessed. This trafficking of haunted items has led to other appalling practices. Some ghost hunters have taken to poaching items from cemeteries. These people steal toys, ornaments, urns, and other mementos from graves and collect graveyard dirt to sell online as "haunted".

The Haunted Collector

One reality TV show capitalizes on the haunted objects fad. Syfy's *The Haunted Collector* stars paranormal investigator John Zaffis, the nephew of "demonologist" Ed Warren (who is best known for his involvement in two cases that later became movies, the *Amityville Horror* and *A Haunting in Connecticut*). Home and business owners who believe they are beset by paranormal activity contact Zaffis and his team. They visit the location, interview the owners, and then investigate the premises to identify and remove the "trigger object". By their theory, spirits attach themselves to objects and become the source of the paranormal activity.

The occupants believe they're experiencing paranormal phenomena, and Zaffis invariably finds a stereotypically haunted item on the premises. He then convinces the owner that the object is causing the disturbances and that for the activity to cease, the item must be removed from the location. Zaffis takes the item and adds it to his John Zaffis Museum of the Paranormal in Stanford, Connecticut, that holds over 1,000 "haunted" objects. Tellingly, the "haunted" objects tend to be valuables, including unique collectibles, antiques, family heirlooms, and jewelry. During the writing of this book I received some reliable insider information. I have it on very good authority that the producers hired several magicians to create effects for the show. They also played tricks on the cast members to lead them to believe that objects were haunted.

Claims of haunted objects are only anecdotal, although they do make for good stories. In the end, "haunted" objects seem to only be haunted by stereotypes, memories, and a belief in the paranormal. As psychologist Robert A. Baker (1921–2005) used to say, "There are no haunted places, only haunted people."

References

Aeliani, Claudii. 1864. *De Natura Animalium Libri XVII.*

Applebome, Peter. 2006. "Our towns; talking to animals in their frequency, and sniffling". *New York Times*. 18 January.

Arnold, K. and Zuberbühler, K. 2008. "Meaningful call combinations in a non-human primate". *Current Biology*. Vol. 18, No. 5, pp. R202–03.

Ayling, Stanley. 1972. *George the Third*. London: Collins.

Bondeson, Jan. 1999. *The Feejee Mermaid and Other Essays in Natural and Unnatural History*. United States: Cornell University Press.

Bondeson, Jan. 2011. *Amazing Dogs: A Cabinet of Canine Curiosities*. Ithaca, New York: Cornell University.

Candland, Douglas. K. 1995. *Feral Children and Clever Animals: Reflections on Human Nature*. Oxford University Press.

Christian Prayer Center, https://www.christianprayercenter.com/aboutus.html

Christopher, Milbourne. 1962. *Panorama of Magic*. New York: Dover.

Dosa, David. 2010. *Making Rounds with Oscar: The Extraordinary Gift of an Ordinary Cat*. Hyperion: New York.

Fitzpatrick, Sonya. 1997. *What the Animals Tell Me: Developing Your Innate Tele-pathic Skills to Understand and Communicate with Your Pets.* Hyperion: New York.

Flournoy, Théodore. 1900. *From India to the Planet Mars. A Study of a Case of Somnambulism.* Harper & Brothers.

Freeman, Richard. 2004. "In search of orang-pendek". *Fortean Times.* April.

Fouts, Roger and Mills, Stephen Tukel. 1998. *Next of Kin: My Conversations with Chimpanzees.* William Morrow Paperbacks.

Gagliano, Monica., Mancuso, Stefano., and Robert, Daniel. 2012. "Towards understanding plant bioacoustics". *Trends in Plant Science.* Vol. 17, No. 6. pp. 323–25.

Grant, R. A. and Halliday, T. 2010. "Predicting the unpredictable; evidence of pre-seismic anticipatory behaviour in the common toad". *Journal of Zoology.* Vol. 281, No. 4, pp. 263–71.

Herman, Louis M. 2010. "What Laboratory Research has Told Us about Dolphin Cognition". *International Journal of Comparative Psychology.* 23, 310–30.

Hertel, Lasse. 1978. "An application of speech processing techniques to record-ings of purported bigfoot vocalizations to estimate physical parameters". MA thesis. University of Wyoming.

Icke, David. 2000. *The Biggest Secret. The Book that Will Change the World.* Bridge of Love. Wildwood: MO.

Jansen, Steve. 2011. "Pet sounds. Animal psychic Sonya Fitzpatrick hears voices – the dog and cat kind". *Houston Press.* 11 May.

Jay, Ricky. 1998. *Learned Pigs & Fireproof Women.* Villard Books.

Josiffe, Christopher. 2011. "Gef the talking mongoose. Meet the strangest media sensation of the 1930s!". *Fortean Times.* January issue.

Kollatz, Harry. 2007. *True Richmond Stories: Historic Tales from Virginia's Capital.* The History Press.

Logan, Nancy. 2012. *The Bigfoot Recordings – The Edge of Discovery.* Narrative of Nancy Logan. Available at: http://www.bigfootsounds.com/experts-point-of-view/nancy-logan/ Accessed April 2012.

Liu, Y., Lillywhite, H., and Tu, M. 2010. "Sea snakes anticipate tropical cyclone". *Marine Biology.* Vol. 157, No. 11, pp. 2369–73.

MacLean, Ali. 2012. "My life with Kitler". *Huffington Post.* 4 April.

McGraw, Walter. 1970. "Gef – The talking Mongoose." In *Psychic Pets and Spirit Animals.* Fate Magazine Editorial. Llewellyn Worldwide.

Moore, Victoria. 2007. Grim rea-purr: The Cat that Can Predict Death. http://www.dailymail.co.uk/news/article-470906/Grim-rea-purr-The-cat-predict-death.html

Mossop, Brian. 1996. "The image of translation in science fiction & astronomy". *The Translator.* Vol. 2, No. 1, pp. 1–26.

Nadzan, Danika. 2005. *How to be a Dog Psychic.* Fair Winds.

Nelson, Scott. R. 2011. "Sasquatch phonetic alphabet and transcription standard: North America bigfoot search". Available at: http://www.nabigfootsearch.com/Bigfootlanguage.html Accessed April 2012.

Newbrook, Mark. 2004. "The aliens speak – and write. Examining alien lan-guages". *Magonia.* 85. July issue.

Nickell, Joe. 1995. *Entities, Angels, Spirits, Demons and Other Alien Beings.* Prometheus Books.

Nidle, Sheldan. 2009. *Meet Your First Contact Team*. DVD. Videotaped Live, 8 November.

Okrent, Arika. 2009. *In the Land of Invented Languages. Esperanto Rock Stars, Klingon Poets, Loglan Lovers, and the Mad Dreamers Who Tried to Build A Perfect Language*. Spiegel & Grau.

Oscar Wilde. 2009. *The Picture of Dorian Gray*. World Library.

Pflumm, Michelle. 2011. "Animal instinct helps doctors ferret out disease". *Nature Medicine*. Vol. 17, No. 143.

Pfungst, Oskar. 1911. *Clever Hans (the Horse of Mr. Von Osten.) A Contribution to Experimental Animal and Human Psychology*. Henry Holt and Company.

Price, Harry and Lambert, R. S. 1936. The Haunting of Cashen's Gap. A Modern "Miracle" Investigated, Methuen & Company.

Rainey, H. J., Zuberbühler, K., and Slater, P. J. B. 2004. "Hornbills can distinguish between primate alarm calls". *Proceedings of the Royal Society of London*. Vol. 271, pp. 755–59.

Randi, James. 1997. *An Encyclopedia of Claims, Frauds, and Hoaxes of the Occult and Supernatural*. St. Martin's Griffin.

Richmond Times-Dispatch. 1927. "Lady Wonder 'mind-reading' mare baffles scientists". 18 July.

Rodwell, Mary. 2010. *Awakening: How Extraterrestrial Contact Can Transform Your Life*. New Mind Publishers.

Romanek, Stan and Allan Danelek, J. 2009. *Messages: The World's Most Documented Extraterrestrial Contact Story*. Llewellyn Worldwide.

Sackman, Douglas Cazaux. 2005. *Orange Empire: California and the Fruits of Eden*. University of California Press.

Seyfarth, R. M., Cheney, D. L., and Marler, P. 1980. "Monkey responses to three different alarm calls: Evidence of predator classification and semantic communication." *Science*. Vol. 210, pp. 801–03.

Sheldrake, Rupert. 1994. *Seven Experiments that Could Change the World*. Fourth Estate, London.

Sheldrake, Rupert. 1999. *Dogs that Know When their Owners are Coming Home: And their Unexplained Powers of Animals*. Crown.

Sheldrake, Rupert and Aimée Morgana. 2003. "Testing a language-using parrot for telepathy". *Journal of Scientific Exploration*. Vol. 17, No. 4, pp. 601–16.

Sheldrake, Rupert. 2004. *The Sense of Being Stared at: And Other Unexplained Powers of the Human Mind*. Random House Digital.

Stollznow, Karen. 2009. "The ballad of Jed (and the pet psychic)". *Skeptical Briefs*. Vol. 19, No. 1. March.

Stollznow, Karen. 2010. "The belief with no name". *The Good Word*. CSI web column. 21 December.

Stollznow, Karen. 2013. *Haunting America*. James Randi Educational Foundation.

Wilson, Ben., Batty, Robert., and Dill, Lawrence. 2004. "Pacific and Atlantic herring produce burst pulse sounds". *Proceedings of the Royal Society of Biological Sciences*. Vol. 271, pp. S95–97.

Wiseman, Richard., Matthew, Smith., and Julie, Milton. 1998. "Can animals detect when their owners are returning home? An experimental test of the 'psychic pet' phenomenon". *British Journal of Psychology*. Vol. 89, pp. 453–62.

Wittgenstein, Ludwig. 1973. (1953) *Philosophical Investigations*. Prentice Hall.

Yule, George. 2010. *The Study of Language*. Cambridge University Press.

Part V

Therapeutic Language

Introduction

Some hypnotherapists believe that speaking to your subconscious can cure illness, unblock forgotten memories, and increase the size of your breasts or penis. Body language experts say they can tell if someone is lying to us. Graphologists teach that our handwriting can be used to diagnose and treat disease, and that the way we dot our i's and cross our t's reveals secret information about our personality. Some therapists believe that if we change the way we speak, it will change the way we think and behave. Will listening to Mozart's music make us smarter? Can the sound of our mother's voice be healing? Does the "brown note" really exist? These chapters explore popular language-based therapies and theories, including graphology, hypnosis, NLP, body language, and speech and sound therapies.

21
Graphology

Graphology is the analysis of the shape, style, speed, size, spacing, and slant of handwriting to uncover information about the author. This is more than simply guessing that a guy is a medical doctor because his writing is illegible. Promoters of graphology believe that it is a kind of X-ray to detect information about personality, behavior, and morality, and to reveal the subconscious mind. It is thought that graphologists are able to determine ethnicity, nationality, and age, and to read a subject's past, present, and future. Proponents claim there are many practical applications for graphology, including its use in a court of law, as a human resources tool, and to diagnose and treat disease.

Never put it in writing

For all of its claims of practicality for business and medicine, graphology is most commonly used for love and relationship readings. I once had a consultation with Jasmin, a graphologist who gave me a "romance reading". Jasmin analyzed a sample of my handwriting and one from my boyfriend. After many hours of examination she determined that we were highly compatible. This was fortunate, because both examples were of my own handwriting (Stollznow, 2003).

Graphology first appeared with the 1611 manuscript *Idengraphicus nuncius* by Prospero Aldorisio. In 1622 Italian physician and philosopher Camillo Baldi also wrote a treatise on the topic. After hundreds of years of practice there is still no single theory of graphology but dozens of different schools of thought. From Graphoanalysis to the gestalt method, the interpretation of style differs across approaches. According to the Morettian method, left-slanted handwriting indicates the person's tendency to contradiction. Graphology also has a tendency to contradiction because the trait stroke method says that left-slanted writing indicates reserve and withdrawal. Graphologists say that no two people have the same handwriting, and this is true. However, no two graphologists offer the same analysis of the same piece of handwriting.

Graphology is the handwriting equivalent of palm reading. It is a favorite of women's magazines where graphologists, who are always "the world's foremost expert", analyze the handwriting of celebrities to gossip about their sex lives. Graphologists believe they can tell a lot about your sexuality from the way you write. Books such as *Lovestrokes: Handwriting Analysis for Love, Sex, and Compatibility*, and *Sex, Lies, and Handwriting* examine our writing to reveal if we are sexually inactive, promiscuous, perverse, frustrated, faithful, or prone to infidelity. Claude Santoy (2005) says that "horizontal clubbed strokes" indicate homosexual or bisexual tendencies in men, and that rapists can be identified by their exaggerated lower loops. If a loop on your "g" or "y" is incomplete, your sex life is also incomplete.

With its apparent quick insights, graphology can be a party trick. My friend Lynn attended a baby shower. Arriving late, she was told that a graphologist was about to analyze the guests' handwriting and she needed to provide a quick sample. Lynn hastily scribbled two sentences onto a scrap of paper and added it to a pile. The graphologist soon selected Lynn's paper and read it aloud. "It is July. It is a hot day outside." With barely a pause she announced, "This writer is a very boring person with no imagination." Lynn was insulted. She had simply written two true statements, the first things that came to mind. The graphologist had clearly based her superficial analysis on the subject matter, rather than the style of the handwriting. Graphologists argue that they analyze handwriting style, although they tend to interpret content instead. Another graphologist may have read Lynn's writing as practical, or honest.

I encountered the same problem during my consultation with Jasmin. My handwriting example was a copy of a poem and so I was labeled as "a creative type of person". My "boyfriend's" sample copied a brainteaser and so the author was described as "a problem-solver" (Stollznow, 2003). Using this simplistic approach many guesses can be gleaned from a piece of writing. A resume showing that an applicant has a degree in geology can be interpreted as the candidate's suitability to scientific pursuits. A person who has remained with one employer for five years can be perceived as loyal and dependable. In this way, content, spelling, misspellings, grammar, and vocabulary are all clues to provide seemingly customized information about a client.

Graphology analyses are often metaphorical interpretations of the visual features of handwriting style. For example, big handwriting supposedly indicates a big ego, while writing that is illegible reveals the author is dishonest and has something to hide (Amend and Ruiz, 1980). The language we use to describe personality overlaps with the way we describe handwriting, so graphologists make simplistic connections. Messy writers are messy people. Writing that is spaced out means that the writer needs more space in life. Leaving a narrow left margin indicates that the writer lives in the past, while those who leave a wide left margin show a desire to move forward and leave the past behind (Lowe, 2007). Presumably, the reverse would be true for Arabic, which is written from right to left, but it's not. (Graphology favors the Latin alphabet, and doesn't account for the thousands of other writing systems in existence.) Alternatively, some analyses are simplistic interpretations of literal features. Trait stroke analysis teaches that missing punctuation shows inattentiveness to detail. The Morettian method says that heavy pressure applied to the page indicates physical strength.

Other analyses give very specific interpretations without providing rationale for the connections that are made. Across the different methods, graphologists offer some very arbitrary interpretations. Amend and Ruiz (1980) say that a leftward or rightward tic on a letter signals sexual frustration, but they don't explain why this is so. Without any justification, Lowe (2007) claims that an unclosed letter "b" indicates the writer is naïve and gullible, while downward hooks inside the letters "o" or "a" show they are untrustworthy. Lowe also says that if the cross on a letter "t" is lasso-like, swinging to the left before returning to the right the writer "suffers guilt feelings and mentally returns to the past, trying to figure out why she didn't handle things better. Often found where a violent death (murder or suicide) occurred close to the writer."

Written all over your face

In 1948, psychologist Bertram Forer gave a personality test to his students. What follows is an evaluation from his test.

Some of your aspirations tend to be pretty unrealistic. At times you are extroverted, affable, sociable, while at other times you are introverted, wary and reserved. You have found it unwise to be too frank in revealing yourself to others. You pride yourself on being an independent thinker and do not accept others' opinions without satisfactory proof. You prefer a certain amount of change and variety, and become dissatisfied when hemmed in by restrictions and limitations. At times you have serious doubts as to whether you have made the right decision or done the right thing. Disciplined and controlled on the outside, you tend to be worrisome and insecure on the inside.

(Forer, 1949)

Cheekily, Forer provided each student with the exact same profile, regardless of their responses in the test. This wasn't an individualized analysis tailored to each student, or even an original one. Instead, Forer copied the text from an astrology book. The students were asked to rate the accuracy of their readings on a scale of 0–5. Amazingly, the average rating was 4.26. The tendency to find personal meaning in vague statements that could apply to many people is now known as the Forer effect. (It is also called the Barnum effect, after hoaxer P. T. Barnum for his famous statement, "We've got something for everyone!") This phenomenon underpins astrology, tarot reading, and also graphology.

Like psychics, graphologists also use cold reading techniques, such as generalizations, guesses, and ambiguous statements. Assumptions can be made about the client on the basis of superficial characteristics, such as gender, age, clothing, language, and body language (Rowland, 2008). Details can be fished for during the reading, when the subject provides personal information unwittingly. Basically, a graphologist tells you what you already know about yourself. Much like a psychic's tarot cards, the client's writing is a tool for the graphologist; the gimmick used to tailor the reading to the client. Most importantly, the client makes personal meaning of the reading.

Graphology can be a type of hot reading too, where personal information about the client is already known. Graphologists often ask for revealing details upfront, including the person's education and occupation. Information about the client might be collected surreptitiously before the reading, or these may be facts that are widely known. Politicians are branded as unfaithful on the basis of their signatures, when these scandals are already known publicly. Readings of famous people are often performed posthumously with the benefit of hindsight. Lowe (2007) says that John F. Kennedy's signature shows he was a "visionary", while serial killer Ted Bundy's writing reveals his "aggression". In her book *Sexual Deviations as Seen in Handwriting* (1990), Marie Bernard says that the Marquis de Sade's handwriting indicates that he was a "sadistic" man, while Liberace's handwriting clearly reveals that he was homosexual.

Graphology readings often do no more than reflect biases and personal views. During the 2005 World Economic Forum, two graphologists snapped up a sample of handwriting penned by then UK Prime Minister Tony Blair. They concluded that Blair was "struggling to keep control of a confusing world". He was "not a natural leader", but "an unstable man who is feeling under enormous pressure". The reading seemed to reflect popular opinion about Blair's personality and problems... until it was discovered that the doodles were actually the handiwork of Bill Gates (Duffy and Wilson, 2005).

I'd like that in writing

Some graphologists believe that illness leaves its mark in our handwriting. Christine Strang (2007) says, "Assuming that whatever conditions exist within a body (psychological, physical or pathological) the brain is aware of the dysfunction and transmits it through the writing." In clinical or medical graphology, handwriting is used as a diagnostic tool. Practitioners claim that a wide range of psychological and physiological illnesses can be detected in our handwriting, including heart disease (Strang, 2007), anorexia nervosa (Beaumont, 1971), cancer (Kanfer, 1973), hypochondria (McNichol and Nelson, 1994), and suicide risk (Mouly et al., 2007). Unfortunately, there isn't any evidence to correlate these conditions with handwriting style.

However, it is true that some conditions can affect our handwriting. Hypergraphia is an uncontrollable compulsion to write. This is often accompanied by an obsession with the shape of the written word. People with hypergraphia will write on anything, from scraps of paper and walls to toilet paper, or even their own skin. They often stockpile massive collections of their writings. It is not a condition in and of itself, but episodes of hypergraphia are associated with neurological conditions such as temporal lobe epilepsy, schizophrenia, and frontotemporal dementia. In posthumous diagnoses, it is believed that a number of famous authors displayed hypergraphia, including Fyodor Dostoevsky and Edgar Allen Poe. Lewis Carroll, the author of *Alice in Wonderland*, most likely had temporal lobe epilepsy and is believed to have shown signs of hypergraphia. Carroll wrote over 98,721 letters during his lifetime. He often used highly elaborate scripts or drew his words as pictures, and he wrote almost exclusively with purple ink (Flaherty, 2004).

Huntington's disease can also affect a person's handwriting. Some patients with this illness exhibit signs of macrographia (Phillips et al., 2004). The size of their writing increases and often becomes irregular and inconsistent. This is caused by a breakdown in the cells of the basal ganglia, which relay sensory feedback about movement. Huntington's disease causes involuntary movements and difficulty in maintaining voluntary movement, so patients can't control the size and shape of their writing.

As young girls, the Brontë sisters Charlotte and Emily played a game in which they wrote in handwriting tiny enough to be read by a toy soldier. Their writing was so small that a magnifying glass had to be used to read it. As adults and novelists, they continued their small writing style. In a condition called micrographia, small writing is a symptom, not a style. This can be a sign of Parkinson's disease and it can appear years before other symptoms are revealed (Contreras-Vidal et al., 2002). Over time, the affected person's writing becomes progressively smaller and more scrawled. To gauge the patient's progress and evaluate the right medication and dosage, doctors perform a test where a digital pad is used to capture the speed and smoothness of motion as a patient writes.

As we can see, some conditions are actually reflected in handwriting, although not those identified by graphologists. Instead, these are neurological disorders, and specifically those that affect muscle co-ordination and therefore movement. These aren't normal stylistic traits; they are observable changes that represent the deterioration of someone's handwriting. This is about how a person's handwriting is affected by sickness, not the way they normally slant their writing or draw their "o's".

Leave no marks

Some believe that graphology isn't only about reading personality but it can also be used to change personality. Graphotherapy teaches that handwriting is "brain writing"; that the brain is responsible for character and handwriting is an expression of our character. Therefore, alter your handwriting and you can alter your personality. Books like *Change Your Handwriting, Change Your Life* (Rogers, 1995) claim that if people change their handwriting style, they can change themselves. Among other things, graphotherapy is said to help people to break their bad behaviors, improve their sex lives, and realize their potential.

These changes are achieved through daily handwriting exercises, similar to those taught in calligraphy classes. These exercises are believed to gradually alter the person's handwriting style. For example, writing with a left slant indicates that the writer is introverted, while a right slant shows friendliness and openness. By their theory, slowly leaning your writing more to the right can help timid people overcome their shyness. Graphotherapists think that handwriting reveals the subconscious mind, so relearning how to write reprograms the subconscious mind.

They say that these ideas are grounded in the theory of neuroplasticity. However, brain plasticity theories are concerned with treating brain damage and learning difficulties through rehabilitation, not retraining writing style to influence personality.

Graphotherapists further claim that if people change their handwriting style using special exercises, they can cure themselves of disease. Some praise it as a cure-all for many unrelated conditions, including allergies, arthritis, cancer, and even baldness! They claim that studies have demonstrated that graphotherapy can treat a range of problems, including drug addictions and borderline personality disorder (de Sainte Columbe, 1972). Despite the hype, there is no evidence to suggest that graphotherapy can successfully cure any condition.

The idea that you can influence your life by changing your handwriting style is similar to a practice in numerology. "Name analysts" advise that people alter the spelling of their names to attract good luck. This may involve a simple modification, most often "i" or "e" is changed to "y", for example, "Karen" becomes "Karyn". For a change of destiny more drastic measures are required, and a completely new name may be recommended. Name changes are especially popular in India, where many Bollywood actors choose to adopt new names or respellings, to which they attribute their star status. Clearly, Suniel Shetty wouldn't have had as much success as "Sunil Shetty", and a change of name was all it took for bus conductor Sivaji Rao to became celebrity Rajini Kanth.

Write or wrong?

Graphology is often confused with questioned document analysis. This discipline isn't about predicating personality; it is the forensic study of handwriting to determine document authenticity. It involves the comparative analysis of handwriting examples and is used in legal disputes to determine if a sample is genuine or counterfeit. Specialists compare an authentic sample with a signature on a check or a handwritten will. They don't rely on the visual inspection of handwriting to determine authorship, but instead they use video comparators, electrostatic detectors, and computer-based image-enhancement programs.

It is also believed that graphology is commonly used in the courtroom. Like psychic detectives who say they've assisted the police with homicide cases, some graphologists claim they've provided evidence as expert witnesses in court. It is true that graphological analyses have been offered as testimony, especially personality assessments and reports of a defendant's physical and mental condition. However, there is not a single case where graphology testimony has been admitted in evidence (Thomas, 2002). Unlike the testimony of questioned document examiners, the graphologists' testimony is not recognized as admissible by the courts. In every historical case in the United States, the courts have ruled that graphology analyses don't produce evidence that is scientifically valid, reliable, and relevant.

Numerous studies and investigations have shown that graphology is more wrong than right (or write). No clear correlation has been found between handwriting behavior and basic personality patterns. Graphologists perform no better than chance in studies where the handwriting samples don't contain content that can be used to make guesses about personality (Beyerstein, 1992). Claims that graphology can determine age, race, and nationality also have no validity, and lend themselves to prejudice. Studies have shown that graphology can determine gender with some accuracy, but even non-graphologists can correctly identify the gender of a writer about 70 per cent of the time (Furnham, 1991).

Computers have made handwriting redundant in many environments, and especially cursive writing. Despite this progress, graphology is still an employment-profiling tool used by thousands of companies in the United States, the United Kingdom, and Europe. This is not to test that the candidate has good penmanship, but to make recruitment decisions, and usually from shortlisted candidates. Selecting the right person for the job becomes a self-fulfilling prophecy because they have already narrowed down their choices to the best people. Employment decisions made on the basis of graphology analyses are discriminatory. However, proponents argue it is non-discriminatory because the practice doesn't judge people on the basis of gender, ethnicity, age, or religion. However, graphology discriminates against people on the basis of a disproven theory.

Using graphology for anything other than entertainment can be a costly mistake. *No One Would Listen* tells the tale of the Bernie Madoff investment scandal. The book shares an interesting anecdote about graphology. Access International, Madoff's largest single client, never performed due diligence before they conducted business with him. They felt this was unnecessary, as they had submitted samples of Madoff's handwriting to a graphologist who had vouched for his honesty and legitimacy (Markopolos, 2011). As we know, Madoff was operating a Ponzi scheme that is now considered to be the largest financial fraud in US history.

22
Speech and Sound Therapies

Pavarotti singing "Nessun Dorma" from Puccini's *Turandot* can reduce people to tears, but can sounds both cure and kill? Can hearing problems be behind depression, dyslexia, and autism? Is there a "brown note" that can cause people to lose control of their bowels? This chapter looks at sounds that are believed to make us smarter, sounds that are soothing, and sounds that are used to inflict suffering.

Voice therapy

Paul Newham believes that good health requires not only a sensible diet and exercise, but also singing. *The Signing Cure* teaches voice movement therapy, a series of exercises based on "vocal healing traditions" from indigenous cultures. Newham (1993) claims the voice is a powerful healing instrument that can be used to tame anger, grief, shame, and other negative emotions.

Another method uses the voice in conjunction with music, drums, quartz crystal bowls, and tuning forks, to return our voices to their "healthy state of resonance".

> We arrive on this planet with everything that we need to heal ourselves, and when we came our voices were rich with all the necessary frequencies to maintain us in a healthy state of resonance. Due to the conditioning of childhood and the suppression of our true thoughts and feelings and the accompanying sounds that go with them, by the time we arrive at adulthood our speaking voice no longer contains the same frequencies it did as a child. Our voice will always reflect our current mental and emotional states of being. When a person feels alive, healthy, happy and abundant, their voice sounds much different than if they are depressed, unhappy, angry or afraid.

> You may notice a difference in your own voice when speaking your truth compared to when you are not, it feels different in your body as well, and from an energetic standpoint the cells of your body are not getting the frequencies they need to stay healthy.
>
> (http://www.cosmicsoundmystery.com/)

Some practitioners claim that voice therapy can cure physiological conditions too. One "certified therapist" in voice healing conducts sessions of singing to reduce stress, ease pain, and create a "cellular level of healing".

> This powerful healing technique which dates back to ancient civilizations and new scientific researches, will enable you to use the power of your voice vibration to improve your health and life. This course is for everybody; the human voice is a very powerful tool. It was not only created for speaking or singing, but also to heal and help each one of us (having a beautiful voice is not relevant) to achieve a state of greater self awareness. Once we get to know our voices with the help of intensive training we will be able to cure ourselves from many disturbing diseases and multiple pains caused by stress, such as insomnia, migraine, abdominal pain, heart problems, sinusitis, cold flu, and more.

There are many names for therapies that claim to harness the healing powers of our voices, including voice therapy, bioacoustics, sound therapy, sound work, and sound medicine. Some practitioners in this field call themselves speech, sound, or voice therapists, but it is not to be confused with speech or language therapy/pathology. Speech therapists work with people who have a wide range of communication and throat-related problems, including stuttering, swallowing disorders, and language difficulties due to neurological conditions or cancer. These therapists work in conjunction with other healthcare professionals, including audiologists and occupational therapists. Nor are they to be confused with vocal coaches, who teach singing techniques and instruct singers and professional speakers how to develop and care for their voices.

We can do some pretty amazing things with our voices. The Discovery Channel TV series *Mythbusters* proved that with the right frequency and volume it is possible to shatter glass with the human voice. However, no note can cure the common cold. It seems that singing may have value but these are personal and subjective benefits. There is no magical power in the words or music; the effects come from inside of us.

The Mozart effect

Like other holistic therapies such as naturopathy, sound therapists claim that we all have a natural healthy state to which we can return via the body's innate ability to heal itself. To get back to this inherent state of health, Alfred Tomatis (1920–2001) experimented with the most seminal of sounds: our mother's voice. Tomatis believed that various conditions are caused when we don't listen properly to our mother in the womb. His theory was that hearing disorders are developed before birth, and are the root causes of many illnesses, including autism, dyslexia, schizophrenia, and depression (Tomatis, 1991, Gilmore, 1999). Tomatis invented a gadget called the "electronic ear" that could simulate the sound of our mother's voice as heard in the womb.

His audio-psycho-phonology method, also known as the Tomatis method, explored the use of music for healing purposes, and he tested his theory with Gregorian chants and Mozart's music. To this day, it is advertised that his listening techniques can treat learning difficulties, help to learn second languages, develop better communication skills, and improve creativity. The approach has had popular acclaim with musicians and actors who believe it helps develop their hearing, speaking, and singing skills. However, these methods and devices haven't been proven in scientific studies. Tomatis had a convenient excuse for this; he argued that the benefits of his methods can't be measured.

By now, the idea of using Mozart's music for therapy might be sounding familiar to you. Tomatis coined the phrase "the Mozart effect" to describe the healing powers of listening to Mozart's music. Author Don Campbell (1997) took this theory further. Campbell claims that prayer and humming healed a blood clot in his brain, and that music can cure anxiety, depression, chronic pain, and even cancer. Then he claimed it can make you smarter. A study by Rauscher et al. (1993) exposed subjects to the first ten minutes of Mozart's Sonata for Two Pianos in D Major. They discovered that this exposure led to a "temporary enhancement of spatial-temporal reasoning". Campbell exaggerated these results, making the claim that Mozart's music boosts intelligence.

In *The Mozart Effect for Children* (2000) he says that exposing children to classical music increases brain development. Campbell's theory was popularized before it could be (dis)proven. The mere claim led then governor of Georgia Zell Miller to issue the parents of newborn children with a CD of classical music (Sack, 1998). A law was passed in Florida requiring that classical music be played daily in state-funded childcare and educational programs. The National Academy of Recording Arts and

Sciences Foundation gave CDs of classical music to hospitals across the country. And in an effort to produce more milk, a dairy farmer in Spain played Mozart during milking time, in what is known affectionately as the Moozart effect (Lee, 2007).

However, Campbell's claims are sales pitches, not science. Numerous attempts to replicate the original results have been unsuccessful, although studies have shown conclusively that listening to Mozart does not enhance intelligence (McKelvie and Low, 2010). (Rauscher has now moved on to studying the effects of Mozart on rats.) In addition, there is no evidence to support Campbell's claims that his therapy treats autism, dyslexia, and attention-deficit hyperactivity disorder. Much like the "we only use 10% of our brains" myth, the belief that "listening to Mozart makes you smarter" outlives its debunking.

Nevertheless, it has spawned an industry. Companies have created mind-expanding music based on this theory. This music uses binaural beats, that is, a different tone is played into each ear. The psychedelic-sounding music will supposedly help boost memory, intelligence, and problem-solving skills. The makers of these audio tracks also claim it can help people to stop smoking and lose weight, and even treat erectile dysfunction. Some say the music can simulate the effects of illicit drugs, or induce out-of-body experiences, lucid dreaming, astral projection, and telepathy. There is some evidence that binaural beats may reduce anxiety (Carter, 2008), but it's hardly mind-expanding news that music can be relaxing. And taste in music is personal and one person's Mozart is another person's Metallica.

Pouring cold water on a theory

According to Masaru Emoto, water likes classical music too. Emoto (2004) believes that the molecular structure of water can be changed by human thoughts, feelings, and words. He freezes samples of water that have been exposed to music and words. Through photography, he shows that positive sounds, prayers, and words like "love", produce beautiful crystal formations. Negative language such as, "You make me sick" creates unattractive, malformed crystals. However, the meanings of words are arbitrary, therefore "love" is not inherently good, and "hate" is not inherently bad, so his followers says that it is the intention that is projected onto the word or song. Water also reveals that classical music is good, while heavy metal music is bad. (In contrast to the *Mythbuster*'s findings that plants like death metal music!) By exposing water to the names of religious and political figures Emoto's method supposedly reveals whether these people are good or bad. Emoto has not subjected his work to testing, and his results seem to be influenced by his own opinions and the connotations of the words or the mood of the music.

Safe and sound

Music isn't always used to soothe the savage beast. Sometimes, it's used as a torture tactic instead. There was a strange soundtrack to the Waco siege of David Koresh and his disciples in 1993. When negotiations failed, the FBI surrounded the Branch Davidian ranch and blasted high-decibel music into the compound to subdue the occupants. The eclectic playlist included Tibetan chants, Christmas carols, bugle calls, and Nancy Sinatra's "These Boots Are Made for Walkin" (Wright, 1995). Koresh fancied himself a rock star, and he retaliated by playing tapes of his own compositions, until the electricity was cut off.

Soldiers also unleashed this rock "n" roll warfare during Operation Just Cause, the US invasion of Panama in 1989 to depose dictator Manuel Noriega. A cacophony of Styx, Judas Priest, Black Sabbath, and a version of "God Bless the USA" was blasted into the papal diplomatic mission, where Noriega was seeking refuge. The Vatican soon put an end to the concert. Closer to home, classical music is pumped into the PA systems of some shopping malls in an attempt to lower crime and deter teenagers from loitering (because Beethoven isn't cool).

Sometimes earplugs aren't enough. Sonic weapons are coming out of science fiction and into use for defense and law enforcement. Instruments such as long-range acoustic devices (LRAD) are used as hailing devices and in crowd-control efforts. A LRAD was even used to deter a group of pirates off the coast of Somalia. High-power sound waves can be used to incapacitate a victim, by causing disorientation, discomfort, and nausea (Miller, 2004). However, sound affects people differently, adding an element of uncontrollability to the use of acoustic weapons.

Ironically, the very technology used to harm might be used to heal. Acoustic lenses are used in defense systems and damage detection in materials, but are also used in biomedical imaging and surgery. Researchers at the California Institute of Technology have created acoustic pulses known as "sound bullets". These could eventually be used to destroy cancerous cells as a kind of noninvasive scalpel that won't damage surrounding tissue (Spadoni and Daraio, 2010). The device is based on the old toy Newton's cradle, and creates concentrated sound waves from ball bearings. In experimental research, sound waves are being used to treat prostate cancer. In one study high intensity focused ultrasound is used to kill cancerous cells and the results are promising. The cancers were treated successfully, with fewer side effects than chemotherapy (Ahmed et al., 2003). Lithotripsy is a related medical procedure that has been around for many years now. This technique uses high-energy shock waves to shatter stones in the kidneys and bladder.

Brownout

This talk of bodily responses to sound may have some of you thinking of the fabled "brown note", also known as the "disco dump". This is the belief that there is an infrasonic frequency that causes "involuntary gastrointestinal motility", that is, a loss of bowel control. The brown note is said to occur between 5 and 20 Hz, although 20 Hz is the lowest frequency that can be heard by most human ears. These low frequency sounds are felt in the body, rather than heard. The TV show *Mythbusters* investigated this claim. A wide range of sub-audible sounds played at high decibel levels were tested on host Adam Savage, but he didn't lose control of his bowels. However, the other members of the team experienced some anxiety and shortness of breath while subjected to the infrasonic frequencies. Just like the urban legends that the voice can heal and that music can make you smarter, it seems that the "brown note" is just a load of hot air.

23
Neurolinguistic Programming

I once graded an assignment for a class in Applied Linguistics. The students had many research topics from which to choose, including NLP. Strangely, one student's essay spoke of "achieving peak performance" and "maximizing one's potential". The paper was brimming with quotes from motivational messiah Anthony Robbins, and discussed methods with registered trademarks instead of references. The student had confused natural language processing with neurolinguistic programming.

It seems that neurolinguistic programming is the better known kind of "NLP". However, it still suffers from an identity crisis. In a bookstore I was directed to multiple categories, "Try New Age ... or Self-Improvement ... or Business ... or Medicine ... or Psychology." Despite the technical-sounding name, NLP has little to do with neuroscience, linguistics, computer science, or other academic fields. These disciplines don't promise to help you quit smoking or lose weight.

NLP was developed in the 1970s by psychology student John Grinder and Richard Bandler, a professor of Linguistics at the University of California, Santa Cruz. The pair created NLP "as a means to investigate and replicate extreme human excellence" (Grinder, 2014). But what does that mean? According to one source:

> NLP is a behavioral technology, which simply means that it is a set of guiding principles, attitudes, and techniques about real-life behavior, and not a removed, scientific theorem. It allows you to change, adopt or eliminate behaviors, as you desire, and gives you the ability to choose your mental, emotional, and physical states of well-being.
>
> (nlp.com)

233

Still confused? Another source describes NLP variously as, "the art of science and communication", "everyday psychology", "commonsense", "a manual for your brain", "the route to get the results you want in all areas of your life", and "the toolkit for personal and organizational change" (Ready and Burton, 2004). If these infomercial-like explanations don't enlighten you, NLP is a controversial and eclectic set of methods for counseling, hypnosis, and communication analysis.

Not-so-linguistic

NLP is based loosely on a broad range of theories and methods. But it has very little to do with linguistics. As Newbrook (2008) says, "Linguistics lecturers have had to tell many new or prospective undergraduates that they will not be studying NLP!" Yet, NLP claims to be heavily influenced by seminal linguist Noam Chomsky. In particular, NLP is said to be inspired by Chomsky's theory of transformational grammar, and his concept of deep structure and surface structure in language (Chomsky, 1965). However, this is intended as theory, not therapy. Chomsky's ideas are theoretical constructs and describe how people speak, they don't tell people how they should speak. Furthermore, Chomsky has either abandoned or modified his ideas since the 1960s. But NLP proponents haven't kept up with modern theory. Other than borrowed terminology, NLP doesn't bear a resemblance to any of Chomsky's theories or philosophies. Moreover, Chomsky doesn't patent his theories.

As noted by Mark Newbrook (2008), NLP more closely resembles the theories of philosopher Alfred Korzybski and linguist Samuel Ichiye Hayakawa. These researchers promoted the idea that thought and behavior are determined by language usage. Therefore, modifying usage can lead to thought and behavioral change. NLP is also influenced by Korzybski's general semantics, a methodology that claims to change behavior through language. (Just like the confusion between neurolinguistic programming and natural language processing, general semantics is not related to semantics, a branch of linguistics that studies meaning.)

Inspired by Korzybski, D. David Bourland (1991) came up with the idea of the E-Prime, short for English Prime. This is a way of speaking that avoids all forms of the copula, that is, the verb "to be", such as the words "am", "is", and "was". This is not like nonstandard English "Where you at?". Instead, E-Prime omits the verb in favor of providing more detailed language. For example, "I am tired" becomes "I need to sleep". Bourland claims that deleting the verb eliminates errors and misconceptions in logic, and allows for speech that is clearer and more precise. However, this is not really the case. My favorite example of using E-Prime is: "Clapton is God" becomes "Eric's fan club pronounced that Clapton has some of the characteristics of God" (Scorpio, 2011).

The idea that thought and behavior are linked to language dates back to nineteenth-century anthropology. Edward Sapir and his student Benjamin Lee Whorf created the principle of linguistic relativity that is best known as the Sapir-Whorf hypothesis. This theory says that language shapes thought and behavior. They believed that different languages promote different world views and therefore lead to different behavior. For example, Hopi speakers perceive clouds as living creatures because "cloud" is an animate noun in their language. Also, Hopi treats time as a single process rather than a sequence, so there is no means of counting periods of time. Conversely, Hopi expresses physics more easily than English, so speakers more readily grasp some principles of modern physics.

As we have seen, NLP claims Chomsky in its pedigree. Ironically, Chomsky's theories often contrast with the Sapir-Whorf hypothesis. Other academics argue that the reverse can be true, that thought and behavior also influence language (Sampson, 1980). Language change is slow and older language may have generated patterns of thought that are no longer current (Newbrook, 2008). For example, "moon" has female gender in French, and "sun" has male gender, while the reverse is the case in German. Of course, French people don't see the sun as "male" today, and German people don't see the sun as "female".

Psychotherapy

NLP is more about psychotherapy than linguistics. It began when Bandler and Grinder learned of the effectiveness of a few famous psychotherapists, and reasoned that observing these therapists at work should identify patterns of practice that could be imitated. This theory expanded to observing and imitating successful people from a variety of backgrounds. This formula became known as "modeling". As O'Connor and Seymour (1993) explain, "NLP is the art and science of excellence, derived from studying how top people in different fields obtain their outstanding results. These communications can be learned by anyone to improve their effectiveness both personally and professionally."

Bandler and Grinder began modeling their hypotheses on research conducted by psychotherapist Virginia Satir, hypnotherapist Milton Erickson, psychiatrist Fritz Perls, and psychologist Paul Watzlawick.

However, with the exception of Satir et al. (1976), they didn't collaborate with these people. Instead, they studied transcripts and videos of their psychotherapy sessions. Therefore, NLP is based on, but not necessarily representative of the research of these therapists.

The NLP umbrella includes the original meta model (modeled after Perls' gestalt therapy) and the Milton model (modeled after Ericksonian psychotherapy). NLP now includes a wide range of (often conflicting) techniques, tools, slogans, and schools of thought. One of their main mottos is, "the map is not the territory" (Lankton, 1980). This is the idea that people think and behave according to their individual representation of the world ("the map"), and not according to the world itself (the "territory"). These maps are determined by our preferred representational system, as learned through our visual, kinesthetic, auditory, olfactory, and gustatory senses (Grinder and Bandler, 1979). Their belief is that we naturally favor one of these senses, and often have difficulty understanding people who favor other modes. For example, auditory people complain that visual people don't listen. Mismatches can result in communication breakdowns between patient and doctor, student and teacher, and husband and wife. The NLP therapist must understand the client's unique "map", and assist them in navigating the "territory".

In practice, NLP involves counseling sessions, hypnotherapy, or self-hypnosis. A major component of NLP involves analyzing the way people speak and recommending guidelines for "improved" communication. One book says, "When you adopt the 'but' word, people will remember what you said afterwards. With the 'and' word, people remember what you said before and after" (Ready and Burton, 2004). NLP also teaches body language theory and that mirroring a person's verbal and non-verbal behavior (e.g., speech, blinking, and breathing) fosters trust and establishes rapport.

NLPs

Today, there is no single NLP. Different approaches are used by different people, and a new client wouldn't know if their NLP change consultant, coach, master trainer, or master practitioner is a Bandler acolyte or a proponent of time-line therapy. Nor is there uniformity in teaching NLP. It is not taught at college (although advocates can be found among university faculty). Instead, NLP is taught at seminars, workshops, and events where participants engage in fire-walking to demonstrate the power of mind over matter (and the principles behind the convection oven). These are the kinds of courses where the teachers push their products, to ensure that if you don't change your life, at least you'll change your bank balance. NLP is the Amway of the mind.

NLP doesn't appear in psychology textbooks. It has made no impact on mainstream academia (Heap, 2008). If their theories were correct, Bandler and Grinder would have made some remarkable discoveries that would have major implications for human psychology. Like many of the theories in this book they skipped a jump in the scientific process: empirical evaluation. As Bandler and Grinder (1979) say about their theory on eye movements:

> As far as I can tell, there is no research to substantiate the idea that there is eyedness. You won't find any research that is going to hold up. Even if there were, I still don't know how it would be relevant to the process of interpersonal communication, so to me it's not a very interesting question.

However, this hasn't stopped them linking themselves to science in name, terminology, and alleged lineage. Even still, NLP enjoys recognition from a number of professions, including psychotherapists and human resources specialists. NLP training is provided to major companies including Hewlett-Packard, IBM, and McDonald's, to public institutions such as NASA, the US Army, US Olympic teams, and in countless secondary schools (Tosey and Mathison, 2010).

Not much is new in the New Age since Dale Carnegie's (1937) *How to Win Friends and Influence People*. NLP is a yet another self-help cult. In the language equivalent of "boosting the immune system" and "providing a sense of well-being", NLP makes many vague claims that it will promote personal growth, and help people to think and communicate more effectively. Ironically, Bandler and Grinder feuded in the 1980s over trademark and theory disputes. None of their countless NLP models, pillars, and principles helped these founders to resolve their personal and professional conflicts.

A frog in your throat

NLP also claims to have therapeutic benefits. Bandler and Grinder's infamous *Frogs into Princes* and other books boast that NLP is a cure-all that treats a broad range of physical and mental conditions, phobias, and learning difficulties, including epilepsy and dyslexia (Grinder and Connirae, 1981). It also promises to cure schizophrenia, depression, and post traumatic stress disorder, and dismisses psychiatric illnesses as psychosomatic.

NLP guarantees to treat serious and chronic conditions rapidly, and often in a single session. It claims to cure phobias in as little as five minutes of therapy: "I've seen a therapist take away a phobia and give it back nine times in a single session without the faintest idea what she was doing" (Bandler and Grinder, 1979). They say the treatment can be so dramatic that it induces amnesia, erasing the memory of bad habits and negative experiences: "Thus, after a session of therapy, smokers may deny that they smoked before, even when their family and friends insist otherwise, and they are unable to account for such evidence as nicotine stains" (Grinder and Bandler, 1981). They also maintain that a single session of NLP can eliminate various eyesight problems, such as myopia, and even cure a common cold. NLP advertisements lure desperate clients with promises that therapists can cure headaches, back pain, snoring, stuttering, blushing, and even cancer.

However, NLP treatments are often simplistic. For example, a remedy for backache is to reinterpret the sensation and description of the pain, "If this is a dull ache, can you change the feeling to a tingle?" (Ready and Burton, 2004). If NLP fails to cure what ails you, they deflect the lack of success to the client. In one case, an NLP practitioner attempted to treat a client with terminal cancer, and attributed the failure of the treatment to the client's lack of desire to heal and determination to succumb to the illness (Stollznow, 2002). This client responsibility is also used to rationalize social problems. NLP believes that poverty is a state of mind,

> Your unconscious can't process negatives. It interprets everything you think as a positive thought. So if you think, "I don't want to be poor", your conscious mind focuses on the "poor" and because it doesn't do negatives, the thought becomes "I want to be poor". Being poor then becomes the goal in your unconscious mind.
>
> (Ready and Burton, 2004)

The law of attraction movement has since adopted this philosophy.

NLP is also full of contradictions as another principle is, "there is no failure, only feedback". Therefore, if one NLP method doesn't produce the desired results, the client is urged to simply "try something else" because "you create your own reality". But the many methods are perceived as NLP's strength, not a weakness, and as choice, not inconsistency. They don't think it necessary to prove the efficacy of NLP because, in their belief, something will work. NLP helps those who help themselves, if it helps at all.

The results are in

NLP works; if we believe the abundance of anecdotal evidence and testimonials, but not if we read the scientific literature. Michael Heap examined 63 studies into NLP and found that its theories do not stand up to scrutiny (1988). Sharpley (1984) reviewed 15 NLP studies and determined that "there are no data reported to date to show that NLP can help clients change". In a follow-up synthesis of 44 studies, Sharpley (1987) found that 61.4 per cent of studies showed no support of the claims of NLP. The author concluded:

> There are conclusive data from research on NLP, and the conclusion is that the principles and procedures suggested by NLP have failed to be supported by those data... Certainly research data do not support the rather extreme claims that proponents of NLP have made as to the validity of its principles or the novelty of its procedures.

Nothing has changed since 1987. Witkowski (2011) reviewed a whopping 401 published papers on NLP, showing that only 9.5 per cent of studies support the theories and effectiveness of NLP techniques. Nineteen per cent were partially supportive, while the majority (71.5 per cent) of studies were non-supportive. Witkowski concludes, "The present review suggests that enough evidence has been collected to announce a final verdict now: NLP is ineffective both as a model explaining human cognition and communication, and as a set of techniques of influence and persuasion." For all of its fairytale promises to turn "frogs into princes", after the kiss of NLP, the frogs remain frogs.

24
Hypnosis

> Imagine now that you're on a lovely, secluded stretch of beach, there's no one around for miles and it's a beautiful warm summer's day. You lie down on the soft white sand, and you can hear the sound of the water gently lapping up to the shore; the sky is a lovely shade of blue and there's not a cloud in sight. The sunlight sparkles on the beautiful deep blue sea and everything is so tranquil, so peaceful, so restful. And imagine that as you lie there on the soft white sand, listening to the waves, and feeling the sun on your body, that you undo your top and let the sun to your body. And as you lie there you can feel the warmth of the sun bathing your body, and imagine the heat from the sun warming your breast area, making your breasts warm and tingling.
>
> (http://www.hypnoticworld.co.uk/scripts/
> breast_enlargement.html)

No, this isn't a reader story from Penthouse Forum. This is a hypnosis script for breast enlargement. Without breast augmentation surgery or a padded bra, merely reading, hearing, or thinking these words is believed to have the power to effect genuine and permanent breast enlargement.

Hypnotherapist Wendi Friesen claims her system of hypnosis can increase a woman's chest size by up to four inches and 1–2 cup sizes in just 8–12 weeks (Friesen, 2011). Her technique involves face-to-face sessions of hypnosis, or listening to her pre-recorded sessions in which she describes scenarios that suggest her client's breasts are gradually growing in size. Friesen offers various theories about how this works. She is enabling the connection between mind and body, reprogramming cells, stimulating the hypothalamus, or increasing the blood flow to the breasts. The increase in breast size may be created by the power of subconscious desires, or perhaps the patient has overcome sexual issues from the past. Only your mind stands between you and bigger breasts.

Stage hypnotist David Knight (2014) also claims that women can increase the size and firmness of their breasts through mind power. He guarantees that his clients will enlarge their bust by up to two cup sizes by undergoing hypnosis with him. He explains that a woman's breasts "go through a period during puberty in which they change dramatically. The same process can be reinstated at any time in a woman's life by using hypnosis." But hypnosis isn't only for the ladies. Various therapists say this same method can be used to increase penis size and cure baldness.

Keeping abreast of things

Friesen, Knight, and other therapists only offer testimonials as proof that hypnosis induces breast growth. A small number of studies (Willard, 1977, Staib and Logan, 1977, Williams, 1974) support the claim, but they were flawed by self-reporting and a lack of controls for factors such as diet and exercise, and the experiments were not blind. The studies weren't conclusive, but instead called for further studies, "With future development, this procedure could become a desirable alternative to surgical methods of breast augmentation" (Staib and Logan, 1977). The research is also old. Many decades later, there have been no findings that support the claims, and hypnosis is still not a viable alternative to breast augmentation surgery. Changes in breast size are physiological and linked to fluctuating hormones, weight, and body fat.

In effect, the claim is that language and thought can effect physiological change. Willpower, hypnotic suggestion, visualization, and persuasive language will not affect breast or penis size. As a general rule of thumb, hypnotherapy may be able to assist with some psychological conditions, but not physiological states. Hypnosis scripts for increasing breast and penis size are simply New Age magical spells.

You are (not) under my control

Historically, hypnotism is a part of many rituals and ceremonies across cultures, including the Australian Aboriginal, Native American, and African. Trance states often involve singing, chanting, invocation, and storytelling for religious, social, and healing purposes. As a therapy, hypnosis dates back to the eighteenth century. Franz Mesmer (1734–1815) was an Austrian physician who practiced an early form of hypnotherapy, but his methods were completely different to modern hypnosis. Mesmer believed in the "animal magnetism" of animate objects, and used magnets to unblock invisible fluids in his patient's body. Once the "fluid" returned to a normal flow, the patient was then miraculously cured. Mesmer is most famous for providing the etymology for the word "mesmerize".

Milton Erickson (1901–80) was another pioneering psychotherapist whose techniques are more familiar to modern readers. Ericksonian hypnotherapy included the use of indirect suggestions over directives, for example, "You can lose weight" instead of "You will lose weight". Erickson also used therapeutic metaphor, which involved telling symbolic stories to influence patients to achieve their goals. He was also known for some unconventional techniques, such as encouraging overweight patients to gain more weight as a kind of reverse psychology. During "double binds", he issued conflicting orders to emotionally distress a subject into submission. He is most famous for using shock inductions, especially his handshake inductions. Erickson would interrupt a handshake by grabbing or pulling a subject's wrist to confuse, surprise, and overload them into a more suggestible state.

Forms of hypnosis appear in many unexpected areas. Shock and persuasion tactics are used by charismatic leaders during motivational exercises, evangelism, faith healing, speaking in tongues, and other spiritual, New Age, and religious rituals. As an empowerment exercise, motivational guru Anthony Robbins uses suggestion and invokes his authority to encourage his followers to walk across a bed of hot coals. Reverend Bob Larson presents fire-and-brimstone sermons and theatrical exorcisms of his "possessed" congregation. Temes (2004) explains that "a subject is bombarded with bewildering terms and instructions, it rattles clients so much that they let down their guard and go with the flow".

You're getting very sleepy...

There are lots of myths and misconceptions about hypnosis that overrate and distort its true capabilities. We tend to think of the stereotypes, like the hypnotist with the compelling voice who swings a pocket watch over a patient and says "Look into my eyes, you are getting very sleepy...". Alternatively, we think of entertainers who hypnotize subjects to cluck like chickens or think they're strippers. But hypnosis is not magic. The therapist can't control the mind of the patient into losing self-control or becoming a zombie. That is the realm of stage hypnosis, a murky mix of role-playing, amateur acting, and plants in the audience.

Hypnosis is also touted as a panacea. It is believed to be a cure-all for anxiety, depression, obesity, and more. There is evidence that it can help a patient help themselves to reduce phobias and manage pain. However, there are many nonclinical therapists who use modalities of varying legitimacy, and make outlandish claims. Others claim it can cure cancer, recall repressed memories, and allow us to revisit our past lives and preview our future lives.

Look into my mesmerize

Clinical hypnosis is very different. It is a series of therapeutic techniques using verbal suggestion, self-hypnosis, and visualization to benefit a variety of conditions. Since 1958, clinical hypnosis has been accepted as an adjunct therapy by the American Medical Association, and the American Psychiatric Association (APA). It is recognized in several areas of healthcare, and practiced by physicians, psychiatrists, psychologists, and dentists.

Current studies have produced some evidence that hypnotherapy is real. Researchers have found that areas in the prefrontal cortex, particularly the anterior cingulate cortex, change their activation patterns during hypnosis (Spiegel, 2006). These are the parts of the brain involved in attention, error detection, and resolving conflicts. Hypnosis can be described as a state that involves highly focused attention, increased relaxation, and heightened suggestibility. The subject presents a lowered blood pressure and heart rate, while being awake and fully alert.

We enter into a state similar to a mild trance on a daily basis, when performing automatic tasks such as reading, watching television, or driving (Shenefelt, 2009). But not everyone is hypnotizable. There are various hypnotic induction scales to determine suitability to hypnosis, such as the Stanford hypnotic susceptibility scale. Not everyone wants to be hypnotized either. Undergoing hypnosis is a verbal and behavioral agreement between therapist and patient. The best subject is one who is motivated, but not resistant, not under the influence of drugs, or suffering from a mental health condition.

A study by Lee et al. (2007) suggests that hypnosis can alter our perceptual and sensory experiences. The study exposed patients to color and greyscale images under hypnosis. The researchers discovered that if the patients were told they were shown color, the brain regions involved in the visual processing of color were activated, even if they were viewing the greyscale images. When they were told they were being shown greyscale images, the activation of the color processing regions decreased, regardless of which images appeared. It seems that, under hypnosis, the subjects were responding to the suggestions, rather than the images.

Overall, it is difficult to distinguish hypnotic suggestion from suggestion alone, and researchers need to identify the distinct neurological signature of hypnosis. Despite these questions, some nonclinical therapists claim to be able to treat a wide range of conditions. Dr Andrew Weil (Weil and Gurgevich, 2005) says, "No condition is out-of-bounds when it comes to the effective use of hypnotherapy." But this is overstating the physiological capabilities of hypnotherapy. Hypnotherapy is not about using the mind to fix the body; it is about using the mind to fix the mind.

Some therapists have strange ideas about hypnosis and its abilities; for example, the idea that achieving weight loss and smoking cessation is just about connotation, thus invoking negative words like "diet" and "quit" will result in failure. Instead, empowering and euphemistic language should be used, such as "give yourself permission to be smoke free" (Hathaway, 2003). Hathaway also offers the following simplistic visualization technique to treat cancer.

> Develop a mental image of what your cancer looks like and feels like, and an image of what your healthy body looks and feels like. Once the two images have been created, you push the wellness image through your mind, forcing the negative one out. A very effective image is to visualize gray cells and healthy cells. The healthy cells chase the gray cells out of the body. As the healthy cells chase the gray cells out, feel your body getting healthier and healthier, and feel the cancer shrinking smaller and smaller. If you respond to colors, select negative and positive colors, and run the positive color through the negative until the negative one is gone.
>
> (netplaces/hypnosis.com)

Clinical hypnosis may benefit cancer patients indirectly by way of pain management. It may also reduce the anxiety and depression associated with chronic conditions. The jury is still out on the capabilities of hypnotherapy. Research shows that when people are hypnotized before a painful procedure the areas of the brain that process pain become less active (Spiegel, 2004, Accardi and Milling, 2009, Jensen, 2006, Thornberry et al., 2007). Studies also demonstrate that hypnotherapy may be useful to reduce post surgery pain and accelerate recovery from surgery (Spiegel, 2007, Wobst, 2007). Hypnotherapy may be an effective tool in pediatrics, for lowering anxiety, distress, and discomfort in children (Saadat and Kain, 2007, Kohen and Zajac, 2007). Hypnotherapy has also been shown to be effective for weight loss, when used in conjunction with lifestyles changes such as diet and exercise (Irving, 1996). However, there is no evidence that hypnotherapy can treat drug or alcohol abuse, and while many studies have mixed results, the Cochrane Collaboration, a body that reviews controlled trials, has concluded that hypnotherapy alone is not effective for smoking cessation (Singh and Ernst, 2009).

The way we weren't

The confusing thing is that all hypnotherapists use this same title, regardless of whether they are clinical or prone to dangerous pseudoscience. One of the best ways to find out if a hypnotherapist is credible or not is to ask if they practice repressed memory therapy or past-life therapy. If they do, then the answer is probably "no". Hypnosis came under scrutiny with the repressed memory therapy scandal of the 1980s and 1990s. This is the theory that painful memories, especially negative childhood memories, are forgotten due to dissociation or delayed remembrance. Under hypnosis, these memories can supposedly be retrieved and the effects treated. However, these "repressed memories" aren't memories at all but a combination of patient confabulations and false memories implanted by the therapist. This is known as false memory syndrome. The use of guided imagery, suggestion, and leading questions can all generate fantasies, and the recollection of second-hand experiences.

This phenomenon prompted a spate of false claims of childhood abuse, satanic ritual abuse, and alien abductions. It also lead to the convictions of many innocent people. As human memory expert Elizabeth Loftus (1995) reports, "Individuals are being imprisoned on the 'evidence' provided by memories that come back in dreams and flashbacks – memories that did not exist until a person wandered into therapy and was asked point-blank, 'Were you ever sexually abused as a child?' " Under hypnosis, suggestive interrogation can powerfully influence a susceptible subject and lead them to fabricate memories. But there is no way of differentiating a true memory from a false memory without corroborating evidence (APA, 2011).

Hypnosis is often combined with spurious New Age beliefs and practices. These include the use of pendulums and automatic writing, and theories of astral projection, out-of-body experiences, and reincarnation, which underlies past-life regression therapy. Instead of regressing the patient to a past experience, this therapy claims to regress them to a former life. These therapists believe that our talents, interests, and dysfunctions in this life are borne of experiences in past lives. In order to overcome our problems we need to revisit those lives to find their source and heal the traumas.

Some psychics also practice past-life readings. To appeal to the client's ego, it is usually claimed that everyone was famous in a past life. I was once told that I had been Marie Antoinette! Hewitt (2009) issues a caution to inexperienced hypnotists.

> You should not attempt to regress someone until you have become a reasonably experienced hypnotist. This is because an inexperienced operator can cause the regression to a traumatic and unpleasant experience for the subject. For example, suppose you regress a person to a past life just at the moment he or she was being beheaded? That could be a terrifying moment for your subject because it is a real experience.

The real world danger is that past-life regression therapy works the same way as repressed memory therapy. Both create false memories, but it is even easier to fabricate past lives without having to provide proof. In the few examples where we have evidence, such as the Bridey Murphy case, (Chapter 7) the explanations come back to false memories. The same goes for a new fad known as future life readings. Goldberg (2006) conducted a future-life reading for former TV talk-show host Jerry Springer.

> During the latter part of the 21st century, Jerry will be a rancher/farmer named Bobby, working in Montana. He is married and has four children. Bobby is involved with a government project to raise crops on the moon. He will be killed at the age of 60 when his craft crashes during a return trip to earth.

In repressed memory, past-life, and future-life therapies, practitioners are teaching their own personal beliefs to clients who are being diagnosed and treated for induced fantasies.

25
Body Language

"When you run your hands through your hair like that it makes me think you're flirting with me", a colleague once said to me. Someone's been reading a book about body language. "Maybe I'm not flirting, but I'm getting my hair out of my eyes, or detangling my hair, or it's a nervous habit, or I have dandruff, or I'm readjusting my wig. There are many possible reasons for any action." But not everyone believes this is so.

Linguistics, kinesics, and semiotics are among the disciplines that observe and describe gesture and other forms of nonverbal communication. On the other hand (excuse the pun), body language is the New Age, self-help interpretation of behavior. Self-styled body language therapists promote themselves as experts at reading posture, stance, facial expressions, and other body movements. Authorities on body language claim to decode our thoughts and feelings, disclose innermost desires, unlock the powers of intuition, provide searing insights, expose secrets, and uncover the hidden meanings behind our behavior. They believe that when we hide the truth with our language, our body language ends up doing the talking instead.

They style themselves as behavioral scientists or detectives who see clues in our cues, inspired by Sherlock Holmes and TV shows such as *Lie to Me*. Charismatic speakers offer themselves as body language specialists, such as "Mr and Mrs Body Language" Allan and Barbara Pease, authors of the "communication bible" *The Definitive Book of Body Language*, and "body language expert" Tonya Reiman. They are motivational speakers, authors of self-help books, and gossipmongers in tabloids and on the talk-show circuit. They analyze photographs of celebrities to guess who's sleeping with whom, and predict who's breaking up. They interpret footage of political debates, speeches, and interviews to uncover underlying meaning and detect deception.

With the help of these body language specialists, you can be a success. Buy their books, attend their seminars, follow their programs, systems, and methods and you too can harness these techniques to achieve your goals. They will provide you with the tools you need to give you confidence, to catch a liar in the act, to ace that job interview, to attract love, and to stop sending out those "wrong messages". Some fear that body language is so accurate that reading people's behavior is an invasion of privacy, or a type of manipulation. Pease and Pease (2004) even claim that body language interpretation is a "sixth sense".

(Don't) read my lips

Proponents of body language theories are basically saying that there is standardized meaning in the way you sit, stand, and walk. There is significance in how you shake hands, lick your lips, or run your hands through your hair. Like a visual polygraph test, they believe that answering a question and touching your nose a certain way, or an involuntary subtle shift in your eye, betrays a lie. Crossing your arms indicates defensiveness, or a lack of openness. Rubbing the stem of a wine glass suggests that subconsciously, you want to rub something (or someone) else.

Body language gurus promote the use of their techniques in conjunction with other alternative therapies, including NLP, color therapy, and feng shui. For example, one practitioner warns, "Cashmere and cotton, for example, are soft and inviting, suggesting that the wearer is a gentle soul. Hard materials, like leather or boiled wool, keep others at a distance" (Hagan, 2008).

Body language theory promotes many unconventional ideas. Pease and Pease (2004) claim that idioms such as "get it off your chest", "put your best foot forward", and "kiss my butt" demonstrate the importance of body language to communication. However, research into conceptual metaphor reveals that body metaphors are also used to talk about machines, computers, cities, and nations (Goschler, 2005). The point is that other body metaphors such as "mouth of a river" and "heart of the city" don't mean that body language is important to geography.

Another theory is that we need to listen to our bodies because literal body pain has figurative significance. This idea is based in the sympathetic magic that we've discussed throughout this book. Identifying physical pains and seeking out idioms associated with those body parts can help reveal the underlying psychological issue. For example, ear pain can indicate that "we don't want to hear something" being said to us. Chest pain means that the sufferer is harboring a problem and needs to "get something off their chest". Tension in our neck and shoulders means we are "shouldering our responsibilities". Pain in the testes might mean the individual is cowardly and "has no balls"! (Benor, 2005).

Written all over your face

Some advocates believe that body language can do more than reveal if someone is sexually attracted to us. Bioenergetic analysis promotes the idea that physical illnesses reflect psychological issues. This body psychotherapy involves reading posture, gestures, and expressions to diagnose clients, and treating them using exercise, movement, and vocal expression (Lowen, 1994). These therapists believe that body language techniques can heal conditions of the mind, including anxiety and depression, and even prevent and treat physical conditions, such as cancer (Lowen, 1993, 1994, Robonson, 1978). This therapy is based on the work of unorthodox psychoanalyst William Reich, who invented the cloudbuster, a device that allegedly produces rain using orgone energy. Like Reich's methods, bioenergetic analysis places great emphasis on sex-obsessed Freudian theory, including dream interpretation, the Oedipus complex, and slips of the tongue.

Similarly, applied kinesiology claims to diagnose disease through body movement. Not to be confused with kinesiology, the scientific study of human movement, applied kinesiology was devised by George Goodheart (1918–2008) to evaluate physical and mental health. The method involves a manual muscle test in which a practitioner exerts pressure on the patient's outstretched arm to gauge the strength and steadiness of the resistance. Treatment is prescribed on the basis of this response. Unsurprisingly, the cure is usually appropriate to the underlying modalities used by the practitioner. Applied kinesiology stems from chiropractic, but acupuncturists, naturopaths, massage therapists, and even multi-level marketers, use it to promote their own treatments and products. Some also use it as a form of divination, especially as a "lie detector" test to gauge whether a statement is true or false. The test is a highly subjective measurement, and controlled trials have shown that the claims of applied kinesiology are inaccurate. Applied kinesiology is dangerous, as it can generate a false diagnosis and prescribe ineffective treatments for a condition that didn't exist in the first place (Singh and Ernst, 2009).

A bone to pick

Sensational late-night infomercials that tell us that we only use 10 per cent of our brains, and similarly body language theory claims that a mere 7 per cent (or 10 per cent, 15 per cent, 20 per cent, or 50 per cent) of our communication is verbal. I once taught a university course in Verbal and Nonverbal Communication and was expected to say that human communication consists of 93 per cent body language and only 7 per cent language. But I couldn't find any evidence to support this statement. There has been much research on this topic, although no study has shown there is a precise ratio of verbal to nonverbal communication.

This myth is based on research by Albert Mehrabian (1971, 2009) who speculates that face-to-face communication is comprised of three elements: words, tone of voice, and nonverbal behavior. In his 1971 study he found that interaction could be broken down into 7 per cent words, 38 per cent tone, and 55 per cent gestures, expressions, and other nonverbal acts. This has become known as the '7%-38%-55% rule'. However, Mehrabian's theory was developed on the basis of just two tests in which participants listened to recordings of speech and judged the feelings of the speakers. Therefore, the results aren't generalizable in any way, but body language supporters applied the findings to *all* communication.

Books about body language are full of such sound bites and urban legends. They refer to studies and authors who support their theories, but they don't cite them, and they name-drop irrelevant research to validate body language. Body language books brag that Charles Darwin promoted body language theory and they reference his 1871 publication *The Descent of Man and Selection in Relation to Sex*. However, they misinterpret and overextend Darwin's arguments. All he did was mention the importance of gesture and sign language, and suggest that they are relevant to the origins of language.

Losing face

Many body language advocates believe in the universality of the meaning of body language. For example, Tonya Reiman (2008) has developed the Reiman rapport method, a "ten step process to master universally pleasing body language". This is also the basis of psychologist Paul Ekman's research. Ekman has conducted extensive research into human facial expressions. His 1972 study claims that there is a small inventory of expressions that are biologically universal to all humans. This list of "basic emotions" includes anger, disgust, fear, happiness, sadness, and surprise.

Ekman's work has produced valuable research on facial expressions, but current studies don't support the idea of distinct emotions and facial expressions (James and Fernandez-Dols, 1997). Facial expressions are not restricted to a small set. Furthermore, a smile isn't an invariable sign of happiness. For example, Amrozi, the Indonesian terrorist known as the "Smiling Bomber" demonstrated that a smile can also signal confidence and defiance. There are immense differences in expressions, gestures, and behaviors across cultures, and individuals.

Tell me lies

In a study of behavioral cues, Ekman and O'Sullivan (2004) claim to have discovered 29 truth "wizards". These people are presented as "geniuses of lie detection". These findings led to the use of behavior-detection officers by the US Transportation Security Administration for the screening passengers by observation technique (SPOT) program. However, the SPOT methodology isn't supported by scientific evidence, and nor is Ekman's work which isn't peer reviewed. He says he doesn't publish his findings anymore because enemies of the United States follow his work closely (Weinberger, 2010). Bond and Uysal (2007) independently examined Ekman's findings and concluded, "Analyses reveal that chance can explain results that the authors attribute to wizardry." A report by Hontz et al. (2009) adds, "Simply put, people (including professional lie-catchers with extensive experience of assessing veracity) would achieve similar hit rates if they flipped a coin."

Ekman is often called the "lie detective". He has written many books on lie detection and he claims to be the inspiration for the TV show *Lie to Me*. However, the opening credits state, "The following story is fictional and does not depict any actual person or event." Lie detection is the bread and butter of body language. Julius Fast (1970) author of the seminal book *Body Language*, says, "Your body doesn't know how to lie. Unconsciously it telegraphs your thoughts as you fold your arms, cross your legs, stand, walk, move your eyes and mouth."

In body language theory there are many systems and methods to spotting a liar. These involve using intuition, and reading eye movements and micro-expressions. Liars are said to rub their eyes, grab their ears, scratch their necks, touch their noses, and cover their mouths when they lie (Pease and Pease, 2004). In more sympathetic magic, liars touch their ears because they "don't want to hear" the interrogation. In one study, researchers linked lying to increased pupil size, lip pressing, and higher voice pitch (DePaulo and Morris, 2004). They also concluded that liars take longer to answer questions, they talk less, and their stories are less logical and less plausible.

The computer program Linguistic Inquiry and Word Count analyzes text. Its creators claim to have devised a linguistic profile of deception. They have allegedly uncovered speech markers that distinguish between true and false stories with a 61 per cent accuracy rate (Newman et al., 2003). According to their findings, liars use fewer first person pronouns (e.g., "I" and "me");. they use more negative emotion words (e.g., "hate" and "sad"); and they use fewer exclusionary words (e.g., "except" and "but"). They conclude that liars are less complex, less self-relevant, and more characterized by negativity. Despite all of these intriguing studies and claims, liars cannot be identified reliably by their language and behavior. Before condemning someone for lying, we require more evidence than a missing pronoun or someone rubbing their eyes. Gestures, facial expressions, and written and spoken language can have multiple meanings, and only serve as hints, not proof.

Love is another popular topic for body language readers. Pease and Pease (2004) claim that men and women exhibit unmistakable courtship gestures. When a female approaches, a man might straighten his tie, or smooth his collar and hair. If he's really keen he might adopt the aggressive "thumbs in belt" gesture that highlights his genital region. According to the authors, females use these very same gestures, and many more. They are overtly flirtatious, and employ such brazen moves as running their fingers through their hair, tossing their hair, exposing their wrists, rolling their hips when they walk, keeping their handbags in close proximity, and fondling a cylindrical object. Again, there is great variance in the possible meaning of all of these behaviors. We need to be extremely cautious in viewing body language as anything more than entertainment, as the consequences may be embarrassing, confusing, or even criminal.

Over my dead body

Nonverbal behavior certainly has important meaning, and we are highly receptive to this kind of communication. The claims of body language enthusiasts seem plausible on the surface, and appear to be insightful clues. However, as Hartley and Karinch (2007) state, "few people today can read body language well". This is because there is no formula for understanding behavior, and no invariable meaning of a gesture, expression or movement. Every act has numerous possible meanings and causes. The meaning of our body language is subject to context, intent, and interpretation. It is influenced by culture and socialization, and differs at the individual level.

Some conditions really can affect our body movements and the way we interpret the body movements of other people. People with Asperger's syndrome or autism often have problems imitating and understanding abstract gestures. They can have joint attention deficits, that is, it can be difficult for them to share a visual experience using eye gazing and pointing (Dawson et al., 2004). Autistic children don't always make eye contact during conversation. Even if they are listening and understand what is being said, their attention and focus can appear to be elsewhere. Their gestures may be more abstract too. For example, pointing to a cookie may mean that a child is hungry, but not necessarily hungry for the cookie. People with these conditions also interpret body language differently. These cases further suggest that there is no standardization in the use and interpretation of body language.

Reading body language is simply about interpretation. It is guesswork, opinion, and prediction, and it is open to misinterpretation and misunderstanding. The analogy to "reading" is helpful. Interpreting body language is another type of cold reading, or a form of body divination to predict thought. Consulting a body language book is similar to asking a psychic, "Does he like me?" or "Is she lying to me?". It's another quick fix for a complex problem. For all of its nuances and ambiguity, verbal language is a more explicit and effective method for communicating complex concepts than body language.

Reading body language is a superficial, subjective, and unreliable practice. It is potentially risky too. So be careful the next time you approach the woman who seems to be looking at you and stroking the stem of her wine glass provocatively. You might just get that wine thrown in your face.

References

Accardi, M. C. and Milling, L. S. 2009. "The effectiveness of hypnosis for reducing procedure-related pain in children and adolescents: a comprehensive methodological review". *Journal of Behavioral Medicine*. August, Vol. 32, No. 4, pp. 328–39.

Ahmed *et al.* 2009. "High-intensity-focused ultrasound in the treatment of primary prostate cancer: The first UK series". *British Journal of Cancer*. 1 July 2009.

Amend, Karen Kristin and Ruiz, Mary Stansbury. 1980. *Handwriting Analysis*. The Career Press.

APA (American Psychological Association). 2011. "Questions and answers about memories of childhood abuse". Available at: http://www.apa.org/topics/trauma/memories.aspx# Accessed 01/06/2011

Aydin, S., Odabas, Ö., Ercan, M., Kara, H., and Agargün, M. 1996. "Efficacy of testosterone, trazodone and hypnotic suggestion in the treatment of non-organic male sexual dysfunction". *British Journal of Urology*. Vol. 77, pp. 256–60.

Bandler, Richard and Grinder, John. 1975. *The Structure of Magic: A Book about Language and Therapy*. Science and Behavior Books.

Bandler, Richard and Grinder, John. 1979. *Frogs into Princes*. Real People Press.

Beaumont, P. 1971. "Small handwriting in some patients with Anorexia Nervosa". *British Journal of Psychiatry*. Vol. 119, 349–50.

Benor, Daniel. 2005. *How Can I Heal What Hurts?* Wholistic Healing Publications.

Bernard, Marie. 1990. *Sexual Deviations as Seen in Handwriting*. The Whitston Publishing Company.

Beyerstein, Barry and Beyerstein, Dale. (eds). 1992. *The Write Stuff: Evaluations of Graphology – The Study of Handwriting Analysis*. Prometheus Books.

Beyerstein, Barry. 1990. "Brainscams: Neuromythologies of the New Age". *International Journal of Mental Health*. Vol. 19, No. 3, pp. 27–36.

Beyerstein, Barry L. and Beyerstein, Dale F. (eds.) 1992. *The Write Stuff: Evaluations of Graphology, The Study of Handwriting Analysis*. Prometheus Books.

Beumont, P. 1971. "Small handwriting in some patients with anorexia nervosa". *British Journal of Psychiatry*. Vol. 119, pp. 349–50.

Bond, Charles and Ahmet, Uysal. 2007. "On lie detection 'Wizards' ". *Law and Human Behavior*. Vol. 31, No. 1.

Borg, John. 2008. *Body Language: 7 Easy Lessons to Master the Silent Language*. Prentice Hall Life.

Bourland, D. David and Paul Dennithorne, Johnston. 1991. *To Be or Not: An E-Prime Anthology*. International Society for General Semantics.

Campbell, Don. 2000. *The Mozart Effect for Children: Awakening Your Child's Mind, Health, and Creativity With Music*. Harper Collins.

Campbell, Don. 2001. *The Mozart Effect: Tapping the Power of Music to Heal the Body, Strengthen the Mind, and Unlock the Creative Spirit*. Quill.

Carnegie, Dale. 1937. *How to Win Friends and Influence People*. Simon and Schuster.

Carter, C. 2008. "Healthcare performance and the effects of the binaural beats on human blood pressure and heart rate". *Journal of Hospital Marketing & Public Relations*.

Charny, E. J. 1966. "Psychosomatic manifestations of rapport in psychotherapy". *Psychosomatic Medicine*. Vol. 28, pp. 305–15.

Chomsky, Noam. 1965. *Aspects of the Theory of Syntax*. MIT Press.

Contreras-Vidal, J. L. et al 2002. "Adaptation to changes in vertical display gain during handwriting in Parkinson's disease patients, elderly and young controls". *Parkinsonism & Related Disorders*. Vol. 9, No. 2, pp. 77–84.

Dabbs, J. M. 1969. "Similarity of gestures and interpersonal influence". *Proceedings of the 77th Annual Convention of the American Psychological Association*. Vol. 4, pp. 337–38.

Darwin, Charles. 1981. (1871). *The Descent of Man, and Selection in Relation to Sex*. Princeton University Press.

Dawson, Geraldine, Toth, Karen, Abbott, Robert, Osterling, Julie, Munson, Jeff, Estes, Annette, and Liaw, Jane. 2004. "Early social attention impairments in autism: Social orienting, joint attention, and attention to distress". *Developmental Psychology*. Vol. 40, No. 2, pp. 271–83.

DePaulo, B. and Morris, W. 2004. "Discerning lies from truths: Behavioural cues to deception and the indirect pathway of intuition". In Granhag, P. A. and Strömwall, L. (eds) *The Detection of Deception in Forensic Contexts*. Cambridge University Press, pp. 15–40.

Dresbold, Michelle with Kwalwasser, James. 2006. *Sex, Lies and Handwriting. Top Expert Reveals the Secrets Hidden in your Handwriting*. Simon & Schuster.

Dresbold, Michelle and Kwalwasser, James. 2008. *Sex, Lies, and Handwriting: A Top Expert Reveals the Secrets Hidden in Your Handwriting*. Free Press.

Duffy, Jonathan and Wilson, Giles. 2005. "Writing wrongs". *BBC News Magazine*.

Ekman, P. 1972. "Universals and cultural differences in facial expressions of emotion". In Cole, J. (ed.) *Nebraska Symposium on Motivation 1971*. Vol. 19, pp. 207–83. University of Nebraska Press.

Ekman, Paul. 1999. "Basic emotions" In Dalgleish, T. and Power, M. (eds) *Handbook of Cognition and Emotion*. John Wiley & Sons.

Emoto, Masaru. 2004. *The Hidden Messages in Water*. Beyond Words.

de Sainte Columbe, Paul. 1972. *Grapho Therapeutics: Pen and Pencil Therapy*. Paul de St Columbe Center.

Fast, Julius. 1970. *Body Language*. Simon & Schuster.

Flaherty, Alice Weaver. 2004. *The Midnight Disease: The Drive to Write, Writer's Block, and the Creative Brain*. Houghton Mifflin Harcourt.

Forer, B. R. 1949. "The fallacy of personal validation: A classroom demonstration of gullibility". *Journal of Abnormal Psychology*. Vol. 44, pp. 118–23.

Friesen, Wendi. 2011. Breast Enlargement Hypnosis DVD. wendi.com Accessed 20 October 2011.

Furnham, Adrian. 1991. "Write and wrong: The validity of graphological analysis," In Kendrick Frazier (ed.) *The Hundredth Monkey and Other Paradigms of the Paranormal*. Prometheus Books, pp. 200–05.

Gilmore, Tim. 1999. "The efficacy of the Tomatis method for children with learning and communication disorders: A meta-analysis". *International Journal of Listening*. Vol. 13, 1999.

Grinder, John. 2014. http://www.johngrinder.com/

Grinder, John and Bandler, Richard 1979. *Frogs into Princes: Neuro Linguistic Programming*. Real People Press.

Grinder, John and Bandler, Richard. 1981. *Transe-formations: Neuro-Linguistic Programming. TM and the Structure of Hypnosis*. Real People Press.

Grinder, J., Richard, B., and Connirae, A. (eds) 1981. *Trance-Formations: Neuro-Linguistic Programming and the Structure of Hypnosis*. Real People Press.

Goldberg, Bruce. 2006. *Self-Hypnosis*. Career Press.

Goschler, Juliana. 2005. "Embodiment and body metaphors". *Metaphorik* online Journal. September. Available at: http://www.metaphorik.de/09/goschler.pdf Accessed 02/10/2011.

Hagan, Shelly. 2008. *Everything Body Language Book: Decipher Signals, See the Signs and Read People's Emotions Without a Word!* Adams Media.

Hartley, Gregory and Karinch, Maryann. 2007. *I Can Read You Like a Book*. Career Press.

Hathaway, Michael. 2003. *The Everything Hypnosis Book*. An Everything Series Book.

Heap. M. 1988. "Neurolinguistic programming: An interim verdict". In Heap, M. (ed.) *Hypnosis: Current Clinical, Experimental and Forensic Practices*. London: Croom Helm, pp. 268–80.

Heap, Michael. 2008. "The validity of some early claims of neuro-linguistic programming". *Skeptical Intelligencer*. Vol. 11, pp. 1–8.

Hewitt, William. 2009. *Hypnosis for Beginners*. Woodbury, Minnesota: Llewellyn.

Hontz, C. R., Hartwig, M., Kleinman, S. M. and Meissner, C. 2009. "A credibility assessment at portals, portals committee report". *Hypnotic World*. Available at: http://www.hypnoticworld.com

Jensen, M. and Patterson, D. R. 2006. "Hypnotic treatment of chronic pain". *Journal of Behaviour Medicine*. Vol. 29, No. 1, pp. 95–124.

Kanfer, Alfred. 1973. "You are what you write. Several scientific studies". In Hartford, Huntington (ed.) MacMillan Publishing Co.

Kirsch, Irving. 1996. "Hypnotic enhancement of cognitive-behavioural weight loss treatments: Another meta-reanalysis". *Journal of Consulting and Clinical Psychology*. Vol. 64, No. 3, pp. 517–19.

Knight, David. 2014. http://www.davidknight.net/breastenlargement.htm

Kohen, D. P. and Zajac, R. 2007. "Self-hypnosis training for headaches in children and adolescents". *Journal of Pediatrics*. Vol. 150, No. 6, pp. 635–39.

Korzybski, Alfred. 1933. *Science and Sanity: An Introduction to Non-Aristotelian Systems and General Semantics*, Englewood, NJ: The International Non-Aristotelian Library.

LaFrance, M. and Broadbent, M. 1976. "Group rapport: Posture sharing as a nonverbal indicator". *Group and Organisation Studies*. Vol. 1, pp. 328–33.

Lankton, S. 1980. *Practical Magic*. Cupertino, CA: Meta.

Lee, J., Spiegel, D., Kim, S., Lee, J. H., Kim, S. I., Yang, B., Choi, J., Kho, Y., and Nam, J. H. 2007. "Fractal analysis of EEG in hypnosis and its relationship with hypnotizability". *International Journal of Clinical Exp Hypnosis*. Vol. 55, No. 1, pp. 14–31.

Lee, Rebecca. 2007. "The Moozart effect". Available at: http://abcnews.go.com/Technology/. Accessed 05/11/2011.

Loftus, Elizabeth. 1995. "Remembering dangerously". *Skeptical Inquirer*. 19 April, Vol. 2, pp. 20–29.

Lowe, Sheila. 2007. *The Complete Idiot's Guide to Handwriting Analysis*. New York: Alpha.

Lowen, Alexander. 1993. *Depression and the Body: The Biological Basis of Faith and Reality*. Penguin.

Lowen, Alexander. 1994. *Bioenergetics: The Revolutionary Therapy That Uses the Language of the Body to Heal the Problems of the Mind*. Penguin.

Manifesting Mind Power. Voice Healing. www.manifestingmindpower.com/voice%20healing.htm. Accessed 04/20/2011.

Markopolos, Harry. 2011. *No One Would Listen. A True Financial Thriller*. Wiley.

Markopolis, Harry. 2012. *No One Would Listen: A True Financial Thriller*. John Wiley & Sons.

McKelvie, Pippa and Low, Jason. 2010. "Listening to Mozart does not improve children's spatial ability: Final curtains for the Mozart effect". *Developmental Psychology*. Vol. 20, No. 2, pp. 241–58.

McNichol, Andrea and Nelson, Jeffrey. 1994. *Handwriting Analysis: Putting it to Work for you*. McGraw Hill.

Mehrabian, Albert. 1971. *Silent Messages* (1st Ed.). Wadsworth.

Mehrabian, Albert. 2009. *Silent Messages – A Wealth of Information About Nonverbal Communication (Body Language)*. self-published.

Miller, Christa. 2004. "Can a crying baby stop a riot?" *Law Enforcement Technology*. Vol. 31, No. 3, March, pp. 8–14.

Mouly, S., Mahé, I., Champion, K., Bertin, C., Popper, P., De Noblet, D., and Bergmann, J. 2007. "Graphology for the diagnosis of suicide attempts: Discussion". *International Journal of Clinical Practice*. Vol. 61, No. 3, pp. 411–15.

Newbrook, Mark. 2008. "Linguistic aspects of 'neuro-linguistic programming' ". *Skeptical Intelligencer* 11, 27–29.

Newman, Matthew L., Pennebaker, James W., Berry, Diane S., and Richards, Jane M. 2003. "Lying words: Predicting deception from linguistic styles". *Personality and Social Psychology Bulletin*. Vol. 29, No. 5, pp. 665–75.

Newman, Paul. 1993. *The Signing Cure. Introduction to Voice Movement Therapy*. Rider & Co.

O'Connor, J. and Seymour, J. 1993. *Introducing Neuro-Linguistic Programming: Psychological Skills for Understanding and Influencing People*. United Kingdom: Thorsons.

O'Sullivan, M. and Ekman, P. 2004. "The wizards of deception detection". In Granhag, P. A. and Stromwall, L. A. (eds) *Deception Detection in Forensic Contexts*. Cambridge Press, pp. 269–86.

Pease, Allan and Pease, Barbara. 2004. *The Definitive Book of Body Language*. Bantam Press.

Phillips, J. G. et al. 2004. "Characteristics of handwriting of patients with Huntington's disease". *Movement Disorder*. Vol. 9, No 5, pp. 521–30.

Rauscher, F., Shaw, G., and Ky, K. 1993. "Music and spatial task performance". *Nature*. 365 (6447) 611.

Ready, R. and Burton, K. 2004. *Neuro-Linguistic Programming for Dummies*. John Wiley & Sons, pp. 10–11.

Reiman, Tonya. 2008. *The Power of Body Language: How to Succeed in Every Business and Social Encounter*. Gallery Books.

Robonson, Margot. 1978. "Visual, imagery, bioenergetics and the treatment of cancer". *Energy and Character*. Vol. 9, No. 1, pp. 2–12.

Rogers, Vimala. 1995. *Change Your Handwriting, Change Your Life*. Celestial Arts.

Russel, James and, Fernandez-Dols, Jose. 1997. *The Psychology of Facial Expression*. Cambridge University Press.

Saadat, H. and Kain, Z. N. 2007. "Hypnosis as a therapeutic tool in pediatrics". *Pediatrics*. Vol. 120, No. 1, pp. 179–81.

Sack, Kevin. 1998. "Georgia's governor seeks musical start for babies". *The New York Times*. 01/15/1998.

Sampson, Geoffrey. 1980. *Schools of Linguistics*. Stanford University Press.

Santoy, Claude. 2005. *The ABCs of Handwriting Analysis: The Complete Guide to Techniques and Interpretations*. Da Capo Press.

Satir, V., Bandler, R., and Grinder, J. 1976. *Changing With Families: A Book about Further Education for Being Human*. Science and Behavior Books.

Schrock, Karen. 2007. "Fact or fiction? An opera singer's piercing voice can shatter glass". *Scientific American*, http://www.scientificamerican.com/article/fact-or-fiction-opera-singer-can-shatter-glass/.

Scorpio, Dan. "E-Prime tutorial". Available at: http://www.angelfire.com/nd/danscorpio/ep2.html. Accessed 11/21/2011.

Sharpley, Christopher F. 1984. "Predicate matching in NLP: A review of research on the preferred representational system." *Journal of Counseling Psychology* No. 31, pp. 238–48.

Sharpley, Christopher F. 1 January 1987. "Research findings on neurolinguistic programming: Nonsupportive data or an untestable theory?" *Journal of Counseling Psychology* Vol. 34, No. 1, pp. 103–07.

Shenefelt, Philip. 2009. *Hypnosis – Applications in Dermatology and Dermatologic Surgery*, www.emedicine.com.

Singh, Simon and Ernst, Edzard. 2009. *Trick or Treatment. The Undeniable Facts about Alternative Medicine.* Norton.

Spadoni, Alessandro and Daraio, Chiara. 2010. "Generation and control of sound bullets with a nonlinear acoustic lens", *Proceedings of the National Academy of Sciences.* Vol. 107, No. 7230.

Spiegel, D. 2004. "Hypnosis: Brief interventions offer key to managing pain and anxiety". *Current Psychiatry.* Vol. 3, No. 4, pp. 49–52.

Spiegel, D. 2006. "Wedding hypnosis to the radiology suite." *Pain.* Vol. 126, No. 1–3, pp. 3–4.

Spiegel, D. 2007. "The mind prepared: Hypnosis in surgery". *Journal of the National Cancer Institute.* Vol. 99, No. 17, pp. 1280–81.

Staib, Allan and Logan, D. R. 1977. "Hypnotic stimulation of breast growth". *American Journal of Clinical Hypnosis.* April. Vol. 19, No. 4.

Stollznow, Karen. 2002. "This little piggy". *The Skeptic.* Vol. 22, No. 3, Australian Skeptics.

Stollznow, Karen. 2002. "Healing by the sea and in the mountains". *The Skeptic.* Australian Skeptics, pp. 38–43.

Stollznow, Karen. 2003. "Graphology: Write or wrong?" *The Skeptic.* Vol. 23, No. 3, Australian Skeptics.

Strang, Christina. 2007. *Handwriting in the Early Detection of Disease.* Available at: http://www.christinastrang.co.uk/downloads/final_edition_paper.pdf Accessed 11/23/2011.

Surovell, Hariette. 1987. *Lovestrokes: Handwriting Analysis for Love, Sex, and Compatibility.* Harpercollins.

Temes, Roberta. 2004. *The Complete Idiot's Guide to Hypnosis.* 2nd Edition. Alpha.

Thomas, John. 2002. *Graphology Fact Sheet. North Texas Skeptics.* http://www.ntskeptics.org/factsheets/graphol.htm

Thornberry, T., Schaeffer, J., Wright, P. D., Haley, M. C., and Kirsh, K. L. 2007. "An exploration of the utility of hypnosis in pain management among rural pain patients". *Palliat Support Care.* Vol. 5, No. 2, pp. 147–52.

Tomatis, A. A. 1991. *The Conscious Ear: My Life of Transformation through Listening.* Station Hill Press.

Tosey, P. and Mathison, J. 2010. "Neuro-linguistic programming as an innovation in education and teaching". *Innovations in Education & Teaching International.* Vol. 47, pp. 317–26.

Weil, Andrew and Gurgevich, Steven. 2005. *Heal Yourself with Medical Hypnosis: The Most Immediate Way to Use Your Mind-Body Connection.* Audiobook. Sounds True.

Weinberger, Sharon. 2010. "Airport security: Intent to deceive?" *Nature.* Vol. 465, No. 7297, pp. 412–15. Available at: http://www.nature.com/news/2010/100526/full/465412a.html. Accessed 07/31/2011.

Whitehead. W. E. 2006. "Hypnosis for irritable bowel syndrome: The empirical evidence of therapeutic effects". *International Journal of Clinical and Experimental Hypnosis.* Vol. 54, No. 1, pp. 7–20.

Willard, Richard. 1977. "Breast enlargement through visual imagery and hypnosis". *American Journal of Clinical Hypnosis.* April. Vol. 19, No. 4.

Williams, James. 1974. "Stimulation of breast growth by hypnosis". *The Journal of Sex Research.* November. Vol. 10, No. 4, pp. 316–326.

Witkowski, Tomasz. 2011. "A review of research findings on neuro-linguistic programming". *Scientific Review of Mental Health Practice.* Center for Inquiry.

Wobst, A. H. 2007. "Hypnosis and surgery: Past, present, and future". *Anesthesia and Analgesia.* Vol. 104, No. 5, pp. 1199–208.

Wright, Stuart. 1995. *Armageddon in Waco: Critical Perspectives on the Branch Davidian Conflict.* University of Chicago Press.

Conclusions

This book has explored many mythical, mysterious, and magical beliefs and practices that involve language. From past-life regression to predicting the future, they all require some aspect of communication, whether that's spirit writing, reading rune stones, speaking in tongues, or listening for voices of the dead.

We've discovered that there are often natural explanations for these supernatural claims. It simply makes more sense that a woman is acting than channeling a 35,000-year-old spirit warrior. It's more likely that it's a scam than a wealthy prince wants to share his billions with you. It's unlikely that Bigfoot can talk when he hasn't yet been discovered.

No matter how many times I tried as a kid, falling asleep on a book wouldn't result in me absorbing its contents because the only way to understand a book is to read it. Language is meant to be heard forwards, not played backwards, and we should listen to the words actually being said. Instead of trying to talk to the dead, language should be used to keep memories of our loved ones alive.

The facts are a consolation to the folklore. It is comforting to know that merely hearing a song won't drive the listener to suicide, and that we can't be turned into a newt by a spell. It is a relief to know that there's no note which can make us lose control of our bowels, and that breaking a chain letter won't lead to destruction and death. A negative prayer said against us won't reach a higher power, but a prayer said for our health and well-being shows that someone cares about us.

Why are we so apt to believe these unusual stories and theories? Everyone speaks a language (or more), and so everyone has a personal stake in language. As speakers, we feel suitably qualified to speak knowledgeably about language. However, our views and attitudes are often based in belief, bias and desire, but not in fact. This gives way to a lot of myths and misconceptions about language, and this book has attempted to dispel some of these. However, believing in the myths doesn't make us stupid, it just makes us human.

In this way, these strange stories reveal the universality of the human condition. We looked at ancient curses carved on tablets that were cast to make money, cure sickness, win a court case, or win the love of a man or a woman. Then we considered the modern popularity of candle burning, prayers, and affirmations used for these very same purposes. These similarities suggest that whether living in ancient Greece or modern America, as humans, we are bound together by common experiences across time and space. A predisposition to believe is an inescapable feature of being human.

Beyond the myths we've unearthed some incredible truths, and found that fact is often stranger than fiction. It's astonishing that a brain injury can cause someone to switch from one language to another. It's amazing that our handwriting can reveal certain illnesses. Why must a horse be psychic to be clever, when she is already so clever that she interprets subtle cues from her trainer? The natural is infinitely more interesting than the supernatural, and there is still much wonder left for us in language.

When we cast off the belief that language has mysterious and magical powers, we find that language has many real world powers. Language expresses our emotions, feelings, and thoughts. It's the voice of our hopes, dreams, and imagination. It's a vehicle to share ideas about knowledge, music, and art. It is used to create poetry, plays, and books; to write stirring lyrics to a song and to pen a love letter. Whether it is handwritten, typed, signed, or said, language is the way we establish and maintain friendships and relationships. It celebrates our experiences and the milestone moments of our lives; it is used to pronounce a couple as married, to name a baby, to say our greetings and goodbyes, and to tell our friends and family that we love them.

Language does have power, but it isn't mythical, mysterious, or magical. Language has the power we give to it.

Index

Printed and bound in Great Britain by
CPI Group (UK) Ltd, Croydon, CR0 4YY